How to Write About Africa

How to Write About Africa

COLLECTED WORKS

Binyavanga Wainaina

EDITED BY ACHAL PRABHALA

ONE WORLD
NEW YORK

2024 One World Trade Paperback Edition

Copyright © 2022 by The Estate of Binyavanga Wainaina
Editorial material copyright © 2022 by Achal Prabhala
Introduction copyright © 2022 by Chimamanda Ngozi Adichie

The Acknowledgments on pp. 345–47 constitute an extension
of this copyright page.

All rights reserved.

Published in the United States by One World, an imprint of Random House,
a division of Penguin Random House LLC, New York.

ONE WORLD and colophon are registered trademarks of
Penguin Random House LLC.

Originally published in hardcover in the United States
by One World, an imprint of Random House,
a division of Penguin Random House LLC, in 2023.

LIBRARY OF CONGRESS CATALOGING-IN-PUBLICATION DATA
Names: Wainaina, Binyavanga, author. | Adichie, Chimamanda Ngozi, 1977–
writer of introduction. | Prabhala, Achal, editor.
Title: How to write about Africa : collected works / Binyavanga Wainaina ;
edited by Achal Prabhala ; [introduction by] Chimamanda Ngozi Adichie.
Other titles: Works
Description: New York : One World, 2023.
Identifiers: LCCN 2023014554 (print) | LCCN 2023014555 (ebook) |
ISBN 9780812989663 (paperback) | ISBN 9780812989670 (ebook)
Subjects: LCSH: Africa. | LCGFT: Essays. | Short stories.
Classification: LCC PR9381.9 .W25 2023 (print) | LCC PR9381.9 (ebook) |
DDC 814.6--dc23/eng/20230329
LC record available at https://lccn.loc.gov/2023014554
LC ebook record available at https://lccn.loc.gov/2023014555

Printed in the United States of America on acid-free paper

oneworldlit.com
randomhousebooks.com

1st Printing

Contents

About the Editor

Achal Prabhala is a writer, filmmaker, and public health activist who lives in Bangalore, India. In 2005, he met Binyavanga Wainaina through Michael Vazquez, the editor at the time of *Transition* magazine, and stayed friends with him across continents, as well as every dazzling phase of Binyavanga's life.

Introduction

I met Binyavanga Wainaina online years ago, when meeting people online was still new. It was on an American writers' website. "Have you read the other African on this site?" somebody wrote to me. So I went searching for the other African. He was from Kenya. We read each other's work and discovered that we both loved Camara Laye and the African Writers Series.

Maybe I sensed even then, so early, that he would become not just a beloved friend but also a kind of partner without a single name: my reader, collaborator, co-literary-journey-taker. Our sensibilities were different. We often disagreed fiercely, and yet I have never since received feedback that I so trusted and respected.

Literature was his god. It fed his roving, luminous curiosity. He thought himself an unworthy practitioner. "I haven't found the language yet," he told me once, about a piece he had been wanting to write for years. He agonized about writing, and his agonized emails were exquisite examples of writing. I admired his sentences, how they seemed to float on the page. I admired his circuitous style, his impatience with any form of constraint, his willingness to lose if it might make him find. And to lose what?

Convention, tepid safety, rules. His writing was full of courage that he would never have called courage, and a kind of emotional integrity that wore itself very lightly.

He loved Africa, in a way that intuitively and intimately understood its shine and its brokenness. This love mattered, because it lay underneath so much of what he wrote. Because his purest joys were literary, he believed in what literature could do, as art but also as history and as a bracing salve to African wounds. He discovered, in his never-ending questing way, stories of Ghana and Zimbabwe and Sudan, stories of dignity and trade and relationships, and he would regale me with them, with an almost childlike delight and also a sadness at how unknown these stories were. He wanted to write them all, and he knew he would be unable to write them all. Sometimes it felt as if he desperately hungered to hasten Africa into its awaiting glory.

I learned so much from him, as a person and as a writer: his humor and mischief, his wit, his generosity, his optimism, his kindness, his astonishing brilliance, his contradictions, his vulnerability, and his open aching humanness. He was one of the greatest minds I have ever known. He was one of those rare people whose unique complexity is so difficult to fully express that I cannot help but resort to boring language: he was an original.

—CHIMAMANDA NGOZI ADICHIE, LAGOS, JULY 2022

The First Story

The first story I ever wrote was in 1995. Or 1996. Or it could have been as early as 1993 or 1994. It was set in a heaven where Africans went to die. I am desperate to find it. I remember the lead character was called Jango. There was a sentence in it about his mind being like a "helium balloon." It was published on some website that mostly American writers frequented called purification.com. Is there no way of recovering it?

—Binyavanga Wainaina

The first short story Binyavanga Wainaina ever wrote was published in 1996. More than two decades later, he wrote to me, desperate to find it. His memory, I will note, was misleading: purification.com does not exist. The amateur writing community he submitted his work to was Pure Fiction, which published him in an indelicately titled section called the "Electronic Slush Pile."

He was not ashamed of his humble literary origins.

Binyavanga was twenty-five years old at the time. He wrote the story on a shared desktop computer at a backpackers' hostel in Cape Town, and sent it in from a dial-up connection at the internet café in its basement. When it was published, the Earth did not move. It would take a few more years of effort before he could break into newspapers and magazines, and several more to attract the attention of the world's leading literary publications.

If you were looking for clues to his eventual literary success, however, you could do no better than to begin with this story. "Binguni!" is an ambitious fantasy of spirituality, sexuality, discovery, and death, but strikingly unlike any other young writer's attempt to grapple with life's big questions. It's a declaration of character: insouciant, honest, and unpretentious, suffused with wit and charm, tinged by a yearning to connect, and bathed in the glow of limitless possibility that his early life, much like the early internet, once offered.

1

Binguni!

Two goldfish were arguing in their bowl: "If there is no God, who changes our water every week?"

Allotropy: (ə-ˈlä-trə-pē) *n*. The property of certain elements to exist in two or more distinct forms.

I

Dawn, December 27, 1999

Jango had often pictured his imagination as a helium-filled balloon, rather than one containing air. As he rose above the wreckage of the car, a whole-body feeling came over him. His life had ended, the string was cut, and his imagination was free to merge with reality. He felt immensely liberated—like he was flexing muscles that had not been used in a long time.

Oh, to stretch! His body felt loose-limbed and weightless, and his mind poised to soar. How could he have stayed in cramped earthliness for so long? How could he have forgotten this feeling? Had he not once danced with stars and had dalliances with gods?

Was he dreaming? Or was this part of some spectral past life? He felt no trauma of the type normally associated with violent death. Right now, he was rather piqued that he had missed out on the nonstop partying that was taking place all over the world. He hugged himself and found that his body seemed intact. He found it odd that he did not seem to feel the trepidation he would have expected if there was a possibility that he was destined for Pastor Vimba's "LAKE OF FIYYRRE!," which starred a leering Red Devil and promised "EEETERNALL DAMNATIONNN!" He giggled at the thought. "Tsk, tsk, Jango," he said to himself. "You're getting above yourself!"

Oddly enough, right now the thought of going to "Heaven" and spending eternity dressed in white robes, blissfully ensconced behind Pearly Gates while drinking nectar or listening to harps, was depressing. After spending most of his life in Johannesburg, and especially after the hedonism of the past few days, the "fires of hell" acquired a certain appeal.

There was another possible destination, though. His father's mania—to become an esteemed ancestor, as Zulu tradition dictated. Yet he could not visualize himself tolerating eternity as an "Outraged Ancestor," imposing droughts and plagues on disobedient descendants and anybody else who happened to be in the vicinity. Ancestor worship was a religion his father had tried to drum (quite often literally) into his head, and it was one he had discarded with relief. The concept of ancestors scrutinizing and guiding people's lives had always inspired images of power-mad old voyeurs playing African roulette (giggle, giggle . . . whom shall we play with next—Rwanda?).

What if one descended from a long line of assholes?

He thought to himself that if he had a choice, he would not mind being dispatched to some sort of Spectral Cyberspace, if such a fanciful place could exist. Hmm, yes. Maybe he was on his way to a place where nobody would dictate to him how to live his life.

Oops.

Afterlife.

Pah! Banish the thought. There were probably harp-playing Censors lovingly denying souls/spirits/whatever their daily fix of Ambrosia if they did not conform.

As he floated with a sort of predetermined aimlessness, he delighted in his new rubber-bandy self, vaguely wondering why he seemed to have carried his body with him. Surely his real body was still getting intimate with the mangled metal of his car?

He looked down at the surrealistic African vista below him. It was as if, as the Earth relinquished its pull on him, he relinquished all the trauma that he expected to have felt after the accident—relinquished all the weighty emotions and burdensome responsibilities that did not endear themselves to his new weightless self.

Or maybe he was still stoned from the party.

Around and below him, the Earth had decided to stake its claim. A sudden gust of wind whipped itself up into a frenzy of anger, and lightning seared the ground. Thunder roared as if backing up the sky's claim on him. Massive, engorged clouds lay low and gave birth to reluctant raindrops.

This drama had no physical effect on him. It seemed that he was in a dimension beyond Earth now. He could not remain unmoved by her mourning, though. As the wind wailed in fury, he mimicked it, roaring his farewell to her.

Meanwhile, fast asleep at her home in Diepkloof, Soweto, Mama Jango moaned as the cloud of unformed premonition that floated past her house darkened her pedestrian dreams. A shadow of loss chilled her briefly. Later she would wonder, and trusty Pastor Vimba would come up with a satisfactory supernatural explanation.

Meanwhile, exultation welled in Jango as he looked below him and saw the grand panorama of the storm-enlivened city. A powerful love for what had been his adopted home for twenty-seven years overwhelmed him. Wordsworth's famous sonnet, a personal favorite, came to mind, and he laughed, stretching his arms wide and bellowing:

Earth has not anything to show more fair:
Dull would he be of soul who could pass by
A sight so FUCKING touching in its majesty:
This City now doth, like a garment, wear . . .

Suddenly a force lifted the flat veld and highways as if they were merely a tablecloth and swallowed them. In no time everything earthly below him—the mine dumps, squatter camps, towers, domes, theaters, and temples of Johannesburg—disappeared the same way. Evaporated by something that seemed to have no substance or form.

Jango found himself surrounded by nothingness.

And all that mighty heart is lying still.

Stasis.

Silence so absolute, it screamed louder than anything he had ever experienced.

The sensation was terrifying. Utter nothingness surrounded him. There was no light, no darkness, nothing to feel or touch. Unearthly cold imprisoned his body. He began to shake and shudder, but soon even his shudders became sluggish and eventually ceased. He was immobile.

In the absolute silence, he could not tell whether he was still floating. An excruciating numbness began to spread all over his body. Soon his body lost all feeling. He lowered his eyes to see what was happening, and to his horror saw that something was eliminating it with a devastating silence.

As if it had never been there.

Finally, only the feeling that his mind was present remained, and it screamed into the nothingness to make itself heard. It tried all manner of activities to convince itself that it would be all right, but waves and waves of self-doubt assaulted it as it found nothing to compare or process. Nothing to perceive.

Not even an echo.

Shutdown began in some areas of his mind, and the rest reacted by exaggerating their most recent functions. "Oh, shit! This is it!" he thought frantically to himself. "This is how it ends." Huge, terribly distorted images thrust themselves to the forefront of his consciousness as it tried to resist the terrible finality of its surroundings. Now all that remained were the screams of tortured metal, flashing lights, his crazed screams, and the smell of feces and smoke. His mind accepted these gratefully as evidence that there was existence, that he did exist. These scenes played themselves over and over as the shutdown continued undeterred, becoming more and more scrambled and indecipherable as more functions shut down.

Then there was just nothing.

II

> Is it a kind of dream . . . following the river of death downstream?
>
> —Art Garfunkel

Something enveloped him luxuriously. Light, or a beginning of awareness?

Starting with his toes, he tingled with it and it spread until every part of him glowed with its warmth. It was the strangest feeling, as if he had been re-created as light—his shape a memory of his earthly body. Nothingness still surrounded him, but he was now a spiritual glowworm, cocooned in what he could think of only as a life-fire. Every part of him took flame, as his body-memory emphatically affirmed and embraced his being. Tiny raptures exploded all over his mind—life thrills and memories concentrated into tiny capsules of pure feeling.

Again, his recent trauma seemed to have had no major effect on him. He did not want to try to understand it. He felt so good.

Children dressed in all manner of cultural pajamas floated past him, playing in their dreamscapes as if this place was home.

Again, that feeling of acquaintance with this place struck him. This time he was sure that, at some early part of his life, he had straddled this place and Earth without conflict. Oh, to bathe in this light again!

He felt a fleeting sadness that these children would soon be tethered to life on Earth as its chains embraced them with ever-increasing possessiveness. Don't wake me up, Mummy!

"Enjoy it while you can, kids," he thought.

He looked above him and saw his naked body mirrored and magnified in a huge translucent gelatinous mass that covered the sky. Saw the long black limbs, the chunky muscle. The hated feet were stretched taut. Saw the face, a rictus of anticipation. Then his eyes trampolined the soft large lips and clambered up the jutting mountains that were his cheekbones, scratching themselves against his toothbrush stubble on their way up.

Looking down from the summit, they were hypnotized by two large eye-pools below. Irresistibly drawn to their twins, they dived off the cliff into themselves and his soul swallowed them.

Light! Oozing out of the mirrored eyes. Light stained brown with their color lit the cloud, dazzling Jango with its brilliance. Oh, the ecstasy! It was his light! His essence! He could feel it coming alive in his body, burning its way up from his feet to his neck, roller-coastering through the pathways of his mind, setting them alight with its force, then blazing out of his eyes to meet its reflection. They made contact, and the universe around him exploded.

He was somewhere else.

His eyes took time to adjust to the light. He was in a world that seemed comprised of nothing but living color. Dancing light was all around him. Heavenly shadows? Directly in front of him, a small tornado of light twisted itself and took on the shape of a person. Then it began to fade and assumed more human features.

An old man had materialized before him. An extremely sour-faced old man. His hair was waist long and in dreadlocks. He wore a three-piece suit, complete with bowler hat. Instead of a tie, there was what looked like a desiccated human ear at the end of a leather thong around his neck. The old man was squatting, African-fashion, and hovered three feet in the air, fiddling with the ear as though it was some kind of talisman.

It was around this time that it occurred to Jango that this was no Heavenly Emissary. His helium balloon began to lose altitude.

Bleak, bitter eyes turned to face him.

"Ah, you're the newcomer," he began. "I presume my accent is comprehensible to you. I learned it in anticipation of your arrival. Let me see . . . Black, English-speaking, Dekaff, I believe you would call it . . . er . . . with a slight urban Zulu accent . . . car accident on the Johannesburg–Pretoria highway. Pity about the BMW . . ."

Jango did not find this dour-peeping Thabo amusing. Was that really a human ear? A white man's ear? Did they not have a Public Relations Department here? This man was more bitter than malaria medication. Yup, no chance this was Heaven. Oh, shit! This was either Hell or Rwandan Rouletteville.

"Hima Tata!" he burst out. "Where is this place and who the—er—Heaven are you? Is this some sort of celestial prank?"

Malaria Face adopted an even sourer expression—if that was possible. "I have often thought so. I am Kariuki, and you are now in what we call African Binguni, part of the Otherworld. Souls here have complete freedom to explore just how mad they can be. You would not believe what perversions prowl in this place. I left Binguni in disgust. Nothing is sacred to these immoral Immortals. I am waiting to be transferred to African Presbyteria; you'd do well to do the same. Their harp band is famous all over the heavens!"

Jango shuddered. Any place this anally overburdened bodypart collector did not like was probably his kind of Heaven. This African Binguni place sounded like fun.

A thin smile distorted the old man's features. "I understand you are one of the highlights at the millennial celebrations; they have chosen you for their insane new experiment. I do not envy you. Now enough chitchat: I will summon Mshale on the Supernet, and he will take you to the millennial festivities."

"Wait a second: who is Mshale and what experiment?"

The Churl harrumphed: "He is one of your ancestors, a disreputable pervert even by the standards here. Now shut up—they will explain all to you. My work in this hellhole is finished."

One of the floating cloudlike things turned into a large screen. With considerable surprise, Jango recognized what looked like a poached version of the Netscape Navigator on the screen. The only real difference was that "Binguniscape" was what was written in the left-hand corner. Jango dazedly wondered what they did about copyright as he watched Kariuki reach out a hand and scribble on the screen:

HTTPS://AFTERLIFE

And a website appeared on the screen:

WELCOME TO THE HEAVENLY WEB! THIS MESSAGE
IS SPONSORED BY THE SUPPLIERS OF COMPUTER
SOUL-STUFF TO BINGUNI

Kariuki mumbled, "Can't be bothered to learn drumsong compuspeak," and wrote "AA.JangotoMshale@AncestralFair" on the screen. Jango was unable to express his astonishment as he suddenly found himself surrounded by darkness.

First to appear was a blue light that slowly formed itself into a banner reading: WELCOME TO THE MILLENNIAL ANCESTRAL FAIR.

Then the ground began to unravel itself: an unrolling carpet of hard, unrelenting African earth, briefly tinted blue by the now fading light of the banner. Grassland, acacia trees, and scrub covered the ground. In the distance, Jango could see a feeding herd of wildebeests and zebras. A minuscule shaft of light appeared on the horizon, growing rapidly and becoming the sun. Its bright white light drowned the banner, then it turned red and sunset burned the ground and trees with its color. On the horizon, the light shadows danced, numinous mirages of humanity. From a distance Jango heard drums beating, and they grew louder—seeming to be coming from closer and closer. He stood still in fascination as this supernatural Cyberdrama unfolded.

As he dazedly wondered who designed this Supernatural Website, an enormous bellow interrupted the download, and it was followed by a string of curses in a combination of Zulu, English, and a language Jango didn't even know existed. Somewhere in the background he could hear music.

"HAYIBO! THAT FUCKING KARIUKI'S DONE IT TO ME AGAIN!"

The voice sounded much closer now, and a body had begun to materialize next to Jango. The huge sweating figure that appeared in front of him could only have been the Notorious Mshale, his great-grandfather. Dressed like a cross between Elvis and a Hollywood version of "What an African Warrior Should Look Like," he wore a leopard-skin loincloth that had ridden up his thigh, leaving the head of a huge dangling penis clearly visible below the hem. A leather waistcoat studded with rhinestones barely covered his heavily muscled torso. His hair was dreadlocked, pomaded, and piled on his head—sort of an Elvis-becomes-a-Rastafari hairdo.

The man even wore blue suede shoes.

Mumbling to himself in Zulu, he tugged the hem of the loincloth down and rearranged his organ. "Damned internet!" he boomed. "It really does pick its moments. One day soon I'll get revenge on that prig of a Gatekeeper!"

"Hello, Tat'omkulu. I am Jango."

Mshale laughed. "Do I look like a grandfather to you! Call me Mshale. I don't stand on ceremony. Sorry about my outfit—I was performing a striptease for some maidens from Arabian Binguni. I understand that you're another one who doesn't speak Zulu, eh? You don't know what you're missing, *bhuti,* it is the sexiest language in Binguni. Yo! You should hear me doing Elvis in Zulu—the man himself has come to Binguni to see me perform!"

Jango, the free-thinking, "anything goes" liberal, was beginning to feel a tad conservative and old-fashioned. What would his "the Ancestors are governing your morals" father have to say about this rock-and-roll-in-the-hay ancestor?

"How did you die by the way?" Mshale asked.

"I had attended a druggy New Age bash, one of those 'I love the whole world' millennial parties, and on the way home my car somewhat overeagerly decided to hug a lamppost—at 150 kilometers an hour . . ."

"And the rest is Ancestral, eh! Hayibo! You're lucky to have such a glamorous death! Would you believe the blasted flu killed me! Me! The great Induna, lover of all women! Come on, we don't have much time. I have a roomful of maidens baying for my presence. Let's get to the party!"

Jango's hand was grabbed by a huge, horny paw. Mshale mumbled something in Zulu and their surroundings disappeared.

Before any scenes appeared before Jango, the smell assaulted him, pungent and tropical, the smell of a marketplace or a marriage feast. Frenzy, sweat, musk, and sensual heat—the smell of abandon.

The noise followed. It was loud and disorganized. He could hear laughter, conversation, and song, in a bewildering assortment of languages. It did not sound like anything Jango had ever encountered. It was as if he could hear every individual's input and everybody's drone all at once. The sheer intensity of it was unnerving, and his mind struggled to unscramble the confusion. Soon, amid the gibberish, he could hear snatches of sounds that his consciousness could make sense of.

"SALE! SALE! ENHANCE YOUR GLOW, SURF MY NEW SOULSITE FOR THE BARGAIN PRICE OF ONLY TWO HU-MANITIES OF PAIN!"

"SPECTRAL SEX . . . CHECK OUT WHAT MY GENE-MEMORY HAS COME UP WITH!"

Even a jingle?

"SOUL-SYTE DESIGNS . . . FOR A TRULY SPIRITUAL SITE—SOOUUL SYTE!"

"SIGN UP FOR A COURSE IN THE NIGGAHS' NEW DRUMSONG COMPUSPEAK . . . KEYBOARDS ARE PASSÉ!"

"MAMA SQUEEZA'S SOUL BREW . . . AN UNEARTHLY HIGH!"

Going off to the soul clinic; I haven't been feeling ecstatic lately.

"THE 'PHECAL MATYRS' IN CONCERT! TAKE A TRIP ON THE DARK SIDE!"

"PUTTY & THE BLOWFISH: BODY MEMORY REPAIRS!"

"JOIN THE CYBER-BER QUICKENING! ACHIEVE NIRVANA!"

"EXPERIENCE PURE AGONY . . . RECENT ARRIVALS FROM RWANDA!"

"TIRED OF JOY? TAKE PACKAGE TOUR TO BINGUNI DARK. ECSTATIC AGONY!"

"DUMP SOME PAIN ON A DICTATOR HERE!"

Before he'd had time to get his bearings, they were plunged into a maelstrom of humanity. What seemed to be a crossroad of souls, rushing in all directions, each hindering the other. Faces thrust themselves in his sight as he dumbly followed Mshale. Huge grins as if from convex and concave mirrors surrounded him, laughing, chanting, singing, arguing.

They were illuminated by revelation, faces overcome with amazement, eyes shining with enthusiasm, pupils dilated with joy, love, passion, and intensity. There seemed to be no logic to their appearance. Bodies danced with scant regard for anatomy or physics. A few passed right through him, leaving varied and intimate flavors of themselves in him. With every step, a swarm of locusts went wild in his insides.

The people who passed through his body seemed to infect it

with their exuberance, and he found it hard to contain himself. A flood of hysterical laughter rose, threatening to engulf his control. He clenched his teeth and swallowed it down. It was promptly replaced by nausea. He much preferred that.

"Are you all right, bhuti?" Jango nodded. "Keep yourself together, we're nearly there. The Welcome is usually more restrained, but we're celebrating, and we have been waiting long for you."

Finally, with Jango feeling rather like he had overdosed on something illegal, they arrived at the Millennial Ancestral Fair, or maybe it had found them. Jango was not sure what was where, or if anything was anywhere. "This is a dream," he thought. "I have smoked too much pot and I am tripping."

He did not need to pinch himself, for Mshale's sledgehammer of a hand walloped his back and brought him to a stinging awareness of his surroundings.

"Welcome!" boomed Mshale. "What do you think of this madhouse, eh?"

What a madhouse it was. Unearthly chaos. And its sensory impact was devastating. He felt as if the world he was in was in constant motion; there was no foundation. His senses were being overwhelmed from every direction.

There was no time to absorb or digest the impact, and even if there had been he did not think that he would have made any logic of what was going on around him. It was as if people here expressed themselves with all senses through a multitude of media and dimensions. He could feel communication bypass his conscious mind and flow into his subconscious. Buttons rusty with disuse were pushed, and doors opened to raw, virgin sections of his mind.

What was most terrifying was that, for the first time he could recall, the thin crust that was logic, civilization, reason, and manners was not in control; it had gone off to a far place and was helplessly observing the body it had served so loyally for twenty-seven years being taken over by pure primal sensation.

He laughed wildly, thinking, "Shit, now this is Multimedia!" The laugh turned into a growl, then exploded into an animal screech. His mind was wide open with all the filters gone, and its unprotected core was being singed by uncontrolled input.

From far away he heard Mshale's voice saying harshly, "Sorry, bhuti, hold on for a bit and I will seal you off from this." Amid the pandemonium that surrounded him, he glimpsed a flash of dreadlocks and he felt Mshale's huge arms around his body. Then something that felt like cool water entered his overheated consciousness and covered it. Relief! His mind attempted a brief resistance against this foreign invader, but a deep gravelly voice crooned it to acquiescence. Finally, he felt himself completely surrounded by a pungent maleness. There was an almost sexual intimacy in the feeling that was disturbing. All his five senses could perceive Mshale completely. Coarse facial hair thrusting through skin and a shock of testosterone.

He remained quiescent as his mind calmed down. Mshale's grip on it was solid and nothing penetrated. After a while, Mshale's grip relaxed, and his consciousness began to communicate softly with Jango's.

"This is my fault, bhuti. We were so excited by your arrival, we forgot that you have not been formatted to face us all together."

He chuckled, and Jango shuddered at the soothing vibration of it.

"You should feel complimented; it is not so often I soul-merge with a man."

He could feel that the sinews of Mshale's body intertwined with his as they gripped his body powerfully, calming the violent shudders. He could hear vibrations, and it seemed that somebody was communicating with Mshale, a deeper, more resonant sentience, not as gravelly or harsh.

"Jango," throbbed Mshale, "I have spoken to Senkou. He is

an old soul, the one who chose you for this mission. He will re-place me as your mind's environment; he's better at this than I am."

That elicited a brief flutter of panic. "Relax," a murmur throbbed. "It will be seamless."

He could feel Mshale's essence seep out of him as another replaced him. Initially, it was difficult to discern the flavor of this person as it mingled with Mshale's pungency. Gradually, he had the sense of a deep, almost bottomless personality: it resonated antiquity and calmness. In contrast to Mshale, he could feel little of this person's physical presence. Another difference was the bizarre sensation that certain essences of himself occurred in this person. This part of the foreign consciousness instantly entered Jango's consciousness and merged with its twin, giving him a feeling of peculiar comfort.

"I wish you peace and many raptures."

What a voice. Ripples as a pebble sank in deep waters.

Away in South Africa
and England

In 1991, at the age of twenty, Binyavanga Wainaina moved from Kenya to South Africa. It wasn't wholly intentional. A few years before, two maternal uncles had been recruited to teach at the university in Mthatha (also known as Umtata), the capital of an apartheid-era region called Transkei. Then, his sister Ciru finished school, and their parents decided to send her to university in Mthatha, reassured by the family connections there. Binyavanga, who was already at university in Nairobi at the time, was sent along to accompany her. He enrolled in a commerce degree, hoping to become a chartered accountant.

Years later, writing in the South African newspaper *Business Day,* he described his motives: "I wanted to be a hard-working, middle-class boy from Africa and earn R16,000 a month as a chartered accountant, buy a sixteen-valve car, pretend to fall in love with a yellow-skinned girl who looked like she lived in an R&B video, and pose cool. I had an S-curl, and Xhosa girls told me I looked like Luther Vandross. That made me very happy."

But his dreams of middle-class bliss were short-lived. He missed classes, failed exams, and took to locking himself up in his dormitory room. Worse, having never converted his visa to the right category, he was living in South Africa illegally and getting by on a succession of tourist visas. The study of commerce did nothing for him, but the country—in the final throes of its transition from apartheid to democracy—thrilled him. "Every day it felt as if South Africa would break. Every few weeks in the 1990s, students would gather and march and it was the most beautiful and terrifying thing I had ever encountered," he wrote in *Business Day*.

By the mid 1990s, he was done pretending. He packed up and moved to Cape Town to discover himself, to write—and, mostly, to cook. With the help of an old friend, he took over the café at the Pan-African market, a prominent local institution. When the venture failed, he ran a small restaurant that served food from all over the African continent. His final foray in the food business was a catering operation, which he closed in frustration shortly after one of his clients, a housewife in Constantia—the wealthy Cape Town suburb that was home to both Margaret Thatcher's son and Princess Diana's brother—asked if he could come dressed in a loincloth to bring a dash of authenticity to her fortnightly ladies' lunch.

In many ways, Binyavanga was formed as much by food as by the experience of living in South Africa. It wasn't merely the making and eating of it that excited him, but the living of it; he threw himself into the worlds that food made. He took the cuisine of the Cameroonian coast as seriously as you would expect an ordinary writer to treat French haute cuisine; he elevated despised foods, like offal, to art; and he burnished the everyday rituals of cleaning and cooking and seasoning with a positively erotic sheen.

A few years and several events later, it was time to leave home again to study in England. As the winner of the Caine Prize for African Writing in 2002, he was entitled to study anywhere in England he wished, on the organizer's dime. He chose a writing course at the University of East Anglia, and settled into an interesting relationship with the country that was something of a spectral presence back home. (Binyavanga was born just eight years into Kenya's independence, and his parents grew up as colonial subjects of the British Empire.) By turns delighted, amused, detached, and dismissive, he made his peace with the specter, culminating in a kind of personal triumph when he discovered he preferred the freedom and opportunity of the United States.

2

A Foreigner in Cape Town

Kwerekwere. Derogatory term meaning an African from outside South Africa. Used mainly around Johannesburg, but more recently around the rest of South Africa by Black people.

Kwerekweres are said to be dark and overambitious. We are supposed to be very good at two things: selling things on street corners and *muti*.

Our main crime is stealing jobs and women.

Maghana. Same as above. Used mainly in the Eastern Cape and the former Transkei. Referred originally to immigrants brought into Transkei and Ciskei from Uganda and Ghana as teachers, civil servants, and doctors when the Homelands were given "independence" in 1976.

I had been in South Africa for a year before I first encountered bigotry. I was sitting in a minibus taxi, on my way to Kwa-Makhutha, one of the large townships just far away enough from Port Elizabeth to keep property prices stable and near enough to provide a pool of cheap labor for the large car manufacturers.

A large woman with improbably clear skin stared at me for

most of the way. After a while, irresistibly driven, she asked, "Are you maghana?"

I said, "No. I'm from Kenya."

She smiled and said, "Yuuu! You are *handsome*! You maghana men are so handsome-yuuu, but your women are ugly! They are Black! Black! Black! and they have big muscles!"

Minibus taxis are not big vehicles. If you say something to someone, you speak to fifteen people. A debate erupted in Xhosa, about the ugliness of amaghana.

Then the inevitable question, "What are you doing in our country?"

"I am a student."

One guy asked me if there are nice cars in Kenya, like the ones in Ghana. I said yes.

I wasn't sure where to get off, so I asked. Several people told me they knew the house. On the way there, one of the guys offered me a beer. We stopped at a shebeen and had a few quarts of beer. I wasn't allowed to pay. Eventually, I was taken to my friend's house. They waited until I was safely inside, and we said goodbye.

I have lived in South Africa for ten years. One of the hottest issues right now is the xenophobic treatment of Black African immigrants by Black South Africans. It is an issue that I have tended to avoid.

I have found Black South Africans, from all parts of the country, to be hospitable to a fault. I have made many firm friendships of the best sort. Friendships that have survived adverse times.

Yet many people I know—honest, hardworking people—have been beaten, thrown off trains, verbally abused, even had their documents torn up.

Part of the problem is transference. There is now a Black government, but whites and a near-invisible new class of Black people retain their economic stranglehold on the country: seventy percent of the economy is controlled by five or six companies.

The education system for Black people was among the worst

in Africa. People were taught *nothing* about the rest of Africa. Nothing, that is, unless it involved genocide, cannibalistic dictators, savage tribes, drought, and civil war. The media played the same role.

Until the 1990s, South Africans in general were not allowed to learn about evolution in state-sponsored schools.

So suddenly to have all these well-spoken dark people flood the country—people with many degrees, diplomas, people whom you could communicate with only in English—it was easy to transfer the hate to them.

In the mining cities and towns the problem has been there for much longer. Workers have been imported from Mozambique, Zimbabwe, Lesotho, and Swaziland to work in mines for over fifty years. When workers came to the cities to work, they were segregated according to community. For a long time there weren't any problems. Then the layoffs started. Gold prices plummeted, recession hit. The riots and upheavals of the 1980s encouraged the mining houses to invest more in foreign labor. South Africans were "troublesome."

As workers across the country started to unionize, labor from nearby countries became more attractive. They didn't strike. They would accept lower wages. They were docile.

They could be deported.

The same thing was happening higher up the ladder. For years, well-educated Zimbabweans, Zambians, and Basotho got managerial positions. Academics from all over Africa started getting jobs in the former white universities. Most avoided politics at a time when fence-sitting seemed like betrayal.

To be fair, many African academics supported the idea of a new constitution and free elections. But after the disasters in their own countries, most were against the unions and the proponents of things like nationalization.

We have been there. Done that. We just couldn't afford the T-shirt.

Sadly, many expatriate Africans missed something special. Their fears blinded them to the great changes that were going on. Many failed to see the obvious. The ANC government-in-waiting was far more democratic and organized than the ruling National Party. Black South Africans were not all a bunch of card-carrying union members in red T-shirts. The common understanding among Black opinion was that differences could not be allowed to exist while a Black government was not in power.

Elections came and went. Africa celebrated. Then the refugees and immigrants came streaming in. Today, Hillbrow, once Johannesburg's only multiracial suburb—home to artists, musicians, and thinkers—has become a fortress controlled by Nigerian druglords. Crime is probably higher here than in any other inner-city area anywhere in the world. Crack cocaine has hit the streets, and it seems like every gun in Mozambique's civil war has found itself in South Africa.

These are the inevitable results of poor policing in a country that had no experience in the flip side of globalization. The Nigerians managed, despite their small numbers, to be voluble and flashy enough to take the blame for the whole problem.

The press didn't help any. The country's largest weekly screamed that there were eight million illegal immigrants—statistics that have yet to be substantiated. The liberal white media was full of sob stories about innocent South African girls in jail in Rio after being deceived by their Nigerian boyfriends.

Somehow, the fact that the Chinese triads and Russian mafia are the main players in this trade managed to escape wide coverage.

The more liberal papers, relieved that Black people were now being seen as bigots, became the champions of the poor downtrodden Africans. By 1999, having a darker than usual skin or an unfamiliar accent could get you picked up by police and deported.

Most expatriate Africans I know have been harassed at one time or another. A well-known TV and radio personality was once picked up at night, together with his wife and children, and left at the Zimbabwe border. His bank accounts were frozen.

It is common for people's papers to be thrown away or burned. It has become a great cash cow for policemen.

While the issue got hotter and hotter, many pertinent facts got lost in the hysteria.

The rest of Africa has been by far the largest investor in South Africa since 1994. It is also South Africa's largest trading partner.

Seventy percent of tourist arrival to South Africa is from the rest of Africa, a fact that manages to escape the marketing strategy of the South African Tourist Authorities. Most Africans who come to Johannesburg come to stock up on goods to sell in their home countries. They spend *billions* of rand every year buying anything from luxury cars to ladies' panties.

Most of the immigrants—legal or otherwise—don't bother to look for employment. They arrive with small amounts of capital and start small businesses, many of which employ South Africans. At Greenmarket Square in Cape Town there are eighty-nine traders from the continent. They employ two hundred South Africans. Most immigrants don't plan to settle in South Africa. They send most of their profits home, mostly in the form of South African goods. When they have acquired a degree of financial security, most go back home.

South Africa's borders are very difficult to man. It is estimated that seventy percent of illegal immigrants who are deported to Zimbabwe and Mozambique are back in South Africa the next day.

Although unemployment remains a big problem (over fifty percent in some places), Black South Africans have enjoyed unprecedented income growth for the last fifteen years. The Black middle class, which was near nonexistent in the early 1970s, is now by far the largest middle class in the country. Times are not so bad.

Many Black professionals are benefiting from this. Many Black people can speak up to five languages. This gives them many advantages over whites in the job market.

One of the more distressing issues has been South Africa's eagerness to issue visas to people like Mobutu's generals and their families. In exchange, they brought a chunk of Congo's foreign reserves into the country.

A couple of years ago, I had a beer with a Congolese musician in Johannesburg. I asked him why he came to South Africa. He said to me, "I am just following my taxes."

Most whites read these changes as "Affirmative Action," discounting the genuine self-improvement efforts of Blacks. Crime that the police encouraged in the townships in the eighties has now spread to the white suburbs. Whites are now emigrating in droves. It has been estimated that more than ninety percent of white medical-school graduates leave the country before doing their internship.

The logical beneficiaries of this brain-drain would be Black South Africans and qualified Africans. Unfortunately, the South African government still prefers to bring in white professionals in many cases.

White expatriates in South Africa don't get accused of stealing jobs.

3

Food Slut

W hen I started to teach myself about African food, I found myself hitting a barrier: a lack of information.

There isn't even a comprehensive source of information for any of the individual countries in Africa, let alone one covering the diverse foods of the continent.

Searching on the internet proved not much better. On the World Wide Web, where you can have a conversation with an alien or learn everything there is to know about the eating habits of cockroaches, there is hardly any information on African cuisine. All I ended up with were millions of web references to starvation in Sierra Leone and food riots in Somalia.

Then there were the travel stories about runny stomachs and icky food, with the occasional comment by an "Africa expert" like: "There is nothing for the gourmet; most Kenyan cuisine is 'stomach-filling fodder,' mainly a gruelly substance called *ugali* [pap]."

Or: "Outside of the coast, most African food is bland and uninspired."

It is easy to take offense at such statements, and, like many on this continent, I guess my reaction could have been, "Why bother?" It is safer to ignore the whole thing and drink my coffee without caffeine. After all, like many of my generation, having never left this continent, I define myself as a follower of the popular culture of the Western world before I am African. A sad state of affairs but a truth. I blame *Dallas* and *Tom Sawyer*.

Our parents' generation had to painfully disassociate themselves from their cultural womb because it was so impossible to straddle the West and Africa and remain sane. The "progressives" of their generation had to be credible in their new world and that meant looking down upon what the Xhosa call the *abakwetha*.

My generation is not as burdened, but we have found that conforming still does not grant us respectability. That I know what fettucine is doesn't do very much for me.

Also, with the wisdom of emotional distance, we find ourselves philosophically bankrupt. We cannot even define ourselves in "the Western way," because that demands invention, innovation, and discovery, and none of these are humanly possible without roots.

But I didn't want to seek knowledge of African food out of anger. That would only have turned me into one of those Africanist mouthpieces who don't really believe, and I couldn't see myself gulping okra with passion simply because it was a symbol of "Our Great and Demolished Past." I enjoy food too much to insult it that way.

But the knock-knock of the little knowledge that was in my head refused to stop. There were so many things I ate as a child, delicacies prepared lovingly and possessing texture, flavor, and sophistication. So many things that stood out in my mental tastebuds even when I ate the best Italy had to offer.

Some of these dishes are traditional daily fare, like *matoke* (steamed plantain bananas with groundnut sauce). Others are ceremonial. Some are new urban dishes, like *mandazis* (*vetkoek* with coconut or overripe banana) or *kyinkyinga* (beef or liver kebabs with crushed nuts).

But it doesn't stop at the food. In most places in Africa, a meal is a celebration of togetherness, and a guest hasn't "visited" until he or she has eaten. Food is served on a communal platter for all to share, and enjoyment takes precedence over etiquette or small talk.

Yet in mainstream South Africa, and in many parts of Africa, the best cuisine that we have remains in villages and at town-hall weddings and taxi ranks.

And so we find ourselves in a demeaning situation: our cuisine is possessed by tourists. If I was a Martian tourist to South Africa, I would believe that people here subsist on a million variations of butternut soup, kudu, crocodile, and ostrich.

There are the places in Africa whose cuisine is called "great," but, commentators rush to add, Mozambican food has a lot of Portuguese influence, and Zanzibari and other cuisine is really Asian.

Really?

There's no mention of the fact that the same spices that influenced European food in the 1500s (when cloves were worth more than their weight in gold) influenced African food, or that Swahili cuisine has evolved over a thousand years—when will it belong to us?

I even read an article in *Fairlady* which implied that jambalaya is an offshoot of Spanish paella.

Really?

Jambalaya, which is an African word, is originally from West Africa. Eat jollof rice and try to deny that. Cajun cuisine, and indeed modern American cuisine, is very strongly influenced by West African food: peanuts were introduced to America by slaves, as was okra, while gumbo is a West African word meaning "food."

Such cuisine is as much ours as chop suey is Chinese.

Brazilian cuisine, with its use of okra, palm oil, and seafood, is also eerily similar to that of West Africa.

A Cape Town hotelier recently tried to explain to me why he felt he could not put African dishes on his menu. He took pains to explain that he loves pap and was brought up eating it on a farm. "But," he said with a sad expression on his face, "our clients are very discerning and they prefer something upmarket."

Upmarket, he says. It's one of those Capetonian words that can mislead a foreigner. (Another is "stunning," which can mean anything from "absolutely fabulous" to "I really hate this, but, being a Capetonian, I cannot dislike something unless it comes from Gauteng.")

"Upmarket" in this context meant "anything sold to me from somewhere really posh" (read "from outside this continent").

Surely what is uppest-market in South Africa, and on this continent, should be the delicacies we possess! Surely we should let the rest of the world ask *us* what all the excitement is about rather than waiting for it to be approved first by "overseas"!

It has been known for years that *mursik,* a Maasai yogurt, contains certain compounds, including saponins and several steroids, which, research has shown, decimate cholesterol. Apparently this is because of the tradition of mixing milk with cow's blood and a little cow dung (spicing), before storing it in gourds for a week or two. As a result, the Maasai, who traditionally eat mostly red meat, milk, and blood, live without fear of cardiovascular disease. Mursik also happens to be delicious. *Yet you cannot buy it in any Kenyan supermarket or shop.* So what's going to happen? Some American ex–Peace Corps worker will patent the recipe and market it as a wholesome, age-old addition to muesli, and middle-aged yuppies across the United States will fall over themselves to "become a warrior." By the time it's sold to us (at dollar value), it will be "upmarket."

The way I see it, this African renaissance business simply means refusing to undervalue the resources we possess and bringing them into the mainstream, making them a part of our "Western way."

It means being able to buy *morogo* (African spinach) in every supermarket.

It means being able to find as many cookbooks about Ghanaian cuisine as Thai cuisine in our bookshops.

It means having at least *one* cooking program on TV that shows us how to make food from this continent.

And it means having cooking schools that teach people to make *samp* (maize porridge) and beans, jollof rice and *moi-moi* (bamboo stuffed with vegetables and grilled over coals).

Now it would be easy to pass the buck and say, "What can I do about it? It is the fault of slavery-colonialism-apartheid oppression." But my father once gave me life-changing advice: "If you blame somebody for your situation, you deprive yourself of the power to solve the problem."

The reason I love to cook African food and continue to teach myself about it is not really because of all of the above. I just love to create, and there is no better or more "undiscovered" material than on this continent.

We ought to take possession of our culinary heritage. Let us stop calling it "ethnic" to disassociate it from ourselves. Let us make it part of our experience.

Maembe na Pilipili
(Mango and Peri-Peri Salad)
SERVES 8–10

5 sweet mangoes
1 pinch peri-peri
2 bags baby spinach
1 handful roasted red-skin
    peanuts (with skin)

DRESSING

1 pinch crushed fresh
    herbs (oregano, basil,
    and rosemary)
1 teaspoon virgin palm oil
    (peanut oil makes a
    good replacement)
1 tablespoon lemon juice
1 teaspoon honey

TO PREPARE:

Cut mango into bite-sized pieces (do not peel). Sprinkle the fleshy side with peri-peri. Arrange the baby spinach around the mango.

Mix all the ingredients for the dressing together in a container and drizzle over the salad.

Sprinkle the peanuts on the salad.

I had a memorable Kenyan meal at a friend's place in Sandton three years ago. We ate a roast leg of goat, *sukuma wiki* (curly kale), and *mukimo* with *njahi* beans.

There was bottle after bottle of Tusker beer to wash it down. The fresh goat and the njahi beans had been smuggled through Johannesburg airport by our enterprising hostess.

The beer came wrapped in a diplomatic pouch, and the curly kale was hijacked from the fish section at a nearby Pick 'n' Pay (it uses the green vegetables to dress the display). I am told that Pick 'n' Pay cameras in Johannesburg have learned to spot Kenyans as soon as they walk into the supermarket. "Warning to all fish-market staff—you are about to be undressed!"

What had brought me all the way from Umtata for this meal, though, was the mukimo made with njahi beans. There is no bean in the world that tastes quite like njahi.

There are some foods that love to play hard to get. I am not quite sure why. There is a legendary pineapple that sends tons of salivating Ghanaian expats home on holiday more often than they can afford because it does not grow anywhere else in the world.

Njahi is like that. Apart from the fact that she does not seem to grow outside East Africa (where she can still be difficult to find), she is also a very sexist bean. In Kikuyu culture, she is supposed to be reserved only for pregnant or breast-feeding women.

This is a particular taboo I take much pleasure in ignoring. The possible punishments (growing breasts, maybe, or being made to suffer monthly periods for eternity after death) don't bother me. The bean tastes *that* good.

Njahi is grown in the highlands of Kenya, from where the

Kikuyu people come. Legend has it that Gikuyu, the father of the Kikuyu people, settled near Mount Kenya with his wife, Mumbi. They had nine daughters, after whom the nine clans of the Kikuyu are named. I've always been curious about which nine men his nine daughters married. However, legends generally don't explain such things.

The highlands from where the Kikuyu come are better known in South Africa as the White Highlands, where a lot of white mischief took place. Needless to say, the Kikuyu were pissed off about what was going on in their land.

In Kikuyu, the word used for "food" is *irio*. The most basic irio is *githeri*, which comprises whole mealie kernels with beans. When mashed potatoes and shredded pumpkin or sweet potato leaves are introduced into the dish it is called mukimo, of which there are three main types.

Njug' mukimo is made from chickpeas, green mealies, and mashed potatoes. This is probably the original mukimo, as chickpeas are indigenous to Africa. Traditionally, mukimo is made with mealies that have been dried in a granary. This allows the dish to keep for longer but makes chewing difficult, especially since mukimo hardens after a while.

There is now a variety of mukimo made from peas (the ones the English call "mushy peas").

And there is mukimo made with njahi, a black bean that turns reddish when cooked. It has a long white crown that runs along its seam. What makes it so special is its musky and bitter flavor, which combines well with mashed potatoes and ripe bananas. It is said to be loaded with nutrients. I suppose it is because it is both scarce and vitamin-laden that it is reserved for breast-feeding and pregnant women. It is mixed with mashed ripe bananas and a little maize.

Incidentally, bone marrow is also traditionally reserved for mothers-to-be.

Mukimo used to be a complete meal on its own, but these days it is often eaten with a stew or grilled meat.

Mushy Pea Mukimo

SERVES 8–10

6 large mashing potatoes,
  quartered

250 grams split peas

Salt

1 pinch black pepper

2 onions, chopped very
  small

1 pinch curry powder

1 spoonful ghee or butter

1 tin whole mealie kernels

All-purpose seasoning

2 ripe bananas

1 clove garlic, crushed.

1 handful pumpkin leaves
  (or spinach), cut finely

TO PREPARE:

Put potatoes, peas, salt, and black pepper in a large pot and just cover with water. Cook on medium-high heat until the peas are cooked but still crunchy. This should take about 30 minutes.

While they are cooking, in a separate pan, brown the onions together with the curry powder in the ghee (or butter).

Mash the potato mixture thoroughly in the pot, making sure most of the peas get crushed.

Add the mealie kernels, the cooked onions, and the all-purpose seasoning to the pot and mix them in with a wooden spoon.

Mash the banana, mix it with garlic and black pepper, and work it into the mukimo as well.

Spoon two large spoonfuls of the mukimo into a pumpkin leaf.

Shingo Ya Kondoo Na Maziwa Lala
(Lamb's Neck Medallions with Mustard and *Amasi*)

SERVES 8–10

Salt

1 tablespoon English
  mustard

8 medallions lamb's neck

500 milliliters *amasi* (sour
  milk)

2 teaspoons honey

TO PREPARE:

Rub the salt and the mustard into the meat. Mix the sour milk and the honey, then cover the meat with the milk mixture. Marinate overnight.

Brown the medallions in a hot pan. Cook for 10–15 minutes, depending on how you like your meat, making sure to baste it with the remaining marinade so the meat remains moist.

I have never eaten a truffle, but I look forward to my first time.

Why would I look forward to eating something that has had an intimate relationship with a pig's nose? I do not know.

Food is a funny thing.

Right up there in that rarefied area where the haughtiest of gourmet things reside, I guess the test of the ultimate gourmunch is for it to come from the most dubious of backgrounds.

(Did you have a mental picture of a French guy with a big nose just then?—I did.)

It could be a hundred-year-old egg, a green-purple-fungus-ridden chunk of rotten-solid milk, enjoy-or-die kamikaze fish or, my personal favorite, bird's nest soup. My feeling is that if something can sound so utterly unappetizing and still be worth more than its weight in gold, it must be *true ambrosia*.

In the south of Ghana there is a relish called *shitor*.

It is brown.

It has a pungent smell.

It is also, without competition, the most delicious preserve I have eaten.

I'll go further. When made properly, it beats any other seafood preparation I have ever eaten.

I was introduced to shitor as a student in Umtata, South Africa, where there is a large Ghanaian expatriate community. We used to use a spoonful to revive the plastic (Uncle Ben's!) rice in the dining hall.

The main ingredient of the shitor I am familiar with is dried shrimp, dried prawns, or dried freshwater crayfish. I found out, though, that dried fish, dried beef, or dried chicken may also be used.

How shitor is made varies enormously from family to family and from place to place. The common thread is that it is used as a preserve. It is made from sun-dried and fry-dried ingredients and cooked with lots of vegetable oil so that it can be bottled and kept for a long time.

Ernestina Peprah, a Ghanaian expatriate now living in Johannesburg, told me that *shitor* means "pepper" in Ga. The Ga people come from southern Ghana, where the country's capital, Accra, is situated.

Shitor has been eaten in Ghana for a long time. Traditionally it is eaten with *kenkey* (fermented maize-meal cakes), fried fish, and vegetables. It is popular in towns and cities because it is handy and quick. To stretch it further, I mix chopped onions and tomatoes into it. It is also great with *waakye* rice boiled with black-eyed beans.

Cook the beans first and, when they are almost ready, add bicarbonate of soda—it makes them cook faster. Then add the rice to the bean mixture and cook as usual. This dish, which comes from the north of Ghana, is delicious served with shitor.

For me, shitor (the shrimp/crayfish one) expresses itself best in jollof rice, that universally popular West African dish. Mix one spoon of it into plain rice for a combination of flavors to rival the best pasta sauce.

We people from upcountry Kenya have a love–hate relationship with the coast.

It infuriates us how coastal people seem to just lounge on street corners and laugh the whole day; how they close their shops every afternoon to sit under coconut trees and gossip, moving only to follow the shadow of the tree; how they just shrug their shoulders nonchalantly when chaos comes their way.

Their in-your-face sexual confidence makes us feel like prudes. They speak Kiswahili, like we do, but for them conversation is the highest literary form. No clichés allowed; your imagery must be original, and interesting. Never repeat a simile. You are allowed to embellish the truth, insult your audience, be lascivious, even pretend to start a fight to spice up the conversation.

Just *never* be boring (like people from upcountry are).

The Mombasa jeer is calculated to reduce you to jelly. The Mombasa sneer melts the jelly, and you will just ooze away. We upcountry folk tend to be very quiet at the coast. Or we just stick to English. It's safer.

What we love about the coast is that it reminds us of simpler days. Days when we had time to talk—not just to exchange small talk. It makes us feel that we have eaten a bit too much of Europe.

There are generally two ways to avoid ridicule in Mombasa.

The first is to pretend to be from the coast. With dedication, and a lot of practice, you could get it right. *But you will have to keep your practice sessions a secret*. Nobody in Mombasa is afraid to laugh at you—out loud—if they spot your attempts.

The second option is to pretend to be *a foreigner*—from Uganda, South Africa, Upper Azania, anywhere. The coast has a long trading history, and foreigners are adored.

If you're considered a foreigner, your attempts to speak cliché-ridden Kiswahili will be loudly, and earnestly, *applauded*. Women will not look at you slowly from head to toe and sneer. They will giggle and wrap you in a veil of charm. They will find out what goodies you brought, whether you are married or not, and whether you have dollars. They will find out what the weather is like in your country, whether jobs are available, and how visas can be acquired.

The coast is full of Germans and Swiss who came for two weeks and ended up married. They wander about wrapped in kikois and a sexual haze.

I was once told a story about Mzee Kenyatta's (Kenya's first president) first visit to Kwale District at the coast. He met with people and asked, "How come you are so poor? This is a fertile place. How can we help you?"

They looked up at him and replied, "Mzee, Father of our Nation. We believe in development. We believe in progress. We want to develop Kwale. The problem is that it is very hot here. We don't want to ruin our hands. You see we use henna on our hands, and digging will spoil it. So we ask for tractors. If you give us tractors, we will develop Kwale."

Kenyatta looked at them for a long time, saw the elaborate decorations of henna on their soft hands and arms; saw the gold jewelry and the charming smiles. Then he said, "I see. Well, we must develop the Nation. If you want tractors, I will bring Kenya's best tractors here."

The women sang and danced around him. They composed *shairi* (musical praise poems). They surrounded him with perfume and gratitude.

Two weeks later, several bakkie-loads of Kikuyu farmers were delivered from upcountry. Two years later, Kwale was supplying Mombasa with fresh vegetables.

They got their tractors.

After its wit, food is what the coast province is best known for. When I was a child, we would go to the coast every December. My late mother had a Swahili friend, Mama Shimshad, who was the senior wife of a wealthy Swahili merchant. We would always spend a day at her house while my dad dug up golf courses. Cooking would take place for the better part of the day. The kitchen was situated in a walled courtyard at the back of the house. The kids would play, while the women ground, pounded, mixed, stirred, and gossiped.

While cooking for the main meal went on, we ate continuously. We would be plied with sweets, cashew nuts, enormous mangoes sprinkled with peri-peri, cassava crisps, lime juice, mandazis (coconut vetkoeks), *mabuyu* (sweet-and-sour baobab seeds), and peanut-and-caramel sweets. I would always have a pronounced waddle when I went back home.

Mama Shimshad and her co-wives would wear *kangas*—our national wraparound. Every kanga has a slogan or a wise saying. I saw an odd kanga in Cape Town once: the slogan read, "The goat has eaten the carpet."

We would be told stories about genies, strange sea creatures, and ghosts of Portuguese sailors trapped for eternity by the wiles of Swahili concubines. We would hear about black cats that prowled the streets at night looking for randy men to seduce. They would turn into beautiful women and occupy the men's souls.

Mama Shimshad would take us into the Old Town in the afternoon, and my late mother would spend hours haggling and buying fabrics, spices, and Objets de Mantelpiece. I loved to wander around the Old Town on my own. I would lose myself in the narrow streets, harass antiques-store owners by ransacking their stores for two-shilling treasures and one-shilling books. I would safely join street-corner conversations. Nobody would make a child feel uncomfortable.

I learned a lot about human nature on holiday at the coast. Many of my schoolmates disliked the place, or never left the north coast resorts, where the only locals were polite hotel employees.

I learned that the greatest pleasure in traveling is allowing yourself to be vulnerable to the cultural differences. This is the only way to see people as they are, and that is more interesting to me than any beach.

The monsoons have blown many influences on to the Kenyan coast for the last four thousand years. In AD 800, the Shirazi people of Persia introduced Islam to the East African coast. A thousand years later, the Sultanate of Oman moved its capital to Mombasa.

Swahili cuisine today is a melange of African, Middle Eastern, and Indian cuisine. Zanzibar is a puff of wind away, and its spices, together with the fresh ingredients of the tropical coast, form the basis of Swahili cuisine.

The range of seafood at the coast is quite spectacular. Rock lobster, oysters, tiger prawns, squid, octopus, shark, rock cod, sea bream, grey mullet, crab, sailfish, tuna, and so on.

Much of the food is grilled, baked in leaves or fried in a *karai*—a Kenyan version of the wok.

Plantains, yams, okra, cassava, various wild greens, spinach, and brinjals (eggplants) are also eaten. Coconut milk is used in most dishes. It tends to give the curries a creamy texture. Pishori rice (similar to Basmati rice), originally from Pakistan, and *roti* (chapatis) are the staple dishes.

Coconut Milk: First Press

Split coconut in half over a bowl, drain coconut water into the bowl, and set aside.

Remove flesh from shell and grate finely. You can use a blender. Place grated coconut into cheesecloth and twist as hard as possible to squeeze out the milk.

Open cloth, pour coconut water inside, and repeat the process.

Coconut Milk: Second Press

Place the remaining grated coconut in a bowl and pour a little boiling water on it.

Repeat the process.

This milk will be weaker, and is good for curries and sauces.

Coconut Spinach
SERVES 4

2 tablespoons vegetable oil
30 grams finely chopped onion
50 grams chopped fresh ginger

¼ chili, seeded and chopped
125 grams coconut milk— first press

½ kilogram of spinach,
   stalks removed,
   washed, and torn into
   large chunks

1 pinch salt

TO PREPARE:

Heat oil in a stewing pan, add onions, ginger, and chili. Fry briskly.

Add coconut milk and bring everything to a boil.

Add spinach leaves and salt. Cover and simmer for 5 minutes.

Crayfish in Coconut Turmeric Sauce

SERVES 4

4 large crayfish
30 grams butter
1 bunch fresh *dhania*
   (coriander leaves)
Salt
1 pinch of freshly milled
   black pepper

SAUCE

30 grams butter
60 grams onions, chopped
½ teaspoon turmeric
   powder
20 grams garlic, crushed

5 grams ginger, peeled and
   grated
½ chili, pounded in mortar
   till paste-like
2 cardamom seeds,
   crushed
30 grams fresh coriander
   leaves, finely chopped
1 pinch salt
Black pepper
500 milliliters first-press
   coconut milk (if lazy,
   buy coconut cream)

TO PREPARE:

Make the sauce: Heat the butter, then glaze the onions. Add the turmeric, garlic, ginger, chili, cardamom seeds, and coriander leaves.

Cook gently at low heat for 5 minutes.

Add salt, pepper, and coconut milk, and simmer for 20 minutes.

Serve with steamed rice, coconut spinach, roasted sweet potatoes, and tomato and onion salsa.

Swahili Braised Chicken

SERVES 4

15 grams garlic, crushed

15 grams fresh ginger, grated

2 tomatoes, sliced

1 green bell pepper, seeded, sliced

1 medium onion, chopped

Juice of 2 limes

1 large chicken, in pieces (2 breasts, 2 legs)

2 tablespoons oil

Salt and black pepper

400 milliliters coconut milk (first press)

TO PREPARE:

Blend garlic, ginger, tomatoes, pepper, onions, and lime juice until smooth.

Skin chicken, season with salt and pepper. Brush with oil and grill on a charcoal grill until crisp and brown on all sides.

Put a saucepan on the grill (find a place where the heat is low), pour in remaining oil, and fry the blended spice mix. Then add the coconut milk and simmer together for 10 minutes. Place the grilled chicken pieces in the sauce and bring back to boiling point. Simmer till the chicken is cooked through. Serve with rice or rotis.

I had always thought of myself as a "writah," as opposed to a journalist. Not for me the sordid, news-grabbing, fresh-scandal-sniffing lifestyle.

Oh, how we lie to ourselves. Somewhere between the abattoir and the smelly tripe butchery, it hit me that I am a journalist but with a different beat. My job is to investigate why Nigerians refuse to have garlic in their *ogbono* stew. Or whether one can dry shrimp for shitor relish in an oven or grill. One can't, and the process leaves one's kitchen smelling like a burnt fish market for days. I know.

These were the thoughts that passed through my mind as I watched the butcher wrap my smelly story—perforated sheep's stomach—in an editorial on "Cape Crime Gangs." I rushed home to cook it before the fat seeped through to the borrowed car's seats.

Now that I have whetted your appetites, I will lead you through the gruesome process of preparing my favorite dish, *mutura*. Mutura is the Kikuyu equivalent of Icelandic *slátur*, *träipen* from Luxembourg, Ukrainian *krov'yanka*, Irish blood sausage, and so on.

This, I guess, is where all the queasy vegetarians, and carnivores who think that meat is grown in cellophane-covered containers, depart. Those of you who insist that those vast cold rooms with hanging carcasses are just places where mafia dons do business, and French movie directors film sex scenes, will not survive this article.

There are various appetizers that Kikuyus adore: after harvest, fresh roasted or boiled white mealie cobs and roast sweet potatoes are common, while roast groundnuts are very popular in season.

On Sundays, though, a couple of slices of mutura are the only way to get the appetite going.

You see, Kikuyus, and more recently other Kenyans, are voracious carnivores at weekends. It is no coincidence that Kenya's best-known restaurant is called simply The Carnivore.

We call roast meat *nyama choma* or *nyamchom,* and on weekends herds of Kenyans leave the city and head upcountry to eat meat at family-friendly beer gardens. At the top end of the market, these places have swimming pools, fun fairs, and even golf courses. At the bottom end, there's beer, meat, and a psychotic barmaid.

Nyama choma is not prepared in the same way as a barbecue. The meat is not cut up into chops or steaks, but rather one goes to a butcher and picks the part of a hanging carcass one wants. Ribs, as well as whole leg, are especially popular.

Nyama choma is served with beer. Outside Nairobi, beer is served at room temperature, not because there are no fridges (even where they would normally be hard to find, Coca-Cola is generously provided) but because Kenyans love warm beer. It might be over 100 degrees outside, but we won't want our Tusker cold.

Why? Blame the British.

Or, on second thought, blame the Romans for colonizing the British and teaching them to sell inappropriate technology like straight roads, sunscreen, boiled mushy veggies, and Mr. Bean.

I once had an argument with a Kenyan barman who tried to tell me, with a straight face, that keeping beer in the fridge made it go flat.

The first time I tried to prepare mutura in Durban, my hosts assured me I'd be able to find tripe in the supermarket at a nearby mall. I searched but could not find the tripe.

Eventually, I noticed a pair of cling-wrapped nappies sitting next to the pickled tongue. Either this was tripe or there was an illegal alien who needed to be deported to the baby section. Yuk!

It reminded me of the nickname we gave tripe as children: towels. We hated it.

Fortunately, only adults are allowed to eat mutura—when one is able to drink a pint of beer without turning green, the palate is considered sophisticated enough to appreciate mutura.

I didn't think supermarkets would take the name "tripe" quite so literally. For any self-respecting Kikuyu, passing those chemically cleaned, baby.com things is like trying to convince a Dutch dairy farmer that those Day-Glo yellow plastic packages in the dairy section are called cheese.

Is it really good for us to be so very sanitized? Why are we so afraid of real food?

Admittedly, tripe has, er, contents, and should therefore be washed thoroughly. It should also be cooked thoroughly and must be fresh. Most Africans and Asians consider tripe, the head, hooves, and so on to be the real delicacies in an animal.

So I ended up in Woodstock (Cape Town's ethnic butchery suburb—they take all comers: halal, kosher, Greek, African) checking sheep stomachs like a Supermarket Towel Buyer. I also managed to secure some bargain intestines to help with the stuffing.

Then for the blood.

Where to find blood at short notice in Cape Town?

I was turned away at the abattoir, which was good because I would rather not know what goes on in there. Fortunately, many Kenyans don't eat blood in their mutura, so I decided to make a bloodless sausage.

In anthropological papers, the Kikuyu are often referred to as vegetarians. I adore anthropological papers, especially those written by really concerned ex–Peace Corps workers. How many people get to read about themselves as anthropological specimens? It's like watching a B-movie with yourself as the star.

Most of our food is vegetarian, but our long interaction with the Maasai has influenced our diet. The Maasai, as mentioned earlier, have a traditional diet that is composed almost wholly of red meat, milk, and blood, and their mursik is very similar to mutura. It is gourmet yogurt—smoky, very thick, and really creamy.

Let's make some mutura! (Now Isaac, a friend, informs me that, strictly speaking, mutura made of stomach is called *n'dundóro*, but, like most Kenyans, I will call it mutura.)

Mutura

Any chopped-up pieces of tripe you favor	½ teaspoon chopped garlic
1 sheep's stomach of approximately 200 grams	1 tablespoon oil
	750 grams boneless forequarter of beef
Salt and pepper	1 cup blood—there's always the neighbor . . .
3 tablespoons chopped onion	250 grams liver
	1 green chili, chopped

TO PREPARE:

Clean the chopped tripe and the stomach thoroughly. Boil the tripe in salt water for half an hour. Fry onions and garlic until onions are golden brown. Allow to cool. Cut the beef and liver into small cubes. Mix with blood and season with salt, pepper, and chili. Place mixture in the uncooked stomach and tie both ends firmly. Grill. Slice to serve.

We're at the coast of Sierra Leone. The weather is like steam rising from a boiling kettle. Pores are open, and sweat is welcome. Unlike cooler places, where sweat has the flavor of something fermented, here it is the sheen of every limb. Sweat is only a perfume when fresh, free-flowing. It is the only air-conditioner that works.

Cold things, iced things, are silly here. They just give you the illusion that you are chilled, before heat overwhelms you with a vengeance.

Pots stir in the midday heat. The kitchen is in the courtyard; kids are playing. Somebody is grinding chili. I have often wondered why chilis get hotter the hotter a place is. To get you to sweat, I guess.

From the Congo River to Nigeria, palates embrace musk and any other flavors that mimic the most sensual smells of the body. Yams. If potatoes ever were in heat, this is what they would taste like.

This is not vanilla turf. Mangoes rule, as well as bananas of varieties that would astound anybody from the temperates—in the tropics bananas are not one flavor but many. The conformity of plantation control restricts itself to cash crops for export. A fruit and vegetable market has a lushness that is almost obscene to the uninitiated. I have frequent visions of lemon-faced missionaries sticking to apple preserves. I am sure most would find market day as alien as an orgasm.

Fruit and vegetables are grown by small-scale farmers. Markets are controlled by women, and it is they who organize the movement of produce from far-flung areas to small villages that turn into mini cities on market day. Fruit is never sold by the way it looks but by flavor. Most people who are used to supermarket fruit will be nauseous when they see how splotchy most varieties of banana look. No banana is quite so devoid of taste as that flawless, evenly ripening one available in Western supermarkets.

Smoked fish, dried prawns and shrimp, and freshwater seafood, especially crayfish—and all kinds of sauces—are popular. Over two hundred types of fish are eaten in Nigeria. The less bland the fish the better.

Prawn palaver is one of the most decadent dishes I have ever tasted. This dish, common in Nigeria and Sierra Leone, for me typifies the decadence of classical West African cuisine.

The sun rises to haggling, knee-deep in water. Mama versus the fisherman. The fisherman is in knee-length shorts, his muscles tanned deep copper by salt, sun, and fresh fish. Mama has bulk, great hips, and the determination of children on her side. They are neighbors and friends, but this is business.

She has spotted the fish she wants. She grabs it, examines it, and tosses it back to the boat, making sure it slaps his shin. She turns away as if to seek better shoals. He is irate.

"How dare you disrespect me, a man, like this? Me, whose wife took care of your kids when you were away at your parents. Check this fish out. Can anybody smell where the fattest ones run better than I can? Me, whose father showed him how to charm fish into jumping into my boat?"

"Ha, you, a man! Who saw you asleep outside your homestead, drunk with palm wine last week? Who saw you running out of your house while your wife chased you with your gutting knife!"

"But you heard us that night, didn't you?" he says, his voice now gravel and okra. "You heard a real man satisfy the wife? Did you see her smile the next day? Did she whisper to you how fishermen do it?"

She hesitates now. The sun is getting hotter, and sweat is starting to run down her breasts. Her husband is usually snoring loudly when the fisherman arrives home, ripe and lusty, veins tumescent and washed with sweat.

The fish suddenly looks very appealing in those hands that surely would never shy at the most potent womanly flavors—

Then she spots the prawns. He has obviously traded fish for them with another fisherman and plans to use them at home.

Her power kicks in. He hasn't sold much today. He is late home. Her cleavage is now gleaming with sweat. She looks him straight in the eye, while she fishes for her purse in her bra.

Ten minutes later, the prawns are soaking in brine. The fish will be eaten for breakfast by her husband. Prawn palaver for supper will guarantee a night even the fisherman will envy.

The morning household spot the prawns, and will salivate the whole day in anticipation of supper. Dad has other ideas.

When making prawn palaver, or any other sauce in West Africa, onions are a much-appreciated ingredient, but must remain an invisible texture. They have been ground soft and salted lightly. The chilis have been slow-burning in oil and tomato purée for a few days.

And that's not all.

The peanuts have been pounded into a paste, resembling commercial peanut butter. Not the same, though. No additives.

Anybody who has eaten peanuts from an African market can never get the plastic taste of supermarket peanuts from their mouth. There is the flavor of the soil in these nuts, and the smoky aftertaste of good charcoal.

The smoked fish is gnarled, pared down to just flavor. The wispy, weightless nature of smoke has been sealed, ready for release in the stew.

Smoke becomes a spice.

Jollof rice, boiled yams, fried plantains, and bitter-leaf greens are also being prepared. Jollof rice is a savory dish on its own, like paella. It comes in about as many variations as there are people in West Africa. It is always red, though, from tomatoes.

It is early evening, and at the shebeen across the road the men are drinking palm wine, that incomparable drink that is tapped from a tree trunk, and is resistant to any attempts to bottle it.

All are nibbling kola nuts, breadfruit seeds, and alligator-pepper seeds.

There is no real attention paid to the cooking until the onions across the neighborhood start to sizzle. There is a brief silence, then animated conversation begins. Last rounds are ordered.

The anticipation is the beginning of the celebration.

The other condiment is music. They say music is what mathematics dreams of being.

Cooking is communal. There are no recipe books or precise mathematical measurements dictated by old-time monks trying to control a market. Women sing songs as they work. The rhythm of the song, its structure, is older than the elders know. Its lyrics change with the seasons, fashions, and generations. The sole purpose of this music is to turn the work and the food into a harmony. The leader sings; the rest respond. Grinding motions, stirring motions, all join the movement of the song.

The background instruments are drums or a small FM radio, cracking and hissing with the rap-like speed of a soccer commentator.

The children relieve the tensions. The younger ones have complete freedom. There are many threats that children have to face, but never that their existence threatens adults.

Always on the fringes, and around dark corners, the teenagers flirt, sulk, preen, and strut, full of hormone-ridden murmurs and giggles.

Her husband worked for many years for a Lebanese man and acquired the taste for garlic and ginger. After the two join the onions they are followed by the crayfish powder. Then the tomato and chili mixture, and next the peanut paste. Kids are ushered away as the creamy sauce begins to splatter. The heat is reduced, and the smoked fish goes in. A little water is added as the sauce begins to thicken. The spinach, finely chopped, is stirred in. Then some thyme and salt are added. The prawns are the last ingredient. Everybody has been watching the prawns in the basin from the corner of their eyes. They go silent for a second when the prawns are in the pot.

It is ten minutes to supper.

Prawn Palaver

2 tablespoons oil

1 medium onion, finely chopped

3 cloves garlic, crushed

1 medium-sized ginger root, grated

1 tablespoon dried crayfish or prawn powder (if available)

200-gram tin of tomatoes, chopped

2 tablespoons organic peanut butter (with no added sugar!)

500 milliliters water

1 sprig thyme

Chili pepper and salt

500 grams spinach, fresh or frozen

1 small piece smoked fish (for flavor)

500 grams fresh or frozen prawns

TO PREPARE:

Put oil in a heavy-bottomed saucepan. When hot, add the onions, garlic, ginger, and crayfish powder (if using). Wait for the onions to go translucent. Then add the tomatoes. Cook on a high heat, stirring for 5 minutes. Reduce heat to moderate and add peanut butter, creaming well into the sauce with half of the water. Stir well and allow to cook, bubbling gently, for 8–10 minutes, stirring.

Add remaining water, thyme, pepper, and salt. Wash and finely chop the spinach (if fresh), stir into sauce, and allow to cook on a moderate heat until sauce is thick (20 minutes).

Add the smoked fish and drained prawns. Stir and cook for 10 minutes more.

Serve with boiled yams and steamed rice. For a salad, have grated carrot with lemon juice, brown sugar, and olive oil dressing.

Most South Africans imagine it is money, war, or dire poverty that sends hordes of kwerekweres across the border into South Africa. It is not.

We come here for the junk food.

You cannot imagine how tortuous it is to spend your whole life watching people on TV eating burgers, pizzas, and Kentucky Fried Chicken in their own homes. Imagine a country where junk food is delivered to you! Where kids are allowed to eat it! Bliss.

Meanwhile, we have to make do with hundreds upon hundreds of varieties of fresh vegetables, nuts, fruits, grains, and so on. Oh, the horrors of living in Africa.

When I arrived in South Africa, I stuffed myself full of all those goodies, and then discovered something depressing. I actually like fresh vegetables, nuts, fruits, grains, and so on. I call it the Immigrant Let-down Syndrome. It usually kicks in after the first six months of living the Western dream.

I remember walking into the fruit-and-veg section of a supermarket and seeing all those perfect-looking apples, those immaculately arranged bananas, and realizing how very fascist food is in South Africa. Variety and taste have been completely sacrificed on the altar of military management of stock.

To us kwerekweres, these sections are like *Baywatch* babes. Good to look at but low on flavor. So we end up creating vast underground mafias that trade huge amounts of ethnic food. These come into the country packed between boxes of curios, clingfilm-wrapped in suitcases, and cleverly disguised in the wonderful invention called hand luggage.

The market my mother shops at daily is a place teeming with hundreds of vendors selling a huge variety of fresh produce. The produce is so fat, it bursts out of its skins. Plantain bananas; splotchy skinned, super-sweet bananas; bananas that remain green when ripe; even red bananas. It is a nice, democratic market. Every veggie has a right to be displayed. Every ethnic-minority vegetable is protected by the constitution of our very liberal stomachs.

My theory is that the West transferred all its suppressed fascism to its supermarkets. It makes a lot of sense when you think about it. The humble greengrocer disappeared after the Second World War, when democracy really began to thrive. Shame on you all, putting your fresh produce through so much trauma for your own selfish desire to be free.

While we are on the subject of things political, I must confess that we do have a dictatorial vegetable in Kenya. The humble kale has colonized us more completely than the British, or even *Dallas,* ever did. I suppose it is because she is more of a modern guerrilla-type veggie. No greenhouse barracks or pretty troop formations for her. You see, she grows everywhere.

She loves backyard gardens, street-corner vendors, boarding-school kitchens, and housewives' handbags. She attacks unsuspecting Kenyans at suppertime, hidden behind a huge mound of ugali while we are watching the weekday news.

We call her sukuma wiki, which means to "push the week." She started off as a veggie we ate with ugali during the week, when we couldn't afford meat. These days she has wormed her way into Sunday supper, between the chapatis and the chicken stew. She has even invaded that favored national dish we call *karanga:* meat fried with tomatoes, onion, and seasoning.

When I last went home, I found her comfortably ensconced between the chips and pork sausage in my favorite takeaway parcel.

For those of you who are laughing at our vulnerability to this plain, humble-looking vegetable, beware! The vegetable queen of camouflage is in South Africa. At first I didn't recognize her. Here, she is all frilly and flirtatious. She calls herself the "curly kale." Being an expert in guerrilla warfare, she knew she would be greatly resisted by the arid rows of neatly uniformed, cellophane-protected spinach. So she came into the market as window dressing, seducing the uninformed, cellophane-protected spinach with her lush green curved and frilly edges.

By the way, for all those difficult-to-convert health freaks out there, Kenyan long-distance runners swear by sukuma wiki and ugali. They carry the stuff to all their marathons and even to the Olympics. So, my soon-to-be colonized friends: if you can't beat her, fry her.

All hail the humble kale.

Sukuma Wiki with Boerewors (Sausage)
SERVES 4

3 bunches curly kale
300 grams *boerewors*
1 medium onion, chopped
    finely
3 teaspoons cooking oil

2 tomatoes, diced
2 teaspoons beef-stock
    powder
100 grams red-skin
    peanuts

TO PREPARE:

Rinse the kale and allow it to drip-dry. Cut out the fleshy part of the stems and tear the leaves into bite-sized pieces.

Grill the sausage briefly, then chop it.

The trick to cooking sukuma wiki is to make sure the mixture is always hot enough to prevent water condensing and pooling at the bottom of the pot. Sauté the onion in the oil in a medium-sized pot, then add the tomatoes to the mixture. Let it cook until the mixture is mushy and beginning to brown, then add the stock.

Put the kale into the pot and turn up the heat. Turn the kale over until it is covered by the tomato and onion mixture. Add the sausage pieces and let the mixture cook for a few minutes. Keep turning the kale pieces over. When their color begins to dull, cover the pot for 2–3 minutes. The kale is ready when it is dark green and still crunchy. Add the peanuts, with their peels, to the mixture and serve with pap.

4

Cured of England

We crawled into Tom's record shop last night, Sbu, Tamara, and I, and soon we were listening to hip-hop and Scottish bagpipes and sixties soul and American folk music and reggae and A Tribe Called Quest. This all happened in a small town, Hay-on-Wye, in Wales, where I have been based for over a month. The awkward selection of music came about because Sbu, who is here from Jo'burg to try to find peace and quiet and karma, happens to be a DJ, as does Tom—and for hours they belligerently tried to outdo each other; and outside the door of this record shop, sheep roam, hills undulate gently, rain pours and pours and pours, and even coughing requires planning permission. A large battered-faced man walks in and hugs Tom, singing, "Arsenaaaaaaawl." He is wearing an Arsenal T-shirt and jeans and is about as inebriated as we all are. His face veers from teary mournfulness (Manchester United beat Arsenal a few hours before) to Karaoke Joy, holding his horny fist like a microphone in front of him, and rapping, and singing reggae, his voice sliding off the register, and Tom's dog starts to whine. He grabs hold of me and hugs me and says, "I love you People! I love all of you!!!!!" He looks at Sbu and says, "Thierry Henriiiii!!!" And

I want to slink away, and he cracks up laughing and says, "I love all you Welsh People."

I walk out of the shop at midnight, into the rain, bagpipes sneering in my head to machine-gun rap lyrics, and the town clock rings, and, for the first time since I came to this tea-cozy-covering, iron-fist country, I am happy.

Hay-on-Wye is a border town. Not really Welsh, not English, startlingly beautiful, it has become a retreat of sorts for people who want to live in an in-between world, to avoid the relentless institutional busy-bodyness of England proper. Richard Booth, the "King of Hay," bought Hay Castle and moved here in 1961 with a dream to build the largest secondhand and antiquarian bookselling center in the world. In the late seventies, Hay declared independence from Britain and hit the headlines all around the world. Much decadence took place behind the castle walls: Marianne Faithfull and other celebrities started to hang out here; the town fathers complained and wore stone faces, while counting the coins that flew in; and today there are thirty bookshops and over a million titles on sale here, and every summer Hay-on-Wye hosts the biggest festival of literature in the UK, and Richard Booth still has the biggest secondhand bookstore in the world, refuses to do business on the internet, and issues titles from his castle.

On the declaration, in 1977, Richard Booth was dressed in his royal robes with crown, orb, and scepter made from an old ball-cock and copper piping. When he was later asked whether the move was serious, he said, "Of course not—but it's more serious than real politics!"

On the Hay Peerage web page, the reasons for Hay's declaration are given: "In a world increasingly ruled by impenetrable bureaucracy, and self-interested big business organizations, the Kingdom of Hay was created as an alternative to embrace the good-humored common sense of ordinary intelligent people, which of course ought to be the basis of good government everywhere, always!"

The history of Hay is the history of Hay Castle. It sits at the highest point of Hay-on-Wye Town. If you stand in front of it, Wales gently undulates in front of you, impossibly green, dotted sheep chewing, and you start to understand words that are impossible to translate into any African language I know, like *cozy*. But the whole of England, and Wales, is a willed place, this landscape in front of me; even its forests and wildernesses are all built in the image of man. It is no coincidence that there are no poisonous snakes; all threatening fauna and flora has been tamed. The castle and its inhabitants have loomed and leered over these valleys like fate. There is nothing stable or cozy even about the history of Hay Castle. Until the Normans came here and built the castle in 1100, there is no sign of settlement. From this time, the Welsh occupied the mountainous areas, and the Normans the lowlands and valleys. In 1215 the castle is thought to have been attacked by King John; in 1231 it was burned by Llywelyn the Great but later rebuilt by Henry III; in 1264 it was captured by Prince Edward; and again burned, this time by Simon de Montfort and Llywelyn ap Gruffudd in 1265; in 1401 it was sacked by Owain Glyndwˆr and in 1460 damaged during the Wars of the Roses.

Around 1700 things seem to settle down a little, and the castle was let out as apartments. In the 1800s it was leased by a succession of vicars. In 1961, following a long tradition of eccentrics in these parts, Richard Booth took it over. And there have been eccentrics here. Legend has it that Maud or Moll Walbee was the giantess who built Hay Castle in one night; she could hurl boulders more than a mile, and she met her end in a dungeon, thrown there by King John, who had her starved. Then there was Reverend Francis Kilvert, who lived near Hay in Victorian times and wrote much about life in those days. He had a quite un-vicarly interest in the female form.

Most locals in Hay are pragmatic, friendly, and unmoved by the dramas of the arty types that descend here from time to time. Property prices have gone through the roof, and there are new housing developments coming up everywhere, which are bought by Londoners looking for second homes. Most locals have been priced out of Hay. Although the town has successfully kept out the chain stores and fast-food franchises, many think that the next few years will determine whether Hay, like all of England and much of Wales, will succumb. In other border towns, cappuccino shops and curios sit on the front lawns of the castles, and the towns fade to near-death when the tourist season stops; it becomes unclear where a living town stops and a twee theme park begins. Richard Booth has fought for years to employ local labor, and most locals are very vocal about keeping the monthly farmers' markets, the weekly market day, and the huge pony sales. Booth's battles are mostly against the deadening influence of institutional Britain: the Arts Council and even the Hay Festival of Literature have had their battles with him, though they seem now to have come to terms.

For a while, I thought that "them thar hills" in the distance were where a true Welshness lived, but so far the hills have produced for me only a software designer who links up to the internet via satellite and a woman I met on the train who edits legal journals. A few weeks ago, drinking coffee at Shepherds Ice Cream Parlor, a Black woman walked in, and we looked at each other with excitement. I wanted to do a *Color Purple* thing and touch her face and say, throbbingly, "Mama! Mama!" Only Marva Lord is way too young and good-looking to be motherly. We shared a coffee, and she asked me if I wanted to attend Black History Month in Hay. I laughed—thinking who will attend, all five Black people in Hay? But I go, and find the hall full, and learn much about Black Welsh History, and we hear some dub poetry with Michael St. George, and dance till morning to Dennis Bovell live and DJ Asif playing Asian hip-hop. I met Atinuke, a Nigerian storyteller of captivating skill who lives in west Wales and has met only two other Black people there. She tells me she loves living in a village where her son can run about freely.

The Wye River glides parallel to the main center of Hay. There is a lovely walk along the river I like to take. I sit on the benches, and from some angles I could be in the Kenyan highlands. There is something disturbing about this landscape, farming sanitized to table-mat prettiness by farm subsidies. When I first came here, it looked to me like this was the image the white settlers to Kenya wanted to re-create, their idea of the Kenyan highlands accomplished. Now, after a few weeks, I miss the untamed gush of Kenyan rivers, the genuine wilderness, the layers of social possibilities, the opaque, unknowable history, unfriendly landscapes spread before you; the differentiated, independent, and contrary way that rural Kenyans have translated our times. I love Hay, but there is only so much of this unbearable niceness of being that I can take.

I have lived in England for most of the past twelve months, and I am leaving in a week—I can't wait. I hate Blair, hate that earnest, snitching, school-prefect voice, hectoring, hectoring. I hate the sullen, limp service in shops and pubs. Most of all I have had enough of the Nannyness of the country: the warning signs everywhere, threatening this bludgeoned citizenry—BEHAVE or you shall be FINED, or charged or, or, or . . .

I have seen *scaffolding* protected by CCTV cameras.

England is drawing a pension: it has a good investment portfolio, brings out its war medals when it needs some money; it pretends vibrancy by creating little retirement-style set-pieces, all carefully controlled, all pretending edginess. Maybe one day, when America achieves its version of self-fulfillment, when there are no fundamentals, or fundamentalists, to adjust, everything will be *cute,* an endless array of humorless white picket fences. A Steve Martin movie.

I went to visit the Notting Hill Carnival. Thinking, "Ah! Here I shall find some vibrancy. Dance. Share time with Black brothers. Leave exhilarated." No. There were more policemen than people, it seemed. The carnival was deemed too exciting to allow people to *participate.* So we stood, in patient Anglo-Saxon lines, and watched the multicolored floats go by.

V. S. Naipaul is disdainful of multiculturalism in the UK. He says immigrants to the UK should have to assimilate. I too am suspicious of multiculturalism—it tastes like Rainbow Nation, a line of bullshit to disguise much grit. But what does it mean to assimilate in England? To chat about George and his Dragon? To adore the Queen Mum? To live politely surrounded by great buildings and museums, not wanting to intrude on the great times of people long dead? Maybe V. S. meant for one to acquire a generic sourpussness; to be fastidious and dislike sex; to live in Surrey and avoid people. Or maybe one could find contemporary English things to latch on to to become a good citizen: Posh and Becks; making art in which toilet paper is splattered on the Union Jack. Or football matches, where real feeling flares to life and violence often follows, as it always seems to when people let themselves be passionate here. Maybe to be English is to hate Blair but to vote for him. Maybe it means to make sex harmless: to call it a bonk, a shag. To make it possible to make nearly naked women of extravagant endowments sexless.

There are things I like and respect about the English. Their ability to find small pleasures, build large internal and personal lives in small places; their grit, their endurance is truly great. I love the way the country sprawls, a messy, organized, incredibly varied place—no singular slogans, no chest-banging nationalism. I like their refusal to take anything seriously. But these things were acquired in more challenging times. Now they seem hollow. So the English make jokes about people in Britain who do have a strong and passionate sense of themselves: the Scots, the Irish, and the Welsh especially. England gave up its own identity to institutions, and people are aware that they lack something. English humor is especially savage when it targets anything with an actual ethnicity.

What England has that is living and great is its institutions. The *National Dictionary of Biography;* the museums; common law; even the National Health Service—thousands upon thousands of great living institutions. These have written inside them the combined intelligence of a country that has had a history much greater than its size. All the passion, all the glory, all the bad, the good, the pungent is invested in these systems. But for people, for an ordinary social life, for the future, England is to be endured. The English, especially the younger English, are bored. This is probably why so many policemen are needed at the Notting Hill Carnival. Institutions mediate everything—and institutions are nervous about having people gather and find their own way of dealing with each other. A newcomer to London finds himself chafing against the weight of these institutions—which mask a totalitarian nature by being polite; which never yield to any request you make that does not suit them. When you have learned to succumb, the city becomes tolerable. So maybe this is what V. S. means: succumb to the dictates of the institutions.

Now, I suspect that it is drugs and football that keep people feeling that things matter. Somebody grabbed me the other day. A chemically enervated acquaintance. He grabbed my shirt and said, his eyes popping, "I want to live! I want to live! Can't live here! I want my children to fart, to be rude. To live!" The next day he waved at me politely. Not a trace of the night before on his face. Kenya is not so great. We can't pay our national bills and will probably never own an empire. But thank God we still have something meaningful to do.

Discovering Home: Essays

In July 2000, Binyavanga Wainaina went home to Kenya. He did not return quietly; instead, he burst into the church where his mother's funeral was being held, surprising his siblings, who thought he was far away in South Africa. Once home, however, there was no going back—he had overstayed his visa by years, making it difficult to return, and he was warmed by the prospect of being with his family. His bereaved father had only recently built the family's permanent home in Nakuru, and his sister June had just given birth to a son. The house was a busy one, the garden offered many immersive delights, and there was enough space for him to skulk, play music loudly, and write.

One year later, he shifted to the Kenyan capital, Nairobi, seduced by the heaving, changing metropolis. Binyavanga had returned home a new man, but to a home that was remaking itself too. He embraced it. He plunged headfirst into street culture, into the very things his previous self, the conservative, cautious, prim young man from ten years ago, would have rejected.

He wrote for anyone who would have him, and especially Rod Amis, the African American editor of *G21*, a pioneering online magazine of world culture, which was based in New Orleans. Amis ran a threadbare operation, but he unfailingly paid Binyavanga a hundred dollars for every piece he published. Every Sunday, once the money had been cashed at Western Union, Binyavanga would celebrate. Sometimes, he booked the sixty-minute package at a Somali-run internet café to talk to new friends from new online writing communities, such as a then unknown writer from Nigeria called Chimamanda Ngozi Adichie.

In 2002 he heard about the recently instituted Caine Prize for African Writing. He scrambled to get an essay published in time to qualify, and decided to go with Amis and *G21*. The Caine Prize organizers immediately rejected his entry. It was an online magazine, they said, and they could only accept entries published in "real" magazines. Binyavanga wrote back a scorching rejoinder, and they folded. He was in. A few months later, he won the award for his essay "Discovering Home," arguably becoming its most famous—and notorious—recipient ever. He used the money from the award to set up a magazine of new writing in Kenya, and called it *Kwani?*, which means "So what?"

It was the beginning of an era.

5

Circumcision

Compared to most teens in Africa, my circumcision was fairly tame. I was twelve. I had completed primary school, and was about to go to boarding school, like most Kenyans at that age.

My dad invited me to play golf with him one Saturday. In the showers afterward, he clapped me on the shoulder and said, "You are a man now. We go Monday."

My big brother spent all of Sunday describing the operation in great detail. The pain, he said, was indescribable. Crying was taboo.

My mum made roast chicken for lunch, and gazed at me proudly throughout the meal. I was allowed two servings of ice cream. My dad drove me to the hospital, and we parked the car.

He lit a cigarette, looked out of the window, and launched into a detailed biological explanation of what girls and boys do, which I mustn't do till I am seventy-seven and married, but, if I do, I must use an—er—condom . . .

His technical jargon was superb, and I finally found out what "Vagina Hygiene" meant. There was a program on the radio that always talked about it, and I thought she and her friend Herpes, Syphilis, and Gonorrhea were bad girls from Greek classics for Adults Only.

This was an excruciating discussion to go through. I was twelve. Twin pillows on a bed were enough to pop the corn. To this day, there is a tree in our old garden, with branches shaped like open legs, that makes me randy.

I had lots of questions that went unasked.

Can I beat up my sister now?

Why can't I drink beer and smoke cigarettes?

How can I control this new, excitable limb? Is Vaseline therapy allowed?

What? What? What is a blow-job? Everybody else seems to know. Maina says he got one. Does she blow on it? Are people actually employed to perform it?

That part (pages 194–96) in that Harold Robbins book, where the woman screams, "I'm coming!"—what does that mean?

We went into the hospital. The receptionist aggravated matters somewhat by saying, rather loudly: "Circumcision, go to Room 14!"

Room 14 was occupied by a KENYAN GOVERNMENT HOSPITAL NURSE. She was chewing gum loudly and nattering on the phone to someone in Bungoma who was tired of her husband's demands and wanted him to take a second wife. Hers apparently had a very small and inactive one, which rarely bothered her gum chewing. I remember wondering what he did to keep it so disciplined. She paused on the phone, looked at me from head to toe, pausing with a smirk at my crotch, and told me to go behind the screen, take off my clothes, and wait for the anesthetic.

Her conversation continued, now in her native Luhya. All I understood was the occasional "Really!" and "You can't be serious!"

All my brother's macho advice had bolstered my courage somewhat: "Er . . . excuse me, madam. Madam, you see, er . . . excuse me, madam."

"WHAT! Can't you see I'm busy!"

"Well, I can't take off my clothes in front of a woman. I am a man now!"

Laughter. A translation into Luhya. More laughter.

A few minutes later a male nurse was found. The doctor, a fussy looking Iranian, kept wringing his hands and saying, "It must come down!"

When I saw the needle, it did. Fast.

I shan't comment on the next half-hour. It was so horrifying, I just felt like laughing.

I left Room 14 with this strange, numb thing hanging on me. I was exhilarated. *So this was it? Pain! What a man I am! I can even walk home (my dad had decamped, promising to return by 3 P.M.).*

I set off. I managed about 400 meters. Then the anesthetic started to wear off.

My dad found me writhing in exquisite sensitivity behind a jacaranda tree.

The first two nights were torturesome. The damned thing burned, and reacted to everything. I couldn't even watch *Roots*.

A week later I managed a bow-legged trip to the Sports Club, where I met Maina, a former classmate. He'd had his done the traditional way. His younger uncles had come bearing gifts of plenty of booze and other illicit substances and had spirited him away blindfolded. His mother had made the prerequisite screams of protest.

In the bush, together with a few other boys, his uncles taught them lots of dirty songs, made them eat earthworms, and built a small hut. They were taught what goes on in the bedroom—*all questions* were answered in raunchy detail. Elders came, told them many secrets and their clan history.

They got secret names that only their age-mates (people circumcised that year) could use. The operation was done three days later. *No anesthetic, just herbs for bleeding.* That night, a bunch of girls came a-teasing to fan the (very hot) flames and left them in exquisite agony.

At dawn, a dip in an ice-cold mountain stream, worse than the operation apparently.

After their return, much revelry, much beer and ganja and many gifts, including cash and a red leather jacket like Michael Jackson's (a gift which defeated the whole purpose).

I was so entranced by his story that I adopted it as mine for many years. *I hope none of my high-school cronies are reading this.*

The age-mate system is still a very powerful networking tool among Kikuyus and related tribes.

The Mau Mau, for example, were dominated by Riika-wa-40 (initiated in 1940).

It isn't uncommon for a Kenyan to tell some upstart, "*Nyamaza, wewe si riika yangu!*" (Which means: "Shut up, you are not of my circumcision-age!")

Black South Africans take this operation very seriously. Zulus don't do it. Xhosa do, and so do Sothos. Xhosas go after high school, on turning eighteen.

Initiates, I am told, are taken for three months to the mountains, where they learn to exist in the wild, build a house, and generally live lives as useful citizens of the community. Sex is discussed at great length. There is no anesthetic. Crying is a humiliation that will last your lifetime. Everybody goes.

I am sure there are more than a million strangled foreskins buried around every December. Doesn't matter if you are Mandela's son or some *nsa-nsa-nsa* from Johannesburg. You must go.

Every December, the WhiteYMedia in South Africa loves to scream about unhygienic practices during circumcision ceremonies. Headlines feature deformed and decapitated dicks. Truth is, there are many initiatives to teach the bearers of the knife basic hygiene. Most of my friends who've been say that all the necessary precautions were taken.

I have learned little about women's initiations. People aren't supposed to talk about these things to the opposite sex. I would imagine that the introductory lecture for Kikuyu women would be, "Now I know up to now we have told you that men are the ones who run things . . ."

When I was working in Maasailand after high school, the excited fifteen-year-old-daughter of my host invited me to her circumcision. I couldn't bring myself to attend.

While at university, I attended the coming-of-age of a daughter of one of our deans. A Zulu. She sat in the sun, her breasts bare, with soft sheep-fat over her shoulders. It was quite amazing to witness. Women sang for her, and she cried and cried with pride.

I still wish I had gone to the mountain.

For the record, Zulu women do not go through any form of genital mutilation.

6

Discovering Home

Chapter One

There is a problem. Somebody has fallen asleep in the toilet. The upstairs bathroom is locked, and Frank has disappeared with the keys. There is a small riot as drunken women with smudged lipstick and crooked wigs bang on the door.

There is always that point at a party when people are too drunk to be having fun; when strange smelly people are asleep on your bed; when the good booze runs out and there is only Sedgwick's Old Brown Sherry and a carton of sweet white wine; when you realize that all your flatmates have gone and all this is your responsibility; when the DJ is slumped over the stereo and some strange person is playing Brenda Fassie's latest hit over and over again.

I have been studying here, in Umtata, South Africa, for five years and have rarely breached the boundary of my clique. Fear, I suppose, and a feeling that I am not quite ready to leave a place that has let me be anything I want to be and provided not a single predator. That is what this party is all about:

I am going home for a year.

So maybe this feeling that my movements are being guided is explicable.

This time tomorrow I will be sitting next to my mother. We shall soak each other up. Flights to distant places always arouse in me a peculiar awareness: that the substance we refer to as reality is really an organization as changeable as the puffy white lines that planes leave behind as they fly.

I will wonder why I don't do this every day. I hope to be in Kenya for thirteen months. I intend to travel as much as possible and finally to attend my grandparents' sixtieth wedding anniversary in Uganda in December.

There are so many possibilities that could overturn this journey, yet I cannot leave without being certain that I will get to my destination.

If there is a miracle in the idea of life, it is this: that we are able to exist for a time, in defiance of chaos. Later, you often forget how dicey everything was; how the tickets almost didn't materialize; how the event almost got postponed; how a hangover nearly made you miss the flight . . .

Phrases swell, becoming bigger than their context and speak to us as *truth*. We wield this series of events as our due, the standard for gifts of the future. We live the rest of our lives with the utter knowledge that there is something deliberate that transports everything into place, if we follow the stepping-stones of certainty.

After the soft light and mellow manners of Cape Town, Nairobi is a shot of whisky. We drive from the airport into the city center.

Around us: *matatus,* those brash, garish public-transport vehicles, so irritating to every Kenyan except those who own one, or work for one; I can see them as the best example of contemporary Kenyan art. The best of them get new paint jobs every few months: Oprah seems popular right now; the inevitable Tupac. The colored lights and fancy horn, the purple interior lighting, the hip-hop blaring out of speakers I will never afford. Art galleries in Kenya buy only the expression for which there is demand in Europe and America—the real artists, the guys who are turning their lives into vivid color, are the guys who decorate matatus.

The matatus swing in and out of gaps, darting into impossible angles, turning the traffic into an obstacle course. Watching them with my no-hurry eyes, they seem like a form of jazz: every trip, finding sophisticated and spontaneous solutions to getting their route accomplished as quickly as possible in Nairobi's aging, colonial road system, designed for a small driving middle class. Public transport must just find a way to make do.

Oh, and they do.

Manambas conduct the movements of the matatu. Hanging out of open doors, performing all kinds of gymnastics, they call their routes, announce openings in the traffic, and communicate with the driver through a series of bangs on the roof that manage to be heard above the music. There are bangs for oncoming allies; bangs that warn of traffic jams ahead; bangs announcing an impending traffic policeman. There are also methods of delivering a bribe, without having to stop.

I see one guy, who is hanging on by his fingernails to the roof, one toe in the open door, inches away from death, letting both hands go and clapping and whistling at a woman who is walking by the side of the road, dressed in tight jeans. She raises her nose and looks determinedly at an electricity pole on the other side of the road.

This is Nairobi. This is what you do to get ahead: make yourself boneless, and treat your straitjacket as if it was a game, a challenge. The city is now all on the streets, sweet-talk and hustle. Our worst recession ever has just produced brighter, more creative matatus.

It is good to be home.

In the afternoon, I take a walk down River Road, all the way to Nyamakima. This is the main artery of movement to and from the main bus ranks. It is ruled by manambas, and their image is cynical, every laugh a sneer, the city a war or a game. It is a useful face to carry, here where humanity invades all the space you do not claim with conviction.

The desperation that is for me most touching is the expressions of the people who come from the rural areas into the city center to sell their produce. Thin-faced, with the large cheekbones common among the Kikuyu, cheekbones so dominating they seem like an appendage to be embarrassed about, something that draws attention to their faces when attention is the last thing they want. Anywhere else those faces are beauty. Their eyes dart about, consistently uncertain, unable to train themselves to a background of so much chaos. They do not know how to put on a glassy expression.

Those who have been in the fresh-produce business longer are immediately visible: mostly old women in kangas with weary take-it-or-leave-it voices. They hang out in groups, chattering away constantly, as if they want no quiet where the fragility of their community will reveal itself in this alien place.

I take the dawn Nissan matatu to Nakuru.

The Kikuyu grass by the side of the road is crying silver tears the color of remembered light; Nairobi is a smoggy haze in the distance. Soon the innocence that dresses itself in mist will be shoved aside by a confident sun, and the chase for money will reach its crescendo.

A man wearing a Yale University sweatshirt and tattered trousers staggers behind his enormous *mkokoteni,* moving so slowly it seems he will never get to his destination. He is transporting bags of potatoes. No vehicle gives him room to move. The barrow is so full that it seems that some bags will fall off on to the road. Already, he is sweating. From some reservoir I cannot understand, he smiles and waves at a friend on the side of the road; they chat briefly, laughing as if they had no care in the world. Then the mkokoteni-man proceeds to move the impossible.

Why, when all odds are against our thriving, do we move with so much resolution? Kenya's economy is on the brink of collapse, but we march on like safari ants, waving our pincers as if we will win.

Maybe motion is necessary even when it produces nothing.

I sit next to the driver, who wears a Stetson hat, and has been playing an upcountry matatu classic on the cassette player: Kenny Rogers's "The Gambler." There are two women behind me, talking. I can't hear what they are saying, but it seems very animated. I catch snatches, when exclamations send their voices higher than they would like.

"Eh! *Apana!* I don't believe!"

"Haki!"

"I swear!"

"Me I heard ati . . ."

Aha. Members of the Me-I-Heard-Ati Society. I construct their conversation in my mind:

"Eee-heeee! Even me I've heard that one! Ati, you know, they are mining oil in Lake Victoria, together with Biwott."

"Really!"

"Yah!"

"And they are exporting the ka-plant to Australia. They use it to feed sheep."

"Nooo! Really? What plant?"

"You knooow, *that* plant—Water-hyak haycy . . . haia. Argh! That ka-plant that is covering the lake!"

"Hyacinth?"

"Yah! That hya-thing was planted by Moi and Biwott and them in Lake Victoria. They want to finish the Luos!"

The driver changes the tape, and a song comes on that takes me straight back to a childhood memory.

It must have been a Sunday, and I was standing outside Ku-kuDen restaurant in Nakuru, as my mother chatted away with an old friend. It was quite hot, and my Sunday clothes itched. Then this song came on. Congo music, with voices as thick as hot honey, and wayward in a way Christian-school tunes hadn't prepared me for. Guitar and trumpet, parched like before the rains, dived into the honey and out again. The voices pleaded in a strange language, men sending their voices higher than men should, and letting go of control, letting their voices flow, slow and phlegmy, like the honey. There was a lorry outside, and the men unloading the maize were singing to the music, pleading with the honey. The song burst out with the odd Kiswahili phrase, then forgot itself and started on its gibberish again.

It disturbed me, demanding too much of my attention, derailing my daydreams. It doesn't anymore.

I am at home. The past eight hours are already receding into the forgotten; I was in Cape Town this morning; I am in Nakuru, Kenya, now.

Blink.

Mum looks tired and her eyes are sleepier than usual. She has never seemed frail, but does so now. I decide that it is I who am growing, changing, and my attempts at maturity make her seem more human.

I make my way to the kitchen. The Nandi woman still rules the corridor.

After ten years, I can still move about with ease in the dark. I stop at that hollow place, the bit of wall on the other side of the fireplace. My mother's voice, talking to my dad, echoes in the corridor. None of us has her voice: if crystal were water solidified, her voice would be the last splash of water before it sets.

Light from the kitchen brings the Nandi woman to life. A painting.

I was terrified of her when I was a kid. Her eyes seemed so alive, and the red bits growled at me menacingly. Her broad face announced an immobility that really scared me; I was stuck there, fenced into a tribal reserve by her features: *Rings on her ankles and bells on her nose, / She will make music wherever she goes.*

Why? Did I sense, so young, that her face could never translate into acceptability? That, however disguised, it would not align itself to the program I aspired to?

In Kenya there are two sorts of people: those on one side of the line will wear third-hand clothing till it rots. They will eat dirt, but school fees will be paid.

On the other side of the line live people you see in coffee-table books. Impossibly exotic and much fewer in number than the coffee-table books suggest. They are like an old and lush jungle that continues to flourish and unfurl extravagant blooms, refusing to realize that somebody cut off the water. Often, somebody from the other side of the line.

These two groups of people are fascinated by one another. We, the modern ones, are fascinated by the completeness of the old ones. To us, it seems that everything is mapped out and defined for them, and everybody is fluent in those definitions. The old ones are not much impressed by our society, or manners—what catches their attention is our tools: the cars and medicines and telephones and wind-up dolls and guns.

In my teens, set alight by the poems of Senghor and Okot p'Bitek, the Nandi woman became my Tigritude. I pronounced her beautiful, marveled at her cheekbones, and mourned the lost wisdom in her eyes, but I still would have preferred to sleep with Pam Ewing or Iman. It was a source of terrible fear for me that I could never love her. I covered that betrayal with a complicated imagery that had no connection to my gut: O Nubian Princess, and other bad poetry. She moved to my bedroom for a while, next to the faux-Kente wall hanging, but my mother took her back to her pulpit.

Over the years, I learned to regard her amiably. She filled me with a lukewarm nostalgia for things lost. I never again attempted to look beyond her costume.

She is younger than me now; I can see that she has girlishness about her. Her eyes are the artist's only real success: they suggest mischief, serenity, vulnerability, and a weary wisdom. Today, I don't need to bludgeon my brain with her beauty; it just sinks in, and I find myself desiring her.

I look up at the picture again. Then I see it.

Have I been such a bigot? Everything: the slight smile, the

angle of her head and shoulders, the mild flirtation with the artist. I know you want me; I know something you don't.

Mona Lisa: nothing says otherwise. The truth is that I never
saw the smile. Her thick lips were such a war between my intel-
lect and emotion that I never noticed the smile.

The artist is probably not African, not only because of the
obvious *Mona Lisa* business but also because, for the first time,
I realize that the woman's expression is odd. In Kenya you will
only see such an expression in girls who went to private schools,
or were brought up in the richer suburbs of the larger towns.

That look, that slight toying smile, could not have happened
with an actual Nandi woman. In the portrait, she has covered
her vast sexuality with a shawl of ice, letting only the hint of a
smile reveal that she has a body that can quicken: a flag on the
moon. The artist has got the dignity right, but the sexuality is
European: it would be difficult for an African artist to get that
wrong.

The lips too seem wrong. There's awkwardness about them,
as if a shift of aesthetics has taken place on the plain of muscles
between her nose and her mouth. Also, the mouth strives too
hard for symmetry, as if to apologize for its thickness. That
mouth is meant to break open like the flesh of a ripe mango;
restraint of expression is not common in Kenya and certainly
not among the Nandi, who smile more than any other nation I
know.

The eyes are enormous, as if the artist was determined to
arouse the sympathy of the viewer, to change a preconceived notion of what a woman is. Skins, with "tribal scars" on her face.
I can see the gaggle of tourists exclaiming: "Ooh . . . such dignity! She's so . . . well, *noble!*"

I turn, and head for the kitchen. I cherish the kitchen at night.
It is cavernous, and echoes with night noises that are muffled by
the vast spongy silence outside. After so many years in cupboard-
sized South African kitchens, I feel more thrilled than I should.

On my way back to my room, I turn and face the Nandi
woman, thinking of the full circle I have come since I left.

When I left, white people ruled South Africa. When I left, Kenya was a one-party dictatorship. When I left, I was relieved that I had escaped the burdens and guilts of being in Kenya, of facing my roots, and repudiating them. Here I am, looking for them again. I know, her eyes say. I know.

Oh, but your land is beautiful!

I've got a part-time job: driving around the Central and Eastern provinces, and getting farmers to start growing cotton again. I have been provided with a car and a driver.

My colleague Kariuki and I are on the way to Mwingi Town in a new, zippy Nissan pickup. The road to Masinga Dam is monotonous, and my mind has been taken over by bubble-gum music, chewing away, trying to digest a vacuum.

That terrible song: "I donever really wanna KILL The Dragon . . ."

It zips around my mind like some demented fly, always a bit too fast to catch and smash.

I try to start a conversation, but Kariuki is not talkative. He sits hunched over the steering wheel of the car, body tense, his face twisted into a grimace. He is usually quite relaxed when he isn't driving, but cars seem to bring out some demon in him.

To be honest, Mwingi is not a place I want to visit. It is a new district, semi-arid, and there is nothing there that I have heard is worth seeing or doing, except eating goat. Apparently, according to the unofficial National Goat Meat Quality Charts, Mwingi goat is second after Siakago goat in flavor. I am told some enterprising fellow from Texas started a goat ranch to service the ten thousand Kenyans living there. He is making a killing.

South African goat tastes terrible. Over the years in South Africa, I have driven past goats that stare at me with arrogance, chewing nonchalantly and daring me to wield my knife.

It is payback time.

This is why we set out at six in the morning, in the hope that we would be through with all possible bureaucracies by midday, after which we could get down to drinking beer and eating lots and lots of goat.

I have invested in a few sachets of Andrews Liver Salts.

I doze, and the sun is shining by the time I get up. We are 30 kilometers from Mwingi Town. There is an intriguing sign on one of the dusty roads that branches off from the highway, a beautifully drawn picture of a skinny red bird and a notice with an arrow: GRUYÈRE.

I am curious, and decide to turn in and investigate. After all, I think to myself, it would be good to see what the Cotton Growing Situation is on the ground before going to the District Agricultural Office.

Ahem.

It takes us about twenty minutes on the dusty road to get to Gruyère. This part of Ukambani is really dry, full of hardy-looking bushes and dust. Unlike most places in Kenya, people live far away from the roads, so one has the illusion that the area is sparsely populated. We are in a tiny village center. Three shops on each side, and a large quadrangle of beaten-down dust in the middle on which three giant wood-carvings of giraffes sit, waiting for transport to the curio markets of Nairobi. There doesn't seem to be anybody about; we get out of the car, and enter Gruyère, which turns out to be a pub.

It looks about as Swiss as one can get in Ukambani. A simply built structure with a concrete floor and simple furnishings, it nevertheless has finish—nothing sticking out, everything in symmetry. I notice an ingenious beer-cooler: a little cavern worked into the cement floor, where beer and sodas are cooled in water. This is a relief; getting a cold beer outside of Nairobi is quite a challenge.

Kenyans love warm beer, even if it is 100°F outside. Since I arrived in these parts, I have had concerned barmaids worrying that I will get pneumonia, or that the beer will go completely flat if left in the fridge for more than twenty minutes.

The owner walks in, burnt salad-tomato red, wearing a kikoi and nothing else. He welcomes us and I introduce myself and start to chat, but soon discover that he doesn't speak English or Kiswahili. He is Swiss, and speaks only French and Kamba. My French is rusty, but it manages to get me a cold drink, served by his wife. She has skin the color of bitter chocolate. She is beautiful in the way only Kamba women can be, with baby-soft skin, wide-apart eyes, and an arrangement of features that seems permanently on the precipice of mischief.

We chat, and I ask her what brought her husband to Mwingi, and she laughs: "You know *mzungus* always have strange ideas! He is a mKamba now—he doesn't want anything to do with Europe."

After the heat outside, the brown bottles, shyly poking their heads out of the Cavern of Cool, are tempting. I stick to soda, though. I have been frivolous enough today.

I can see a bicycle coming a distance, an impossibly large man weaving his way toward us, short, rounded legs pumping furiously.

Enter the jolliest man I have ever seen, plump as a mound of ugali, glowing with bonhomie and wiping streams of sweat from his face. There is (of course) the Kamba expression of mischief on his face—only with him, it is multiplied to a degree that makes it ominous. Gruyère's wife tells me he is the local chief. I stand up and greet him, then ask him to join us. He sits down and orders a round of beer.

"Ah! You can't be drinking soda here! This is a bar!"

He beams again, and I swear that somewhere a whole *shamba* of flowers is blooming.

I try to glide into the subject of cotton, but it is brushed aside.

"So," he says, "you go to South Africa with my daughter? She's just sitting at home, can't get a job—Kambas make good wives, you know, you Kikuyus know nothing about having a good time."

I can't deny that. He leans close, his eyes round as a full moon, and tells me a story about a retired major who lives nearby and has three young wives, who complain about his sexual demands.

So, it is said that parents in the neighborhood are worried because their daughters are often seen batting their eyelids whenever he is about.

"You know," he says, "you Kikuyus cannot think further than your next coin. You grow maize on every available inch of land and cover your sofas with plastic. Ha! Then, in bed! *Bwana!* Even sex is work! But Kambas are not lazy: we work hard, we fuck well, we play hard. So drink your beer!"

I decide to rescue the reputation of my community. I order a Tusker. Cold.

What a gift charisma is. By 11 A.M., there is a whole table of people, all of us glowing under the Chief's beams of sunlight. My tongue has rediscovered its French, and I chat with Monsieur Gruyère, who isn't very chatty. He seems to be still under the spell of this place, and, as we drink, I can see his eyes running over everyone. He doesn't seem too interested in the substance of the conversation; he is held more by the mood.

It is midday when I finally excuse myself. We have to make our way to Mwingi. Kariuki is looking quite inebriated, and now the Chief finally displays an interest in our mission.

"Cotton! Oh! You will need someone to take you around the District Agricultural Office. He! You are bringing development back to Mwingi!"

We arrive at the District Agricultural Office. Our meeting there is blessedly brief, and we get all the information we want. The Chief leads us through a maze of alleys to the best butchery/bar in Mwingi. He, of course, is well known there, and we get the VIP cubicle. Wielding his potbelly like a sexual magnet, he breaks up a table of young women and encourages them to join us.

Whispered aside: "You bachelors must surely be starving for female company, seeing that you have gone a whole morning without any."

We head off to the butcher, who has racks and racks of headless, hanging goats. I am salivating already. We choose four kilos of ribs, and order mutura as an appetizer.

The mutura is delicious—hot, spicy, and rich—and the ribs tender and full of the herbal pungency that we enjoy in good goat meat.

After a couple of hours, I am starting to get uncomfortable at the levels of pleasure around me. I want to go back to my cheap motel room, and read a book full of realism and stingy prose.

No, no, no! says Mr. Chief. You must come to my place, back to the village; we need to talk to people there about cotton. Surely you are not going to drive back after so many beers? Sleep at my house!

Back at the Chief's house, I lay myself under the shade of a tree in the garden and sleep.

Wake up! Let's go and party!

I am determined to refuse. But the light embraces me. By the time we have showered and attempted to make our grimy clothes respectable, it is dusk.

As there is only space for two in the front of the pickup, I have been sitting in the back. I console myself with the view. Now that the glare of the sun is fading, all sorts of things reveal themselves, including tiny hidden flowers of extravagant color—as if, like the Chief, they disdain the frugal humorlessness one expects is necessary to thrive in this dustbowl. We cross several dried riverbeds.

We are now so far away from the main road that I have no idea where we are. This lends the terrain around me a sudden immensity. The sun is the deep yellow of a free-range egg, on the verge of bleeding its yolk over the sky.

The fall of day becomes a battle: birds are working themselves into a frenzy, flying about feverishly, unbearably shrill. The sky makes its last stand, shedding its ubiquity and competing with the landscape for the attention of the eye.

I spend some time watching the Chief through the back window. He hasn't stopped talking since we left. Kariuki is actually laughing.

It is dark when we get to the club. I can see a thatched roof, and four or five cars. There is nothing else around. We are, it seems, in the middle of nowhere.

We get out of the car.

"It will be full tonight," says the Chief. "Month-end."

Three hours later, I am somewhere beyond drunk, coasting on a vast plateau of sobriety that seems to have no end. The place is packed.

More hours later, I am standing in a line of people outside the club. A chorus of liquid glitter arcs high out, then down to the ground, then zips close. The pliant nothingness of the huge night above us goads us to movement.

Some well-known Dombolo song starts, and a ripple of excitement overtakes the crowd.

This communal goose bump wakes a rhythm in us, and we all get up to dance. One guy, with a cast on one leg, is using his crutch as a dancing aid, bouncing around us like a string-puppet. The cars all have their inside lights on, as couples do when they do what they do. The windows seem like eyes, glowing with excitement as they watch us on stage.

Everybody is doing the Ndombolo, a Congolese dance where your hips (and only your hips) are supposed to move like a ball-bearing made of mercury. To do it right, wiggle your pelvis from side to side while your upper body remains as casual as if you were lunching with Nelson Mandela. In any restaurant in Kenya, a sunny-side-up fried egg is called *mayai* tombolo.

I have struggled to get this dance right for years. I just can't get my hips to roll in circles like they should. Until tonight. The booze is helping, I think. I have decided to imagine that I have an itch deep in my bum, and I have to scratch it without using my hands or rubbing against anything.

My body finds a rhythmic map quickly, and I build my movements to fluency, before letting my limbs improvise. Everybody is doing this, a solo thing—yet we are bound, like one creature, in one rhythm.

Any Ndombolo song has this section where, having reached

a small peak of hip-wiggling frenzy, the music stops, and one is supposed to pull one's hips to the side and pause, in anticipation of an explosion of music faster and more frenzied than before.

When this happens, you are supposed to stretch out your arms and do some complicated kung fu maneuvers. Or keep the hips rolling, and slowly make your way down to your haunches, then work yourself back up. If you watch a well-endowed woman doing this, you will understand why skinny women are not popular in Africa.

If you ask me now, I'll tell you this is everything that matters. So this is why we move like this. We affirm a common purpose; any doubts about others' motives must fade if we are all pieces of one movement. We forget, don't we, that there is another time, apart from the hour and the minute? A human measurement, ticking away in our bodies, behind our façades.

Our shells crack, and we spill out and mingle.

I join a group of people who are talking politics, sitting around a large fire outside, huddled together to find warmth and life under a sagging hammock of night mass. A couple of them are students at university; there is a doctor who lives in Mwingi Town.

If every journey has a moment of magic, this is mine. Anything seems possible. In the dark like this, all we say seems free of consequence, the music is rich, and our bodies are lent a brotherhood by the light of the fire.

Politics makes way for Life. For these few hours, it is as if we were old friends, comfortable with each other's dents and frictions. We talk, bringing the oddities of our backgrounds to this shared plate.

The places and people we talk about are rendered exotic and distant this night. Warufaga . . . Burnt Forest . . . Mtito Andei . . . Makutano . . . Maili Saba . . . Mua Hills . . . Gilgil . . . Sultan Hamud . . . Siakago . . . Kutus . . . Maili Kumi . . . The wizard in Kangundo who owns a shop and likes to buy people's toenails;

the hill, somewhere in Ukambani, where things slide uphill; thirteen-year-old girls who swarm around bars like this one, selling their bodies to send money home or take care of their babies; the politician who was cursed for stealing money, and whose balls swell up whenever he visits his constituency; a strange insect in Turkana that climbs up your urine as you piss, and causes much pain for a day or two.

Painful things are shed like sweat.

Somebody confesses that he spent time in prison in Mwea. He talks about his relief at getting out before all the springs of his body were worn out. We hear about the guard who got AIDS, and infected many inmates with the disease deliberately before dying.

Kariuki reveals himself. We hear how he prefers to work away from home because he can't afford the school fees and hates seeing his children at home; how, though he has a diploma in Agriculture, he has been taking casual driving jobs for ten years. We hear about how worthless his coffee farm has become. He starts to laugh when he tells us how he lived with a woman for a year in Kibera, afraid to contact his family because he had no money to provide for them. The woman owned property. She fed him and kept him in liquor while he lived there.

His wife found him by putting an announcement on National Radio.

Some of us break to dance, and return to regroup. We talk and dance and talk and dance, not thinking how strange we will be to each other when the sun is in the sky, and our plumage is unavoidable, and trees suddenly have thorns, and around us a vast horizon of possible problems reseal our defenses.

The edges of the sky start to fray, a mauve invasion of the dark that protects us. I can see shadows outside the gate, people headed to the fields.

There is a guy laying on the grass, obviously in agony, his stomach taut as a drum. He is sweating badly. I almost expect the horns of the goat that he had been eating to force themselves through his sweat glands. His friends take him away in a pickup.

Self-pity music comes on. Kenny Rogers, "A Town Like Alice," Dolly Parton. I try to get Kariuki and the Chief to leave, but they are stuck in an embrace, howling to the music and swimming in sentiment.

Then a song comes on that makes me insist that we are leaving.

Sometime in the 1980s, a Kenyan university professor recorded a song that was an enormous hit. It could best be described as a multiplicity of yodels celebrating the Wedding Vow.

Will you take me (spoken, not sung) / To be your law-(yodel)-ful wedded wife / To love and to cherish and to (yodel) (then a gradually more hysterical yodel): Yieeeeei-yeeeeei MEN! . . . then just Amens, and more yodels.

Of course, all these proud warriors, pillars of the community, are at this moment yodeling in unison with the music, hugging themselves (beer bottles under armpit), and looking sorrowful.

Soon, the beds in this motel will be creaking, as some of these men forget self-pity and look for a lost youth in the bodies of young girls.

Late afternoon: sunlight can be very rude. I seem to have developed a set of bumpy new lenses in my eyes. Who put sand in my eyes? Somewhere, in the distance, a war is taking place: guns, howitzers, bitches, jeeps, and gin and juice.

"Everybody say 'Heeeey!' "

The Chief bursts into my room, looking like he spent the night eating fresh vegetables and massaging his body in vitamins. This is not fair. "Hey, bwana, chief."

Is that my voice? I have a wobbly vision of water, droplets cool against a chilled bottle, waterfalls, mountain streams, taps, ice cubes falling into a glass. Oh, to drink.

"*Pole* about the noise—my sons like this funny music too much." There's somebody in the bed next to me.

Kariuki snores too much.

A Fluid Disposition: Maasailand

August 1995

A few minutes ago, I was sleeping comfortably in the front of a Land Rover Discovery. Now I am woken suddenly, as the Agricultural Extension Officer makes a mad dash for the night comforts of Narok Town. Driving at night in this area is not a bright idea.

It is an interesting aspect of traveling to a new place that, for the first few moments, your eyes cannot concentrate on the particular. I am overwhelmed by the glare of dusk, by the shiver of wind on undulating acres of wheat and barley, by the vision of mile upon mile of space free from our wirings. So much is my focus derailed that when I return into myself I find, to my surprise, that my feet are not off the ground, that the landscape had grabbed me with such force it sucked up the awareness of myself for a moment.

It occurs to me that there is no clearer proof of the subjectivity (or selectivity) of our senses than at moments like this.

Seeing is almost always only noticing.

There are rotor-blades of cold chopping away in my nostrils. The silence, after the nonstop drone of the car, is as clinging as cobwebs, as intrusive as the loudest of noises. I have an urge to claw it away from my eardrums.

I am in Maasailand.

Not television Maasailand. We are high up in the Mau Hills. There are no rolling grasslands, lions, and acacia trees here; there are forests. Impenetrable woven highland forest, dominated by bamboo. Inside, there are elephants, which come out at night and leave enormous pancakes of shit on the road. When I was a kid, I used to think that elephants, like cats, use dusty roads as toilet paper—sitting on the ground on their haunches and levering themselves forward with their forelegs.

Back on the choosing to see business. I know chances are I will see no elephants for the weeks I am here. I will see people.

It occurs to me that if I was white, chances are I would choose to see elephants, and this would be a very different story. That story would be about the wide, empty spaces people from Europe yearn to get lost in, rather than the cozy surround of kin we Africans generally seek.

Whenever I read something by a white writer who stopped by, or lives in Kenya, I am astonished by the amount of game that appears for breakfast on their patios, and the number of snakes that drop into the baths, and the cheetah cubs that become family pets. I have seen five or six snakes in my life. I don't know anybody who has ever been bitten by one.

The cold air is really irritating. I want to breathe in, suck up the moist mountain-ness of the air, the smell of fever tree and dung—but the process is just too painful. What do people do in wintry places? Do they have some sort of nasal Sensodyne?

I can see our ancient Massey Ferguson wheezing up a distant hill. They are headed this way.

Relief.

A week later, I am on a tractor, freezing, as we make our way from the wheat fields and back to camp. We have been supervising the spraying of wheat and barley in the scattered fields my father leases.

There isn't much to look forward to at night here, no pubs hidden in the bamboo jungle. You can't even walk about freely at night because outside is full of stinging nettles. We will be in bed by seven to beat the cold. I will hear stories about frogs that sneak under your bed and turn into beautiful women who entrap you. I will hear stories about legendary tractor drivers—people who could turn the jagged roof of Mount Kilimanjaro into a neat Afro. I will hear about Maasai people, about so-and-so, who got two hundred thousand shillings for barley grown on his land, and how he took off to the Majengo Slums in Nairobi, leaving his wife and children behind, to live with a prostitute for a year.

When the money ran out, he discarded his suit, pots and pans, and furniture. He wrapped a blanket around himself and walked home, whistling happily all the way.

Most of all, I will hear stories about Ole Kamaro, our land-lord, and his wife Eddah (names changed).

My dad has been growing wheat and barley in this area since I was a child. All this time, we have been leasing a portion of Ole Kamaro's land where we keep our tractors and things and make camp. I met Eddah when she had just married Ole Kamaro. She was his fifth wife, thirteen years old. He was very proud of her. She was the daughter of a big-time chief from near Mau Narok. Most important, she could read and write. Ole Kamaro bought her a pocket radio and made her follow him about with a pen and pencil everywhere he went, taking notes.

I remember being horrified by the marriage—she was so young! My sister Ciru was eight, and they played together one day. That night, my sister had a terrible nightmare that my dad had sold her to Ole Kamaro in exchange for fifty acres of land.

Those few years of schooling were enough to give Eddah a clear idea of the basic tenets of Empowerment. By the time she was eighteen, Ole Kamaro had dumped the rest of his wives.

Eddah leased out his land to Kenya Breweries and opened a bank account where all the money went.

Occasionally, she gave her husband pocket money.

Whenever he was away, she took up with her lover, a wealthy young Kikuyu shopkeeper from the other side of the hill who kept her supplied with essentials like soap, matches, and paraffin.

Eddah is the local Chairwoman of the KANU Women's League and so remains invulnerable to censure from the conservative element in the area. She also has a successful business, curing hides and beading them elaborately for the tourist market at the Mara. Unlike most Maasai women, who disdain the growing of crops, she has a thriving market garden with maize, beans, and other vegetables. She does not lift a finger to take care of this garden. Part of the cooperation we expect from her as landlady depends on our staff taking care of her garden.

Something interesting is going on today, and the drivers are nervous. There is a tradition among the Maasai that women are released from all domestic duties a few months after giving birth. They are allowed to take over the land and claim any lovers that they choose. For some reason I don't quite understand, this all happens at a particular season, and this season begins today. I have been warned to keep away from any bands of women wandering about.

We are on an enormous hill, and I can hear the old Massey Ferguson tractor still wheezing. We get to the top and turn to make our way down, and there they are: led by Eddah, a troop of about forty women is marching toward us dressed in their best traditional clothing.

Eddah looks imperious and beautiful in her beaded leather cloak, red kanga wraps, rings, necklaces, and earrings. There is an old woman among them; she must be seventy, and she is cackling with glee. She takes off her wrap and displays her breasts, which resemble old socks.

Mwangi, who is driving, stops and tries to turn back, but the road is too narrow: on one side there is the mountain, and on the other a yawning valley. Kipsang, who is sitting in the trailer with me, shouts, "Aiiii! Mwangi bwana! DO NOT STOP!"

It seems that the modernized version of this tradition involves men making donations to the KANU Women's League. Innocent enough, you'd think—but the amount of these donations must satisfy them or they will strip you naked and do unspeakable things to your body.

So we take off at full speed. The women stand firm in the middle of the road. We can't swerve. We stop.

Then Kipsang saves our skins by throwing a bunch of coins onto the road. I throw down some notes, and Mwangi (renowned across Maasailand for his stinginess) empties his pockets, throwing down notes and coins. The women start to gather the money, the tractor roars back into action, and we drive right through them.

I am left with the picture of the toothless old lady diving to avoid the tractor. Then standing up, looking back at us and laughing, her breasts flapping like a flag of victory.

I am in bed, still in Maasailand. I pick up my father's *World Almanac and Book of Facts 1992*. The language section has new words, confirmed from sources as impeccable as the *Columbia Encyclopedia* and the *Oxford English Dictionary*. The list reads like an American Infomercial: "Jazzercise," "Assertiveness Training," "Bulimia," "Anorexic," "Microwavable," "Fast-tracker."

The words soak into me. America is the cheerleader. They twirl the baton, and we follow.

There is a word there, "skanking," described as: "A style of West Indian dancing to reggae music, in which the body bends forward at the waist and the knees are raised and the hands claw the air in time to the beat; dancing in this style."

I have some brief flash of us in forty years' time, in some generic dance studio. We are practicing for the Senior Dance Championships, plastic smiles on our faces as we skank across the room.

The tutor checks the movement: shoulder up, arms down, move this-way, move-that: Claw, baby. Claw!

In time to the beat, dancing in this style.

Langat and Kariuki have lost their self-consciousness around me and are chatting away about Eddah Ole Kamaro, our landlady.

"Eh! She had ten thousand shillings and they went and stayed in a hotel in Narok for a week. Ole Kamaro had to bring in another woman to look after the children!"

"Hai! But she sits on him!"

Their talk meanders slowly, with no direction—just talk, just connecting, and I feel that tight wrap of time loosen, the anxiety of losing time fades, and I am a glorious vacuum for a while, just letting what strikes my mind strike my mind, then sleep strikes my mind.

Ole Kamaro is slaughtering a sheep today.

We all settle on the patch of grass between the two compounds. Ole Kamaro makes quick work of the sheep and I am offered a fresh kidney to eat. It tastes surprisingly good: slippery warmth, an organic cleanliness.

Ole Kamaro introduces me to his sister-in-law, Suzannah, tells me proudly that she is in Form 4. Eddah's sister. I spotted her this morning staring at me from the tiny window in their *manyatta*. It was disconcerting at first, a typically Maasai stare, unembarrassed, not afraid to be vulnerable. Then she noticed that I had seen her, and her eyes narrowed and became sassy—street-sassy, like a girl from Eastlands in Nairobi.

So I am now confused about how to approach her. Should it be one of exaggerated politeness, as is traditional, or with a casual cool, as her second demeanor requested? I would have opted for the latter, but her brother-in-law is standing eagerly next to us.

She responds by lowering her head and looking away. I am painfully embarrassed. I ask her to show me where they tan their hides.

We escape with some relief.

"So where do you go to school?"

"Oh! At St. Teresa's Girls in Nairobi."

"Eddah is your sister?"

"Yes."

We are quiet for a while. English was a mistake. Where I am fluent, she is stilted. I switch to Kiswahili, and she pours herself into another person, talkative, aggressive. A person who must have a Tupac T-shirt stashed away somewhere.

"Arhh! It's so boring here! Nobody to talk to! I hope Eddah comes home early."

I am stunned. How bold and animated she is, speaking Sheng, a very hip street language that mixes Kiswahili and English and other languages.

"Why didn't you go with the women today?"

She laughs. "I am not married. Ho! I'm sure they had fun! They are drinking muratina somewhere, I am sure. I can't wait to get married."

"*Kwani?* You don't want to go to university and all that?"

"Maybe, but if I'm married to the right guy, life is good. Look at Eddah: she is free; she does anything she wants. Old men are good. If you feed them and give them a son, they leave you alone."

"Won't it be difficult to do this if you are not circumcised?"

"Kwani, who told you I'm not circumcised? I went last year."

I am shocked, and it shows. She laughs.

"He! I nearly shat myself! But I didn't cry!"

"Why? *Si,* you could have refused."

"Ai! If I had refused, it would mean that my life here was finished. There is no place here for someone like that."

"But—"

I cut myself short. I am sensing this is her compromise—to live two lives fluently. As it is with people's reasons for their faiths and choices—trying to disprove her is silly. As a Maasai, she will see my statement as ridiculous.

In Sheng, there is no way for me to bring it up that would be diplomatic; in Sheng she can present this only with a hard-edged bravado—and it is humiliating. I do not know of any way we can discuss this successfully in English. If there is a courtesy every Kenyan practices, it is that we don't question each other's contradictions; we all have them, and destroying someone's face is sacrilege.

There is nothing wrong with being what you are not in Kenya—just be it successfully. Almost every Kenyan joke is about somebody who thought they had mastered a new persona and ended up ridiculous.

Suzanna knows her faces well.

Christmas in Bufumbira

December 20, 1995

The drive through the Mau Hills, past the Rift Valley and onward to Kisumu, bores me. I haven't been this way for ten years, but my aim is to be in Uganda. We arrive in Kampala at ten in the evening. We have been on the road for over eight hours.

This is my first visit to Uganda, a land of incredible mystery for me. I grew up with her myths and legends and her horrors, narrated with the intensity that only exiles can muster. It is my first visit to my mother's ancestral home; the occasion is her parents' sixtieth wedding anniversary.

It will be the first time that she and her ten surviving brothers and sisters have been together since the early 1960s. The first time that my grandparents will have all their children and most of their grandchildren at home together; more than a hundred people are expected.

My mother, and the many relatives and friends who came to visit, have filled my imagination with incredible tales of Uganda. I heard how you had to wriggle on your stomach to see the Kabaka; how the Tutsi King in Rwanda (who was seven feet tall) was once given a bicycle as a present; because he couldn't touch the ground (being a king and all), he was carried everywhere, on his bicycle, by his bearers.

Apparently, in the old kingdom in Rwanda, Tutsi women were not supposed to exert themselves or mar their beauty in any way. Some women had to be spoon-fed by their Hutu servants and wouldn't leave their huts for fear of sunburn.

I was told about a trip my grandfather took, with an uncle, when he was young, where he was mistaken for a Hutu servant and taken away to sleep with the goats. A few days later his uncle asked about him and his hosts were embarrassed to confess that they didn't know he was "one of us."

It has been a year of mixed blessings for Africa.

This is the year that I sat at Newlands Stadium during the

Rugby World Cup in the Cape and watched South Africans reach out to each other before giving New Zealand a hiding. Mandela, wearing the number six rugby jersey, managed to melt away, for one incredible night, all the hostility that had gripped the country since he was released from jail. Black people, traditionally supporters of the All Blacks, embraced the Springboks with enthusiasm. For just one night, most South Africans felt a common nationhood.

It is the year that I returned to my home, Kenya, to find people so way beyond cynicism that they looked back on their cynical days with fondness.

Uganda is different: this is a country that has not only reached the bottom of the hole countries sometimes fall into, it has scratched through that bottom and free-fallen again and again, and now it has rebuilt itself and swept away the hate. This country gives me hope that this continent is not, finally, incontinent.

This is the country I used to associate with banana trees, old and elegant kingdoms, Idi Amin, decay, and hopelessness. It was an association I had made as a child, when the walls of our house would ooze and leak whispers of horror whenever a relative or friend of the family came home, fleeing from Amin's literal and metaphoric crocodiles.

I am rather annoyed that the famous Seven Hills of Kampala are not as clearly defined as I had imagined they would be. I have always had a childish vision of a stately city filled with royal paraphernalia. I had expected to see elegant people dressed in flowing robes, carrying baskets on their heads and walking arrogantly down streets filled with the smell of roasting bananas; and intellectuals from a 1960s dream, shaking the streets with their Afrocentric rhetoric.

Images formed in childhood can be more than a little bit stubborn.

Reality is a better aesthetic. Kampala seems disorganized, full of potholes, bad management, and haphazardness. The African city that so horrifies the West. The truth is that it is a city being overwhelmed by enterprise. I see smiles, the shine of healthy skin and teeth; no layabouts lounging and plotting at every street corner. People do not walk about with walls around themselves as they do in Nairobbery.

All over, there is a frenzy of building. A blanket of paint is slowly spreading over the city, so it looks rather like one of those Smirnoff adverts where inanimate things get breathed into Technicolor by the sacred burp of forty percent or so of clear alcohol.

It is humid, and hot, and the banana trees flirt with you, swaying gently like fans offering a coolness that never materializes.

Everything smells musky, as if a thick, soft steam has risen like broth. The plants are enormous. Mum once told me that, traveling in Uganda in the 1940s and the 1950s, if you were hungry you could simply enter a banana plantation and eat as much as you wished. You didn't have to ask anybody. But you were not allowed to carry so much as a single deformed banana out of the plantation.

We are booked in at the Catholic Guesthouse. As soon as I have dumped my stuff on the bed, I call up an old school-friend, who promises to pick me up.

Musoke comes at six and we go to find food. We drive past the famous Mulago Hospital and into town. He picks up a couple of friends, and we go to a bar called Yakubu's.

We order a couple of beers, lots of roast pork brochettes, and sit in the car. The brochettes are delicious. I like them so much that I order more. Nile beer is okay, but nowhere near Kenya's Tusker.

The sun is drowned suddenly, and it is dark.

We get on to the highway to Entebbe. On both sides of the road, people have built flimsy houses. Bars, shops, and cafés line the road the whole way. Many people are out, especially teenagers, guided hormones flouncing about, puffs of fog surrounding their huddled faces. It is still hot outside; paraffin lamps light the fronts of all these premises.

I turn to Musoke and ask, "Can we stop at one of those pubs and have a beer?"

"Ah! Wait till we get to where we are going—it's much nicer than this dump!"

"I'm sure it is; but, you know, I might never get a chance to drink in a real Entebbe pub, not those bourgeois places. Come on, I'll buy a round."

Magic words.

The place is charming. Ugandans seem to me to have a knack for making things elegant and comfortable, regardless of income. In Kenya, or South Africa, a place like this would be dirty, and buildings would be put together with a sort of haphazard self-loathing; sort of like saying "I won't be here long, so why bother?"

The inside of the place is decorated simply, mostly with reed mats. The walls are well finished, and the floor, simple cement, has no cracks or signs of misuse. Women in traditional Baganda dresses serve us.

I find Baganda women terribly sexy. They carry about with them a look of knowledge, a proud and naked sensuality, daring you to satisfy it.

They don't seem to have that generic cuteness many city women have, that I have already begun to find irritating. Their features are strong, their skin is a deep, gleaming copper, and their eyes are large and oily black.

Baganda women traditionally wear a long loose Victorian-style dress. It fulfills every literal aspect the Victorians desired, but manages despite itself to suggest sex. The dresses are usually in bold colors. To emphasize their size, many women tie a band just below their buttocks (which are often padded).

What makes the difference is the walk.

Many women visualize their hips as an unnecessary evil, an irritating accessory that needs to be whittled down. I guess a while back women looked upon their hips as a cradle for the depositing of desire, for the nurturing of children. Baganda women see their hips as supple things, moving in lubricated circles—so they make excellent Ndombolo dancers. In those loose dresses, their hips filling out the sides as they move, they are a marvel to watch.

Most appealing about them is the sense of stature they carry about them. Baganda women seem to have found a way to be traditional and powerful at the same time—most I know grow more beautiful with age and many compete with men in industry, without seeming to compromise themselves as women.

I sleep on the drive from Kampala to Kisoro.

From Kisoro, we begin the drive to St. Paul's Mission, Kigezi. My sister Ciru is sitting next to me. She is a year younger than me. Chiqy, my youngest sister, has been to Uganda before and is taking full advantage of her vast experience to play the adult tour guide. At her age, cool is a god.

I have the odd feeling we are puppets in some Christmas story. It is as if a basket-weaver was writing this story in a language of weave: tightening the tension on the papyrus strings every few minutes and superstitiously refusing to reveal the ending—even to herself—until she has tied the very last knot.

We are now in the mountains. The winding road and the dense papyrus in the valleys seem to entwine me, ever tighter, into my fictional weaver's basket. Every so often, she jerks her weave to tighten it.

I look up to see the last half-hour of road winding along the mountain above us. We are in the Bufumbira Range now, driving through Kigaland on our way to Kisoro, the nearest town to my mother's home.

There is an alien quality to this place. It does not conform to any African topography that I am familiar with. The mountains are incredibly steep and resemble inverted ice-cream cones. The hoe has tamed every inch of them.

It is incredibly green.

In Kenya, "green" is the ultimate accolade a person can give land: green is scarce, green is wealth, green is fertility.

Bufumbira green is not a tropical green; no warm musk, like in Buganda; nor is it the harsh green of the Kenyan savanna, that two-month-long green that compresses all the elements of life—millions of wildebeest and zebra, great carnivores feasting during the rains, frenzied plowing and planting, and dry riverbeds overwhelmed by soil and bloodstained water. Nairobi under water.

It is not the green of grand waste and grand bounty that my country knows.

This is a mountain green, cool and enduring. Rivers and lakes occupy the cleavage of the many mountains that surround us.

Mum looks almost foreign now. Her Kinyarwanda accent is more pronounced, and her face is not as reserved as usual. Her beauty, so exotic and head-turning in Kenya, seems at home here. She does not stand out anymore—she belongs; the rest of us seem like tourists.

As the drive continues, the sense of where we are starts to seep into me. We are no longer in the history of Buganda, of Idi Amin, of the Kabakas, or civil war, Museveni, and Hope.

We are now on the outskirts of the theater where the Hutus and the Tutsis have been performing for the world's media. My mother has always described herself as a Mufumbira, one who speaks Kinyarwanda. She has always said that too much is made of the differences between Tutsi and Hutu; that they are really more alike than not. She insists that she is Bufumbira, and speaks Kinyarwanda. Forget the rest, she says.

I am glad she hasn't, because it saves me from trying to understand. I am not here about genocide or hate. Enough people have been here for that—try typing "Tutsi" on any search engine.

I am here to be with family.

I ask my mother where the border with Rwanda is. She points it out, and points out Zaire as well. They are both nearer than I thought. Maybe this is what makes this coming together so urgent. How amazing life seems when it stands around death. There is no grass as beautiful as the blades that stick out after the first rain.

As we move into the forested area, I am enthralled by the smell and by the canopy of mountain vegetation. I join the conversation in the car. I have become self-conscious about displaying my dreaminess and absentmindedness these days.

I used to spend hours gazing out of car windows, creating grand battles between battalions of clouds. I am aware of a conspiracy to get me back to Earth, to get me to be more practical. My parents are pursuing this cause with little subtlety, aware that my time with them is limited. It is necessary for me to believe that I am putting myself on a gritty road to personal success when I leave home. Cloud travel is well and good when you have mastered the landings. I never have. I must live, not dream about living.

We are in Kisoro, the main town of the district, weaving through roads between people's houses. We are heading toward Uncle Kagame's house.

The image of a dictatorial movie director manipulating our movements replaces that of the basket-weaver in my mind. I have a dizzy vision of a supernatural producer slowing down the action before the climax by examining tiny details instead of grand scenes.

I see a continuity presenter in the fifth dimension saying: "And now our Christmas movie: a touching story about the reunion of a family torn apart by civil war and the genocide in Rwanda. This movie is sponsored by Sobbex, hankies for every occasion" (repeated in Zulu).

My grandmother embraces me. She is very slender and I feel she will break. Her elegance surrounds me, and I feel a strong urge to dig into her, burrow into her secrets, see with her eyes. She is a quiet woman, and unbending, even taciturn—and this gives her a powerful charisma. Things not said. Her resemblance to my mother astounds me.

My grandfather is crying and laughing, exclaiming when he hears that Chiqy and I are named after him and his wife (Kamanzi and Binyavanga). We drink *urugwagwa* laced with honey. It is delicious, smoky and dry.

Ciru and Chiqy are sitting next to my grandmother. I see why my grandfather was such a legendary schoolteacher: his gentleness and love of life are palpable.

At night, we split into our various age groups and start to

bond with each other. Of the cousins, Manwelli, the eldest, is our unofficial leader. He works for the World Bank.

Aunt Rosaria and her family are the coup of the gathering. They were feared dead during the war in Rwanda and hid for months in their basement, helped by a friend who provided food. They all survived; they walk around carrying expressions that are more common in children—delight, sheer delight at life.

Rosaria's three sons spend every minute bouncing about with the high of being alive. They dance at all hours, sometimes even when there is no music. In the evenings, we squash on to the veranda, looking out as far as the Congo, and they entertain us with their stand-up routines in French and Kinyarwanda, the force of their humor carrying us all to laughter.

Manwelli translates one skit for me: they are imitating a vain Tutsi woman who is pregnant and is kneeling to make a confession to the shocked priest: "Oh, please God, let my child have long fingers, and a gap between the teeth; let her have a straight nose and be ta-a-all. Oh, Lord, let her not have a nose like a Hutu. Oh, please, I shall be your grateful servant!"

The biggest disappointment, so far, is that my Aunt Christine has not yet arrived. She has lived with her family in New York since the early 1970s. We all feel her absence keenly, as it was she who urged us all years ago to gather for this occasion at any cost.

She and my Aunt Rosaria are the senior aunts, and they were very close when they were younger. They speak frequently on the phone and did so especially during the many months that Aunt Rosaria and her family were living in fear in their basement. They are, for me, the summary of the pain the family has been through over the years. Although they are very close, they haven't met since 1961. Visas, wars, closed borders, and a thousand triumphs of chaos have kept them apart. We are all looking forward to their reunion.

As is normal on traditional occasions, people stick with their peers, so I have hardly spoken to my mother over the past few days. I find her in my grandmother's room, trying, without much success, to get my grandmother to relax and let her many daughters and granddaughters do the work.

I have been watching Mum from a distance for the past few days. At first, she seemed a bit aloof from it all, but now she's found fluency with everything, and she seems far away from the Kenyan mother we know. I can't get over the sight of her blushing as my grandmother machine-guns instructions at her. How alike they are. I want to talk with her more, but decide not to be selfish, not to make it seem that I am trying to establish possession of her. We'll have enough time on the way back.

I've been trying to pin down my grandfather, to ask him about our family's history. He keeps giving me this bewildered look when I corner him, as if he was asking: Can't you just relax and party?

Last night, he toasted us all and cried again before dancing to some very hip gospel rap music from Kampala. He tried to get grandmother to join him, but she beat a hasty retreat.

Gerald is getting quite concerned that, when we are all gone, they will find it too quiet.

We hurtle on toward Christmas. Booze flows, we pray, chat, and bond under the night rustle of banana leaves. I feel as if I am filled with magic, and I succumb to the masses. In two days, we feel a family. In French, Kiswahili, English, Kikuyu, Kinyarwanda, Kiganda, and Ndebele, we sing one song, a multitude of passports in our luggage.

At dawn on December 24, I stand smoking in the banana plantation at the edge of my grandfather's hill and watch the mists disappear. Uncle Chris saunters up to join me.

I ask, "Any news about Aunt Christine?"

"It looks like she might not make it. Manwelli has tried to get in contact with her and failed. Maybe she couldn't get a flight out of New York. Apparently, the weather is terrible there."

The day is filled with hard work. My uncles have convinced my grandfather that we need to slaughter another bull, as meat is running out. The old man adores his cattle but reluctantly agrees. He cries when the bull is killed.

There is to be a church service in the living room of my grandfather's house later in the day.

The service begins and I bolt from the living room, volunteering to peel potatoes outside.

About halfway through the service, I see somebody staggering up the hill, suitcase in hand and muddied up to her ankles. It takes me an instant to guess. I run to her and mumble something. We hug. Aunt Christine is here.

The plot has taken me over now. Resolution is upon me. The poor woman is given no time to freshen up or collect her bearings. In a minute, we have ushered her into the living room. She sits by the door, facing everybody's back. Only my grandparents are facing her. My grandmother starts to cry.

Nothing is said; the service motors on. Everybody stands up to sing. Somebody whispers to my Aunt Rosaria. She turns and gasps soundlessly. Others turn. We all sit down. Aunt Rosaria and Aunt Christine start to cry. Aunt Rosaria's mouth opens and closes in disbelief. My mother joins them, and soon everybody is crying.

The priest motors on, fluently. Unaware.

7

Joga of Mathare Valley

My eyes hurt. I'm still not used to having the sun directly above me again. There is a truth in the saying that what you see in Kenya is uncompromising—there is *no* soft focus here.

The Serengeti migration has nothing on Eastlands at rush hour. Eastlands is where the *mwananchi* lives. There is a whole ocean of people, moving like time has run out on them. The wares of a mish-mash of informal traders color the streets. Eastlands has taken on a distinctly Middle Eastern persona since half of Somalia and Ethiopia resettled here. There are bazaars, shops advertising henna, *buibui*-clad women, and lots of miraa on sale. There is a beauty salon whose sign shows Mickey Mouse having his hands hennaed.

I am here because I am bored. Since I came back home four months ago, I have found my feelings for Kenyans somewhat barren. Everybody I know is ten years older, and conversations revolve around nappies and the size of mobile phones.

To most, my dreadlocks and lifestyle in Cape Town are decadent and wasteful. Already tactful moves are being made to get me engaged to somebody, or at least into some kind of respectable relationship. Almost all my peers probe and dig and insist that my life has no fulfillment, no spiritual promise, without baby poo and nappies. Every Saturday afternoon somebody is getting married or being baptized, or there is a baby shower.

I am bored. Bored with the endless political discussions, with going to the same old places, and listening to the same twenty R&B songs the radio stations have been ramming down my soul.

Mathare Valley is Kenya's largest informal settlement. The name is so notorious it strikes terror into any owner of fixed property. It doesn't help that Kenya's only psychiatric hospital is called Mathare too.

Last night I was in a bar. I sat next to a gentleman wearing cowboy boots and a cowboy hat. He turned out to be the Councilor for Mathare. Brits small-talk about the weather; Kenyans used to. These days we small-talk about Daniel arap Moi, our bewildering President, a source of endless fascination. To protect ourselves from revolutionary fury, we speak of him as if he is a well-known, slightly eccentric relation, calling him "Uncle Dan" or "Em-Oh-One."

Unfortunately I had picked probably the one person in Nairobi whose feelings for Moi were still an open wound. By the time we were on our fifth beer, the attacks had become personal.

What do you know about how real Kenyans live? Do you believe what you read in the papers? Don't you know that seventy-five percent of people in Nairobi live in slums like Mathare? Have you ever been to one?

By the time he was finished with me, I felt like an Afrikaner Weerstandsbeweging member in Soweto. I had to see Mathare for myself.

The photographer I am with, J. Wambua, lives here, so I feel fairly safe. Also, this is probably the only place in Kenya where my dreadlocks are likely to be well received. Bob Marley is a god here.

Wambua tells me that Mathare has redeemed itself significantly in Kenyans' eyes since its football team made mincemeat of Kenya's best in the Premier League. Started as a club to keep kids off the streets, Mathare United is now Kenya's leading soccer team.

Just as the sun drops behind the silhouette of the city in the distance, we turn off the main road. We enter another planet.

It is as if we are in a city of paraffin lamps, and there are literally thousands of people milling about. Narrow paths zigzag between shacks. In front of the shacks something is being sold. Meat is grilling, chapatis are doing triple somersaults off flat pans, and vetkoek are spitting with fury. The energy of the place is unbelievable.

There are piles and piles of neatly arranged tomatoes, red onions, mangoes, and kale. Red, yellow, and green bananas hang from ceilings. *Mielies,* Kenya's national snack, are being grilled. There are acrobats, charismatic preachers with mobile PA systems, butchers and fishmongers, secondhand book stalls, bars, and every sort of clothing imaginable for sale. There is not a blade of grass, no trees or bushes.

It is only once I adjust to the frenzy around me that I notice *the art*. It is like the cover of a fantasy novel. I guess nobody needs to buy realism for their walls; it's free here. I notice that most of the better paintings have been done by the same person: Joga. He is sent for, and after fifteen minutes a diminutive young man with uncomfortably naked eyes joins us. There doesn't seem to be a part of him that isn't spattered with paint.

Joga is nineteen. He has only a primary-school education and has never been to an art gallery. He just likes to draw.

He takes us around his favorite works. I can count on my fingers the number of times I have felt beauty so utterly.

When I was eight, we drove through Laikipia during a storm. My face was pressed to the window and a slow brandy warmth spread from the pit of my stomach. I had been through this dusty harsh veld many times, but the thunder and lightning had caught the area unawares, and in the panic of fauna and flora I saw the big picture. For the briefest moment I felt part of something that could not be broken into the sum of its parts. To this day, the smell of rain on dust brings back this feeling of completion.

Joga's best work is of women. He manages to render what they want to look like when they leave a salon, without restricting himself to the usual clichés. He draws plump women; doe-eyed women; tough, strong-jawed women; women all pruned and primed, their hair done just the way that suits them best. Expressions range from orgasmic joy to prim satisfaction.

Mama Njeri, a salon owner, tells me that Joga's signs have brought in a clientele who previously went downtown to get their hair done.

We go into a bar. The average age of customers here is fifty. The language spoken is Kikuyu, not Sheng, the latter that blend of Kiswahili and English spoken on this side of town. The murals on the walls show scenes of drunkenness. Grilled meat and drunkenness. Pastoral humor: cows with overlarge udders, lush milkmaids. The dreams of rural immigrants. Escape here, says the advertisement, sample a little bit of home. I laugh at the drunks. Legless. Joga has drawn them with spaghetti legs.

I've been surprised when Joga has said his works are like photos. Many other people say so too, yet his style is not representative.

He refuses to accept that there could possibly be an objective picture of somebody. Surely people are exactly how he chooses to see them? He therefore refuses to see the difference between his cartoon images, which distinctly reflect the character of the people he portrays, and photographs taken from the perspective of the photographer. It amazes me that he is able to discern this truth with such simplicity—it is one I grapple with often.

Joga is able to draw attention to what people see in other people, even laughing at the silliness of the stereotypes he portrays, but so subtly that his clients never notice. The guy at the telephone bureau will be happy that the picture will bring in professionals, yet Joga manages to show what he thinks of such people: a greedy glint in the eye, a frown of stress, overbright lipstick on a hard face.

Does he like Mathare? Yes, he doesn't plan ever to leave. I look about and imagine him twenty years from now, never lacking a wall on which to hang his vision. I envy him.

8

Hair

Somebody somewhere should start a Museum of Black Hair. If art is about suffering, surely what we darkies go through to keep our hair up to trend is worthy of a biennale.

In the 1970s, the chafe of polyester was not the only torture Kenyan boys had to deal with. There was the *kinyozi*. In my hometown, there was a street full of kinyozis. It was my dad's job to take us to the kinyozi every last Saturday of the month. Normally the prospect of a day out with my dad was filled with pleasure. His wallet was always full of crisp hundred-shilling notes—and he had not read that rule book mothers inherit (together with eyes in the backs of their heads) that says, "Not more than one ice cream and I will not relent even if you bang your head against the window and have a full-blown tantrum in the middle of the market with the ice-cream men looking at me as if I were some sort of child-abuser and anti-ice-cream-communist."

Kids are ruthless, and my dad was mostly a softie, racked with guilt that work kept him too busy to spend enough time with us. But whenever we went to the barbershop, I hated the man. I frequently requested assistance from Jesuschristomiyty, but he always seemed to be busy cloning fish and baking bread.

Kikuyu (my mother tongue, which I speak very badly) can be a harsh and blunt language. Often somebody speaking Kikuyu seems to be sneering at you. It doesn't help that the language is the street language of money in Kenya. Walking into the barbershop, I was always assaulted by wide, crocodile grins and raucous greetings in Kikuyu. The barbers were always in 1950-style military cuts.

On the wall, there would be the ubiquitous side profiles of improbably neat cuts, right next to the large, red NO CREDIT! signs. Pictures of Harry Belafonte (damn you!) and U.S. Marines were popular as well.

James Brown, The Jacksons, Osibisa, or Earth Wind and Fire never have been seen in any African barbershop, and never will be. Bob Marley and Jimi Hendrix had dealings with the devil (just look at their hair: bad for business!). Jesus had a crew cut. Muhammad Ali was okay, but he was a boxer, and boxers were allowed some privileges for having their heads bashed regularly.

In school, only Ali Saleh managed to get away with an Afro. His hair so impressed Liza M., the prissiest girl in school, that she kissed him and showed him her panties. He was an Arab and his hair could grow a couple of inches during break. Besides, he went to the Indian barber, whose only torture was a bottle of coconut oil. Ali frequently came to school reeking of Swahili coconut curry.

I was well known at the barber's. One time I managed to wriggle out of the chair and spent the rest of the week with a halfro. This did not happen again. There was always somebody to hold me down while the barber performed a root canal on my scalp. There were no electric razors in those days. The barber would pick two combs; one small, vomit-yellow round brush with hard, plump bristles. Its job was to *kwaruza* (literally "scratch") the hair back till you looked like Ray Parker Junior.

This phase was known as "plow."

I always had a string of swellings on my forehead after this assault. After this, he would bring out the mzungu-comb, a deceptively delicate and fine-toothed number. Its job was to *fungua* the hair.

This process was known as "harrowing."

It is generally at this point that the human straitjackets were needed. The barber would start the comb at the front and run it through without pause to the back. On more than one occasion a few teeth broke, and the barber cursed the thick jungle that was my hair.

This was just the starter. I really began to holler when the barber rubbed his hands in anticipation as he went up to the shelf lined with rows and rows of gleaming stainless steel. The clipper would be examined in detail. Is it oiled? Are the teeth clear of obstruction?

The fingers would be exercised, knuckles cracked. My head would be forced down, and the combine harvester would begin its work. Of course, it cut in the opposite direction from which you combed your hair.

Those old clippers had no levels. One comb cut all. It would dig into the base of my scalp and start cutting. Every few seconds, it would choke and entangle itself in the forest.

Curses. Screams.

My sister had it much worse. Girls had to have their hair straightened or plaited. Straightened meant a metal comb, like my "harrow," that had sat for some minutes on a gas fire. Plaited meant pulled as high as it would go, woven, and tied with balls and balls of wool or raffia. These would be pulled again and shaped into the fashion of the day. "Pineapple" was okay, but "Mango" slanted sideways, and that meant some extra-special pulling.

Years passed, and then came this skinny little man with breathy lyrics and lots of moans, groans, and squeaks. Breathy lyrics changed the way we farmed our hair. Curly Kit took Kenya by storm. Men found themselves in hair salons, gossiping about conditioners and protein treatments, as the lye slowly fried their scalps. I remember one hairdresser laughing at some screaming men and telling them, "Let it cook. Labor lasts hours."

Public-transport vehicles invested in industrial-strength detergents for their windows. Sales of paper towels went through the roof. Frequent trips to the toilet were necessary to apply "curl activator." Ali's days as the class stud were over. Hair-Glo was much cooler than Patel's Coconut Oil.

The ultimate insult became, "You've got growth." Gelatin left the larder and found its way to bathroom cabinets. Best of all, many kinyozis closed down. Those that remained open had electric clippers, and photos of Michael Jackson trying to pull his crotch out.

Then the Gulf War came, and oil prices rose so high we couldn't afford the grease.

My present dreadlocks horrify my father. To him they mean a descent into drugs and anarchy. He also worries about the insects I am breeding (he worked with pyrethrin insecticides for thirty-five years).

The way he talks, you'd think Black men have never been vain about their hair.

The Kuria and Turkana peoples in Kenya would weave their hair into vast sculptures, which were often supported by wire and shaped with sheep fat and red clay. Men would travel around with a wooden "pillow" shaped like a catapult; its job was to keep the hair fresh while they slept.

Maasai men, to this day, are experts at braiding hair.

Women are supposed to shave theirs clean. In the mid 1980s Maasai braids became very fashionable in Nairobi. Many Maasais in Nairobi worked as security guards. No *moran* will run from a fight, and they can club a moving target on the head from fifty meters.

Girls left their salons and slow-burns in droves, and queued at the gates of factories and Westlands mansions, while Maasai Braves did their hair and advised them about dandruff and scalp rash.

Who said African men don't have a feminine side?

9

Travels Through Kalenjinland

To get a matatu to Baringo, you have to get to Ogilgei—which is the name of a notorious bar, and more: it can be found throughout Kalenjinland, the plains and rifts and mountains and towns; inside State House and its circles, among Special Branch police with their gray shoes and red or white socks, and shiny suits with a KANU party badge near the pocket; and nearly everywhere the two million people, of various related languages and cultures called Kalenjin, whether they be in Texas working for an IT company, or in the hills of Cherangani shaking bones and wearing a cloak of skin for a ceremony, exist. In Nakuru, *ogilgei* means "a lot." Across the road from the bar, just 10 meters away, are fifteen-seater Nissan vehicles that go to various places in Kalenjinland. So this noisy corner, not 20 meters square, is a sort of Kalenjin national nerve center: you can land, dusty and tired, from Texas or Kabartonjo, and ask around in your language for mursik or to be updated on all the latest politics, or negotiate, if your tongue is adroit enough, to meet the President; or a good traditional healer, or a trustworthy doctor, or your missing cousin, or a guy who knows a guy who speaks your language who can find you a tractor to hire, or a friendly policeman to help your court case disappear.

When times are hot and there is conflict with the Kikuyu, this is a place of safety—or danger—for you can hide here, and be hidden, or be sought out. If you stand outside the bar, a soft mist of Kalenjin babble rises. To the outsider it has a slight falsetto, not high, flat—sounds are sharp sticks hitting wood, hard *g*'s and *b*'s are soft porridge, gurgly, and a force defined in secondary-school physics class as a bush or a bull, because that is where *p* becomes *b*.

If there are riots against a perception of Kalenjin threat—which means that people feel that State House is being ethnically xenophobic—people will know to head to Ogilgei. To attack this small place, even with loud banging noises, is to speak loudly to the nation of Kalenjins, and directly to the President.

There have been ethnic clashes here, in 1991 and 1994. We all know Moi and his people were at the center of it: shoring up his support among the Kalenjin by creating paranoia about the Kikuyu, the Luhya—all neighboring tribes. They use the cheapest and most flammable political tactic: the outsiders are out to get you, if you give them an inch. There is enough tinder here, from Kenyatta days and before, when the Kikuyus were seen to benefit disproportionately.

But ethnic clashes never really have to do with the noble quest of the oppressed. In Kenya, it is always the poor who get killed and displaced by the poor, and only to serve the territorial needs of the political elite. If Kikuyu petty traders are kicked out of Maasailand, Maasai politicians can grab their assets.

Those who really steal from Kenyans, in all our political regimes, have never had their wealth challenged. As people become poorer and more desperate, the politicians escalate the paranoia, for fear that, one day, the crowd will stop and turn on them.

Not 10 meters away from Ogilgei, you are in little Somalia, which merges with little Mombasa—because the mosque is nearby—and so spicy things to eat can be found alongside sweets and incense. Behind Mombasa Stores, a Swahili grocer, and right next to the mosque is Nakuru's most famous whorehouse, also referred to as Mombasa Stores. Any teenager knows what you mean when you say Mombasa Stores.

I walk down, past Zoom Zoom, where we used to eat ice cream, past the Rift Valley Sports Club, an ocean of green cricket fields and brown tennis courts marked with white chalk, waiters who have worked there for forty years, and Mwangi, the chef, who has been making cheap English food (fish and chips, shepherd's pie, and others) for forty-six years and who talks about the days when you would be beaten by settlers in Nakuru Town if you were Black and seen wearing shoes within club grounds. Behind the wall are Tipsy and Nakuru Sweet Mart, twin restaurants, one a bakery and vegetarian thali restaurant and the other serving burgers and chips and the best masala chips in the world.

I stop to get a cup of masala tea, and a grimy face with brown smelly teeth presents itself in front of me. "Wainaina!" he shouts. I am embarrassed; I can't remember his name. He is waving a rag—a group of young men have been seated here for thirty years fighting to wash cars. This particular young man has been a street kid since I was a child. He and his brother operate from the market that is two streets down—both are fond of my mother and my brother Jim. He has a new car, Jimmy does, I am informed, and he helped me very much, very much. Your brother, he! He has a good heart. Your mother is very strict, but she always helps, and your brother has a good heart, he never forgets me. You have grown fat . . . you were in Botswana right? No, South Africa, and how is Mandela? An almost empty bottle of glue sticks off the side of his face. Things are rough these days, he says; there are people coming down from Molo and places, the Kalenjins are coming for Kikuyus . . . there are even Maasais hiding in Nakuru . . . are you driving the 505?

I can remember the first day I met him and his brother. I was seven or eight, and it was the first time I had ridden my bike into town, with my brother. I was exhausted, and hating it; my brother loves exercise and I don't. But I loved the idea of being allowed to be next to Jimmy. My lungs were burning as we ped-aled, but my heart was twin purple fluorescent tubes of happi-ness. My sister Ciru and I are like twins, maybe too close for me to feel love so violently. My love for Jimmy, and my desire for approval from him, disables me.

So, by the large patch of loudly trading voices and hooting vehicles opposite the market, we were pedaling furiously when we saw, spread out on the dust, two long bodies in ragged shorts and nothing else. Their ribcages stood out like hills, skin patchy and blackened with dirt, bruises, and scars. In the full heat of the dry, high-altitude day, they were motionless, and my brother turned to me and said, "They are dead," and my heart stopped, my feet flailed, and I toppled, scratched deeply by the bicycle chains. I did not want to look to see if their tongues were hang-ing out, because that was, in our childhood language, the utter confirmation of death. I was squinting at the bodies, when one of them jerked up and red swollen eyes caught mine. I squealed in fear and Jimmy started laughing, not so differently from how he is laughing with me now.

I am not afraid now.

Drama unfolded at Nyandarua County Council on Thursday afternoon when a chief officer swallowed a banker's check for one million shillings only a few minutes after being suspended. Civic leaders were dumbfounded at a special full council meet-ing when the officer grabbed the check and swallowed it. Chaos erupted as councilors wrestled with the officer in a bid to re-trieve the check. Mathingira Ward Councilor Margaret Wam-bugu was bitten as she tried to retrieve the check and was rushed to a local hospital.

—*The Standard*, 1995

The road shoots out into the distance, knobbly gray tarmac, straight and true, and making equal: Nakuru Town; the Agricul-tural Showground; the dead straight line of jacaranda and their morning carpet of mushy purple on rich, brown damp earth;

President Moi's palace and its attached school in Kabarak; plains of grain and cattle; stony, sky land, hot and dry; a pile of lonely casks of fresh milk, slowly souring by the side of the road; another pile of recycled bottles filled with dark beer-colored Baringo honey, waiting for a market that is not coming; an arm reaching out to show off a wriggling catfish to the odd city car; a huddle of schoolgirls, giggling, in purple school-skirts swollen by the wind into swaying polyester lampshades; goats seated in the center of the road just past Marigat Town; dried riverbeds; and the plains of grain and cattle as we head toward Baringo; groups of shining, Vaselined people walking or cycling by the side of the road, to church, sometimes ten or more kilometers away; ten or twelve tribes, three lakes; the whole unbroken line of human evolution here, in the base of the Rift Valley, as I head out to Pokot.

This road was the promise of a president to his people. The honey projects, the milk, the irrigation scheme not far from here that once produced aubergines the size of small pumpkins—all these things failed to make wealth, to find markets. The only durable success is the school, Kabarak High School, which provides some of the best high-school education in the country and has created a meritoclass of Bright Young Kalenjins now in banks, and government, and Wall Street, and teaching at universities all over the world. Moi has invested a lot in education all over Kalenjinland.

I board the early matatu to Kabartonjo at dawn, and get the front seat, next to a plump woman in a thick prickly sweater and a massive handbag. She is reading the Bible and chatting to the driver—in Kalenjin, which I do not understand, but which I love to listen to, the soft *t*'s and baby-softness of it, and how it is spoken always with the mouth yapping up and down in the grip of a full smile, a smile sometimes made poignant by a gap in the bottom teeth some men have, like the driver.

When I was a child there was a season of Sunday drives like

this. My father had committed, one year, to playing golf in every Sunday tournament in the country. So, come Sunday morning, we would be tearing up roads to make tee-off time. Mum hated golf, and golfers—and this whole expedition—and, although we often did not attend church in our hometown, she often insisted we go when we were on such trips, which we hated.

Trips were for other things.

This particular Sunday, the plan was to launch ourselves into a frenzy of splashing and swinging and sliding with fellow golf children and lick tomato sauce and molten Cadbury's chocolate off hot fingers and generally squirm and bliss around.

Uplands pork sausages.

But Mum must find a church first.

We end up in just some corrugated-iron church, and the heat and light are blinding, and people are jumping up and down and singing, what seems to me to sound like voices from an accordion.

I do not know what this religion is. But it is unseemly.

I do not like accordions.

We sit. All hot and in Sunday sweaters and collars and Vaseline under the hot iron roof, and people spit and start, and this is because we are frying, not because God is here. In the front, there is a line of young women dressed in long gowns: bright red and green, with a stiff cone rising outward up their chins. They are bouncing up and down. Up and down. And some of them have rattles, and some have tambourines, and they are singing and sweating in that gritty dusty Kenyan way—not smooth and happy like America-on-television.

And the man in the front stands in the pulpit, sweating and shouting. The Catholic Church I know is all about kneeling and standing when everybody else kneels and stands, and crossing and singing with eyebrows up to show earnestness before God, and open-mouth dignity to receive the bread. Some women will not put out their tongues for the priest—this is too suggestive. They will cup their hands and receive bread, and put the bread demurely into their hands and move back and bend one knee briefly before fading back to their seats, adjusting headscarves before sitting, kneeling, standing. Kneeling. Standing. Massage rosary. Service ends in fifty-seven minutes.

This service goes on and on. Mum is shushing us a lot. Why does she come here? What is she looking for? Jimmy is quiet and seems pained. Mum, dressed in a simple elegant dress, her hair professionally done, with her angular Tutsi face, looks out of place. She does not seem involved; her face is set. People are dressed in wild robes: orange Peter Pan collars, neon-blues and golds and yellows. And I am curious at this clang of music and God. And heat. Why does hot sun music clang?

And, somewhere, things reach a pitch after we have given money, and people are writhing in the heat and shouting in the heat. Words are flowing from their lips, like porridge, in no language I know. Some people just hiccup for twenty minutes. In the front, eyes are closed, tears are flowing, and handmade bottle-top tambourines are rattling at full slapslapslap, the tin-roof church is so hot. And people have stretched to be integrated into this heat and clang. Have found a commitment. Not us, though. Our hot wet breath is making moisture drip down on us from the roof. Some faint. I want to drink. What is she looking for here?

Then—some are moaning, others whisper, music softer, honey-eyed panting, tongues lolling, and the pastor's hands are spread out and he is swaying, and the tambourine is soft, and soon we spill out, and people are talking to each other and shaking hands solemnly, and we go to swim and lick Cadbury's chocolate off our fingers.

We drive past the turn-off to Kabartonjo. There the road rises a few thousand meters in a few minutes. To our left, in the hills up there, is the series of humps called the Tugen Hills that run all the way to Kabartonjo, from where you look down from a great height on the Lukeino Formation, on the lakes of this area, the deep Kerio Valley. On a clear day you can see past Pokot lands to Turkana. The Lukeino Formation has for long been thought to be a good candidate for finding early hominids. The Turkana, who live not far from here in the hostile desert in the north of Kenya, are many things. They are also the world's oldest society, all five hundred thousand of them.

When I got into the matatu this morning, the conductor, a young shabbily dressed man, had been slapping the vehicle, eyes narrowed and shrewd, sometimes urging people on with his hand on their back—sometimes grabbing people from the side of the road, all the time in Kikuyu—bawdy and rustic, laughing hoarsely when somebody shrugged away in annoyance. We left, and he marinated chatter in Kikuyu, and in Kikuyu-accented English.

We had just passed the police post at the industrial area when the driver turned to the young man sitting next to the door in the backseat of the fifteen-seater Nissan and addressed him in Kalenjin, and he replied in the same language. I was so startled I turned back and his eyes caught mine and he laughed, then broke into Kalenjin for the benefit of the passengers, swinging his chin to point at me, laughing softly, his smile now open and friendly, teasing, rather than mocking. I notice this less and less, and often only after traveling. The man's body language and his expressions, his character even, change from language to language—he is a brash town guy, a Kikuyu matatu guy in Kikuyu, and even in Kiswahili. In Kalenjin his face is gentler, more humorous, ironic rather than sarcastic, conservative, eyes more naked to vulnerability. Easier to shock, easier to anger. By the time we pass Kabarak, the newer passengers are helped in with more courtliness and less rush, with things piled on the roof; one older woman is helped in, his eyes respectful.

Some frail old threads gather as the woman sitting next to me sighs, long, in the middle of saying something to the driver; her shoulders slump, and she says, "*Msllp, ai, aliniuthii*"—the *Msllp* a sort of pulling in of saliva—a completely familiar movement, and one I haven't seen in years. The thing about it is how complete it is: it is not just the sound that she has, it is the way her neck swings, her shoulders move up the droop quickly, as she says, Oh, that man! He really offended me, her slack shoulders say, even now she can only soften and succumb to this offense, for, like me, or you, she suggests, we are vulnerable to being offended and being defeated by the offense: and this moves us all, for she has told us all too that she trusts our common reaction enough to know that we would not put up a wall of pride at offense, or begin an escalation of conflicts.

We sigh with her. For a moment we become a common personality, and she is chatting back and forth with people all over the matatu. In the soft quiet following her shrug, if she turns back to me and asks some small intimacy of me, which my individual would not appreciate, my common person will find himself being gracious and open . . . and it occurs to me, just now, that all the movements she presented are, like Ogilgei, a national capital: a small tool that can be used to elicit an act of grace, in any part of this country, where neither our anthem, nor our tax base, nor our language, nor our view of the world is in any way universal.

I look out, and there is a horizontal placenta of cloud, dirty pink and brown, and, somewhere in this distance, shafts of cloud-colored rain are falling; on both my sides there is a wall of blue mountains, the escarpments of the Rift Valley. Some ragged-looking cows stand staring at us stupidly, and there is a trail of goat shit on the road. It comes from every direction—shrapnel climbing up my arms, warm pools at the base of my stomach, a pulse of rising heat in my temples: the feeling of home.

They say, those scientists who know these things, that our smartest nerves are mirror neurons. They fire when we watch sports or watch somebody dancing. Our brains have been this big for two hundred thousand years—most of this time, we have lived within a few miles of where we are right now, the Rift Valley. But it is only forty thousand years ago that the "Big Bang" happened—a sort of critical mass in which tools, tailored clothes, and religion appeared. Some speculate that a genetic change also happened to the brain.

We have become used to thinking that, until we learned to write, human beings struggled to build a scaffolding of knowledge and ideas to carry them, and spread them.

What a defense of good!

That the patterns we spread around, we pass on, as efficiently as title deeds carry realty; we can pass on ourselves through our grace, down generation after generation. We spread even simple motions, movements, defenses, loyalties.

But grace is a funny thing, and I don't mean just the grace that refers to swans. Because if we are sitting together, in this vehicle, and somebody's mirror neurons fail to fire (maybe there is a Bavarian sitting with us) when this woman shrugs and her soft phrase pierces the silence, and group chatter rises, and she begins to speak to the whole vehicle, and this Bavarian person says something poisonous like, "Please shut up, madam, can't you see I am reading?"—and the moment this happens this man senses the small shift and stiffness inside the vehicle, the sudden silence of fifteen chattering mindingownbusinesspeople, and his body is now numb, fingers do not know what to do as they fidget, and his throat clears, gurgling defenses, he knows exactly what mood he has spoiled, but not at all what she said or did, or what that meant. So he may choose to stretch out a hand which we are all so suddenly acutely aware of—it stands outside this common experience—a naked thing wriggling in empty space.

It is scary, and we are tense, as this foreign object reaches forward. Perfectly physically familiar, this hand becomes an immediate animal threat, an inhuman object. It knows this and is tentative, and those long, pale, wrinkled things that spread like a fan from a palm flutter for a moment, and then pat the shoulder of the woman, too hard or too soft, somehow not right, and she jerks sharply with an inhale of breath to catch his eyes, which are jumping now, clueless, and he looks down. And this immediately releases our tension. He mumbles, sorry, sorry, Mama, and there is silence for a moment as we let him marvel with us, at his own bravery, standing naked of mirror-neuron empathy in thorny space and time, and finding his way to us blindfolded.

And somebody, the conductor maybe, and this becomes a truly appropriate word—conductor—will send us all into a new series of patterns by saying, Hello, Mzungu, and jerking about in a deliberately unpatterned way, but close to our idea of foreign Bavarian clumsiness, and we all burst out laughing at this joke with no punchline, constructed only out of movements that are incongruous, a word I am already associating with my brief religious ideology, based entirely on patterns and mirror neurons, and capital places like Ogilgei, and capital people, and conductors.

During these minutes, we climbed up the whole wall of an escarpment, drove past lakes and parks and towns, and these remained invisible as we registered with no conscious attention little sighs and slumping shoulders and a pat on a shoulder. And so I register the irony of a swaying conductor, moving to be righteously German, doing it ever so slightly wrong; he is confident enough in the smallest of signals to suggest that he is not proposing violence by this parody but is defusing awkward patterns, killing their threat. And we all get it—even the imaginary clichéd Bavarian leans back and laughs.

Timing is everything, said Miles Davis.

10

I Hate Githeri

I hate githeri. Four years of it—six times a week in boarding school, with floating bits of cabbage, cracked teeth and gravel, and the dining-hall smell of steaming peeling paint and bubbling giant cookers. After living abroad for ten years, I used to fantasize about boiling githeri; about rude matatu drivers; about bad speakers screaming near matatu ranks; about us Kenyans, who are so bullied by authority figures that we turn on each other instead of on the authority figures.

We miss the old ways. We are terrified about new things—because we have learned to measure with exactitude what we can expect from a president who is a monarch and a parliament whose single aim is to make themselves as rich as the wealthiest class of people in the wealthiest nations of the world.

This is why we, not they, are squashing any opportunity for a meaningful new Kenya—run by professional, sane, feet-on-the-ground people who did not earn their stripes as Affirmative Action Vaseline-faced Missionary School Boys (or their children, cousins, uncles, and godfathers): people who have lived and thrived in a crumbling Kenya and kept their integrity about them; people who have innovative and bold ideas; people who have had their hands on the earth, and their minds in the sky.

One time in South Africa, I was in a cheap country bus, and the driver was drunk. I was terrified, because I was sitting right behind him, and my Kenyan reaction was to pretend it was not happening. I slept. Half an hour later some very rude women—some grandmothers—were screaming. They stood. Picked out the strongest man in the bus and asked him to stop the driver. Eight or nine people surrounded him. He stopped.

The travelers took a vote after some brisk discussions. The driver was dropped off at the nearest police station, and a passenger was appointed to take us to Johannesburg. Many of these women were probably illiterate. Most of this time I was just annoyed. I do not know why I was annoyed. The women were changing a status quo, a way of doing things—good or bad—and maybe this is what annoyed my narrow fearful Kenyan self.

A few weeks after coming home in 2000, I took a matatu (express) from Njoro to Nakuru. It was full, and was not supposed to stop along the way—a privilege for which we had paid forty bob. I had been heaving bags of leek since early morning and was dirty and smelly. We got to the Rift Valley Institute of Science and Technology, and three people were hustled in, elbows in my nose, warm and squirming chicken at my feet, hot breath in my ear—a kiss. A kiss? I'd had enough. I shouted at the guy to put them down. I started to elbow my way out. Behind me, in Kikuyu, speculation was rife, coupled with much nose sniffing as the other passengers made it clear that they were unimpressed with my revolutionary ideas. Who does he think he is? Is he better than us who take this thing? And so on.

The conductor was laughing. In annoyance I demanded my money back and then asked them to drop me off. I could hear passengers laughing as I left in a silly, hot-eared huff.

In Kenya, until we are left naked, we will defend the status quo—much has been made of the five hundred people who earn ninety percent of the government wage bill; much has been made

of the knot of families and connections who have taken ownership of this country—and who are not happy with all the land
they own and all the assets, who will still come into our homes
and take our very last cent as taxes to fund their referendum
campaign, and the elections in 2007. But these days they hardly
need to do this work—a whole population of people will defend
them, will make velvet carpeting for them and ululate for a loaf
of bread. So when I ask a Kikuyu taxi driver in Nakuru, "Is business good?," he says it was better during Moi. I ask him about
the government. He brightens and says, "But he! Kibaki is a wise
one! He is Working!"

For whom? Kenya's rich–poor index has worsened since this
government came to power. Clearly the economy is doing well.

But for what five percent?

"Truly a god. Did you know he was Number 1! From Standard 1 until university! And the way he is confusing Raila?" says
the taxi guy.

"And what has he done for you?"

"Oh! We have been telling them '*Kaa mūcii. Kaa mūcii!*' We
told them we would help them keep the Luos out of Nakuru."

Over the last two years a kind of insanity has overtaken many
Kikuyus. Messiahs have come to "save us" from the "beasts of
the west"—and these "beasts of the west" are, of course, the
problem with Kenya. The same people who had vowed in 2002
to allow a Kenya for Kenyans are now selling Kenya—with their
massive vote—to a bunch of people who do not know the price
of a pint of milk, or care—except when they own the milk-
manufacturing plant that stole machinery from a KCC (Kenya
Cooperative Creameries) that was built with our money.

Neither do they care about the sisal-producing district, where
a whole tribe remain squatters, or the ranch in Laikipia, where
poor people are herded away by the same army and police forces
that are meant to exist to protect them and their sovereignty.
And we are grateful for this love by these people, partly because
they do a little work—nowhere enough to be meaningful for

Kenya, but sufficient to plant flowers on roundabouts and build one school with the CDF (Constituency Development Fund).

The real money, our money, ends up, in now legislated ways, in the pockets of the Fortune 500. Parselelo Kantai calls it the "Vampire State"—and really no state in Africa is as adept as Kenya at misleading its population and channeling all meaningful monies to the few who partner with "international investors" to leave us all bone-dry. This is why even poorer countries, countries with fewer resources and institutions, were able to shed their old guard and we can't.

The Kibaki government, like the Moi government and the Kenyatta government and the ODM (Orange Democratic Movement) possible government, are all cut from the same original cloth. Although we all see Uhuru and Raila and Kibaki as very different people representing very different ethnicities, they are brothers—of the same class of families who feel they have a royal right to rule. They come from the same eras, the same schools, the same social circuits—they battle things out when we are watching—for we validate their power. But within themselves they have no real problem. This is why former enemies always seem to turn around and become friends when they need to be: because they all need each other—they are in a conspiracy to control the history and future of Kenya—which we are told is all about them, their daddies, their cousins and uncles and in-laws. Since they are heroes, it is their natural right to inherit everything. So every five years we troop off to vote for one of them to inherit our assets—for we are their employees, their citizens and slaves, their children, their feudal chattels. And we are happy when they throw extra shillings on the floor for us. It makes us feel good.

What I fear, as a Kikuyu and as a Kenyan, is that the mobile, flexible ambition we had for Kenya is now frozen behind a new dogma chanted by Kikuyus everywhere—that the new *mtukufus* of Kenya are here to stay, and it is these mtukufus who will save Kenya. Again, a new generation fails to invest our hope in ourselves; we do not want to challenge a government to be better; we want to be comfortable with the status quo—and that will send us straight back to 1969. To 1988.

Our aim is not to alienate, or to be "comprehensive"—it is simply to provoke conversation. Our newspapers speak in maidenly terms—like old Victorians about "a certain community." We feel we need to name things—and allow conversations to take place—because it is in these secret in-between places that hate and fear build and thrive, when people start to think that at home their close friends and their families are "plotting against them."

We feel obliged to work toward the end of an era of big men, and their families and children. And the way to do this, I believe, is to question our own hearts.

The hearts of those in power are not in doubt.

11

Who Invented Truth?

Who invented that piece of nonsense called truth? Tired of truth, I am. And metanarratives and more truth and post-colonies. An intellectual world in which each paper rewrites its own perceptual framework; everybody is represented, nobody is real. Sick, I am, of affirming stories about strong brown women; of being pounded into literary submission; patronized beyond humanity. I miss beginnings, middles, and ends. Please bring back the myths and legends—even those about wise rabbits and wicked witches.

Nothing is true. Pick and choose your way. And it helps that there aren't simple, direct ways to places. There are gritty things, hinges to doors we do not want to open, that we want sealed, buried under the vast amount of cowshit we are shoveling in print onto our continent. Let's have things tested again: maybe sung, like Fela did; like Nesta did. If your thing cannot fit into a song, just shut up.

What is the test? Ideas aren't democratic—the value of your ideas can't be measured by how many people understand them. That is nonsense. And, though they have to fit into something, a system, there are no straight lines or building blocks. Only just webs, interlinkages that feed themselves and lead into each other and go nowhere . . . Which writer on this continent has started a movement? A series of aesthetics that has influenced a generation somewhere? A movement that has burned on its own fuel?

I am obsessed, at this point, with a conversation with myself. Writing, a vain pursuit. Everywhere, everywhere, boxes are imposed. Responsibilities. Who is your audience? Who are you writing for? Why are you not writing in your mother tongue? Art is never for art's sake, you tell yourself. Of course it isn't. But art for art's sake is a necessary lie.

Who has perfect knowledge, mastery over their imagination?

I can't be, nor do I want to be, Mr. AllPanAfrica when I write.

As a reader, detest the contrived. I do. The writing that comes with answers before it starts to write. Hate fiction that uses a hammer to ram its message into your head. Why not sing a protest song? Fiction is about creating worlds; if you do not want to do this, go write a thesis.

My country, Kenya, is forty years old. This century, we have had only two seasons of national unity—both lasting only a few months: Independence and the 2002 elections.

What many in and outside Kenya know as tribes did not exist as nations before the white man came. The contracts were different, the social arrangements different. Languages were shared, and agreements and rules. Tribal self-awareness came when people needed to deal with the British, in structures the Brits could recognize and talk to. The Miji, Kenda, Kalenjin, Kikuyu: all words used in the twentieth century to describe peoples who had similar lifestyles and spoke similar languages.

Jomo Kenyatta took the game further when he invented a certain Kikuyu. Before he wrote *Facing Mount Kenya* in England, those of us now known as Kikuyus could not agree on our origins, on how many clans there were. Some said we were descended from the same, some that Gikuyu and his wife Mumbi were the first Kikuyus, and that their nine daughters formed the nine clans. Some insisted the clans were thirteen, some said five. His version of Kikuyu-ness, a mix of missionary education and the experiences of his own village life, became the *idée fixe*. Now we look to his book to find out how to perform wedding ceremonies, to settle debates. Kikuyus, once the most decentralized of decentralized communities, have become raving nationalists. They believe Kenya is their baby: they fought for it, liberated it, built it; and the rest of Kenya is intruding on what was a fine Kenyatta-designed arrangement.

And how do you create a nation out of forty or so tribes? You spend time, as frenziedly as possible over forty years, building a weave of mythology strong enough to bond the pieces together: a grammar, a constitution, mottos. But you fail to do this successfully: only blood creates nations. Only the risk of annihilation makes people abandon the ways they presently use to make sense of the world. But you must try to make this work—we know no other way, so we pretend it works. And wait and see. And become born-again Christians or drunks when things take the wrong course.

A young nation is a bad novel: contrived, trying to push an agenda that cannot persuade readers, trying to impose a tight structure that excludes all reality. The British were beaten into submission before democracy took present-day root; tribal sentiment was beaten out of them; religion embossed in blood; the state fought and beat all comers to establish a complete monopoly of violence over its citizenry. Only then were individual freedoms possible. Yes. Yes. Bad medicine. Let's pray nationalism will die soon, and something more gentle will come by and massage us gently to prosperity. Don't hold your breath.

Uganda, my mother's country, has abandoned complex funeral rites. Kenya, more modern, Western, less Christian, still sticks to traditional funerals, sometimes mixed with Christian services; a funeral can last days, sometimes weeks. So many Ugandans died from AIDS in the late 1980s that it became impossible to justify the expense and time needed to organize a proper traditional or religious funeral. These days somebody dies, and he or she is buried the next day. So far everybody seems comfortable with the idea. But then, you see, Uganda has done the genocide, the civil wars, all the blights that built Europe. It will do what it needs to. And will make the grammar to justify it.

In Kenya we veer from ecstasy to despair. Open societies come with their stresses. People held themselves back, held back their creative instincts in the Moi days; old unresolved hates and grudges that were in suspension for a while have now risen to the surface. We have a gormless president—and, without anybody selling us dreams, we hang in a vacuum, and are able to deal with each other only at a political level in the old, ethnic alliance ways, complete with emerging Godfathers. To be honest, we miss the day when government was opaque; when power was centralized in one man. It is starting to seem that corruption was more manageable then.

François Mauriac said, "There is no such thing as a novel which genuinely portrays the indetermination of human life as we know it." I wonder about this statement. It seems to me that man is adept at fiction. We use the same rhetoric to build nations, justify wars, bond families, make marriages work, keep the attention and loyalties of our cliques. Narrated by any Kenyan you ask, the story of Kenya will not seem different from a historical novel. Characters will rise up; there shall be titanic conflicts, climaxes, and resolutions—the amalgamation of tiny incidents that actually took place are indigestible—and, more important, dangerous.

Computers are fortunate. As the software needed to get things done starts to grind down the hard drive, the body, one needs only to invest in a better computer which can accommodate new technology. I have in mind somebody from the 1950s, in sepia, running at great pace, as Technicolor sweeps up behind him: the story of our times.

Kenyans are simply muddling along, as human beings do, insisting on learning everything the hard way. We live in times when we are all associated, in real time, with everything that everybody in the world is doing; we are aware of the rest of the world. But we sit here, in our 486 computerbodies, watching a world where people speak in gigabytes. With the exception of time, as taught to us, life provides no highways. We make them; we call them "habits." And these paths are often changeable, adaptable. The most stubborn of them are those highways found and drawn in our minds when we are children. Small things, as solid as matter, we keep inside of us to protect us from facts, from the fact that we are tiny things suspended in an enormity we cannot digest or comprehend, and threats can come from anywhere.

As a child, I learned to love novels. They took hold of me at the time the acquisition of language was important: trying to name the world and its incidents. By the age of ten, I had learned to sniff out the useless long descriptive passages, and ignore them. Take the marrow. I more or less kept up this pace. It reduced only when in my twenties I became infatuated by writing.

So part of me is Europe. A place where Man has become his own God, looking down at Himself, and shaking His head sadly. But because God the Man and Man the Man are the same person, they are at an impasse. I have read too much to escape being that kind of a person. So have many Africans. So have many people around the world who are fixed into their past, who cannot adapt. And people who may be seen in other times as near inhuman can take advantage of our times, sublimely, because they are able to blank-slate themselves. They are able to change in a world where changing fast, and without baggage, is a mark of the Hero. David Beckham. The more successful ANC activists were those who were quickly able to shed their past and embrace Randburg . . . and all it stands for.

Nairobi is full of people born generations away from a mud hut who drive into the city every morning, cassette player blaring with motivational tapes, trying to get themselves formatted for work and life and success. Most of the social effort—how you plan your decor, where you drink, what you talk about when you drink—is all planned to fit into a template that you were not brought up in. Many, most even, are unable to blank-slate themselves. They fail, and nobody has sympathy. My peers have friends they have known all their lives. But only in English. When somebody dies in one's family, your friends do not come. They do not know, or want to know, you in your mother tongue; that vast part of you that cannot present itself in a Nairobi bar remains yours and your family's.

I wonder sometimes whether the main problem with the educated classes of our continent is simply this: we want our continent resolved in our own lifetimes. And our continent is not interested. So we contort, and twist ideas around, and blame and create whole new disciplines to understand and explain, when maybe all that is required of us is to document, to simply document our times if we are writers, document in the flawed way that seems true to us in our individual hearts, instead of superimposing with that vile censorious correctness that means nothing, and does nothing, and only makes middle-class Africans feel better about themselves. What matters, what will be useful, will resolve itself in its own good time. And you can be sure it won't be the literature about the strong brown woman who empowered herself without human quirks. I speak here specifically about the writer Edwidge Danticat, whose novels I cannot stand, and other writers of her school.

Do I know what I am saying? No?

Okay.

12

Inventing a City

For those trying to understand it, Nairobi can be a very slippery city. Four years ago I came back after spending a decade in South Africa—my mother had just died, and I was tired of being away from home. But it was difficult to adapt. I found myself living at the edge of Mlango Kubwa, a slum on the east side of the city, in a cheap hostel called Beverly Hills, where college students and the newly employed lived. That first night there was a flood, and I woke up to see my laptop floating in four inches (10 centimeters) of water.

I slipped and slid and fell in love with this city. Mlango Kubwa is all motion—streams of people finding original ways to survive and thrive. You never get the impression there are fixed and rooted institutions (buildings, legal entities) around which people organize. The organization of Mlango Kubwa is hidden in the unhindered toing and froing of people feeling their way through the day.

It was at Beverly Hills that I met Mash (short for Macharia), who reintroduced me to Nairobi. We would walk together down Moi Avenue, the street that leads from Nairobi the international city to the undocumented sprawl of an evolving African city:

people and their small, illegal constructions fronting opaque skyscrapers; secondhand-clothes shacks and rickety vegetable stands; wooden cabinets behind which whispered price-setting over watch repairs takes place in Dholuo, the language of Lake Victoria; shoe shiners and shoe repairers soliciting work by keeping eyes on the feet of passersby. These people tell tall political tales that later turn out to be true.

Mash was in his late twenties. His father had been a wealthy man. He was, to Mash, a man living in English, who believed in education and "fair play." A man who invested a lot of time telling his children to look forward to the West, to progress. Then he died, and at his funeral another wife and three children appeared, as if from nowhere. Mash's father had managed to hide a family for twenty years.

In order to negotiate our complex lives, Nairobi people have learned to have dual personalities. We move from one language to another, from one identity to another, navigating different worlds, some of which never meet.

Mash would go to work in the morning for a tour company, where he spoke good private-school English. In the evening we would cross to Biashara Street in Mlango Kubwa to drink and talk. We would speak in English about philosophy or literature or the formal job market. We would speak in Kiswahili about life in general, about the little things that made up our day. We sought a kind of brotherhood from our conversations in Kiswahili—speaking always in a mock-ironic tone, laughing a lot, being generous about each other's opinions, offering each other drinks and favors in ways we could not in English.

We hide whole lives in the gaps between these forked tongues. This is how Mash's father managed to hide his village family for so long. He was somebody else, somewhere else, in another language. His story is not unusual.

Mash seemed to know everybody and have a thousand deals running at the same time. He had shares in a small shop selling mobile-phone airtime; some weekends he would go upcountry to buy mung beans to sell in Nairobi. Much of the money he made was spent on lawyers. He felt it was his responsibility to restore to his mother items he believed various relatives had stolen from her.

I saw him in action one day in Mlango Kubwa when we stumbled upon a group of women, secondhand-clothes dealers, who had caught a thief—a dirty, disheveled young man, eyes bleary from sniffing glue. A crowd had already gathered. They were ready to beat him to death.

In Nairobi, where the police are the enemy, there are people who take charge in incendiary situations. Mash was masterful. He speaks Kikuyu very well, and he used it now. We, the Kikuyu, place great stock in people who are able to "speak well"—those who can command attention, even change behavior, through the power of their rhetoric.

As the women were about to turn over the thief to some men who had gathered around, Mash addressed the women with a Kikuyu proverb about men not knowing how to deal with difficult situations: "*Maitu, tha cia arûme itirî iria.*" Which means, "Men cannot stop the crying of a baby by suckling it."

The women laughed.

In half an hour they were pacified, confident the case would be dealt with by the government-appointed Chief of the area, and that what had been stolen would be returned. The women then started to banter with Mash, flirting with him. They gave him a free raincoat.

At dusk Mash and I walked lighter. There is something magical about the moment when the light softens and the city stops glaring and people are removed from themselves by this hour of transition: vendors packing away their mobile shops; children cut loose from school, shrieking on their way home; workers on their black Chinese-made bicycles, ringing bells, hurling warnings and threats; people everywhere streaming through alleyways and around familiar obstacles.

On lower Moi Avenue matatus gather, bound for Buru Buru, one of Nairobi's largest and best-known housing projects. The matatus are frenetic, horns chirping loudly like warring tropical birds, yellow lights blinking on their domed foreheads, neon-painted teeth snarling around their snouts, bright-eye headlights gleaming in the dark. Matatus flash urgency, hoot urgency, battling each other to snag passengers in a hurry to go home. But this urgency is fake: the matatus will always wait until they're full, then overfull, moving off only when bodies are hanging outside doors, toes barely in the vehicle. "*Songasonga, mathe, songasonga*" ("Move, mama, move").

The newest matatus have plasma screens to show hip-hop videos. Always quick to find new ways to make money, matatus have managed to embody a look and sound and feel that is particular to Nairobi. Matatu culture has transported new words all over the city and made Sheng trendy. Sheng is a fast-growing creole language based on Kiswahili, with some English words and other words from the many tribes living here. Much of Kenyan rap, which now dominates the airwaves, is in Sheng.

At the bottom of Moi Avenue, Mash and I reached Nairobi's railway station. There would be no city here if the railway had not been built at the close of the nineteenth century. A decade earlier, Kimnyole, the *orkoiyot* of the Nandi nation, warned of the arrival of a white tribe with an iron snake that would change everything. The center of power shifted from the village to this strange concrete thing called Nairobi. But Nairobi offers no time-tested, trustworthy way of living. Kitu-Sewer, a poet and rapper, captures our dilemma, singing: "*Umekwama na mimi ndani ya hizi mashahiri*" ("You and I are trapped inside our traditional poems").

This is the tension that best defines Nairobi: to try (and often fail) to live within the world-views of our traditional nations; to try (and often fail) to be seamless, Western-educated people; to try (and often fail) to be Kenyans—still a new and bewildering idea.

13

She's Breaking Up

Until I was twelve or so, I had various versions of this terrible nightmare.

The sun is high in the sky, and is just warm enough to caress. I am lying like a baby in a wheeled contraption that is rolling gently downhill, on its own momentum. There are people around, and children chasing chickens. It wheels faster and faster. I start to laugh, feathery feelings gathering in my stomach. Something gives, and my laugh seems to infect everybody. We are now a swelling crowd of laughter—accordion-faces swelling up, falling back shakily. Their faces creep over me, filled with swelling and reducing teeth and lips, clownish and rubbery, the laughter wheezes and stretches, echoes and swings and turns, and faces are now just accordion-shapes of fear, looming and falling, and the wheels have softened and bounce on the sounds of jelly. The gathering continues to some climax I can't wait to reach, but which does not come.

I am seven.

Steve Austin. Astronaut. A man barely alive.

I am learning to gulp down, force the marbles back into place. We recite and recite. ABC. 123. At first it is exciting and fleshy. Then is it not, and I am stifling perpetual panic.

Gentlemen, we can rebuild him.

I have not been able to allow a line to be just a line. A letter a letter. Numbers are dreadful. They are hot, dusty, January, and school-time. They have no lubrication, and they chafe and chafe and do not stop.

I should be able to blink and turn those new sounds and recitations into a pattern that skids and ducks and bursts into color; instead they swell into a rising swirl of hell, and lift me and throw me down into a gurgling sink of fear.

They are breaking my world apart. Offering dead little black insects with the promise that I shall see again when they start to make sense.

We have the technology. We have the capability to make the world's first bionic man.

The ability to make moving pictures out of smells and sounds and tastes recedes.

My report cards are terrible. Everybody else seems to find all this easy.

The head of my pencil breaks; I pressed it down to do what it should do, the thing that everybody else can make it do. Stop daydreaming, they say. I can't. Tears drip down onto the page. The pencil slides. I hold it tighter. The teacher is looming; she pushes my pencil back to fit the cushion between my thumb and pointing finger. It bounces back. Upright and stiff. To this day I hold a pen in a death grip. I use a pen or pencil only to doodle. I cannot take notes. I do not take any satisfaction in writing by hand.

The sound of this reality is those cymbals drummers hit, two metal plates cupped together. My reality gleams with sun-on-metal clang-ity. I jump up and down on it, hoping it will yield and bend or open up a hole to elsewhere. Nothing.

There is a fever of crayoning. On walls, paper, encyclopedias, which I call En-Cleo-Padeas. Crayons do not satisfy. They will not fill the whole space inside the outline. Colored pencils work better, and near heaven are the rare, beautiful things called felt pens. You can fill the outline completely.

Years later it will be water paints, which soak into paper and fade and crack. Then those lovely paints from tubes for my birthday, and a four-week holiday of heaven, painting mountains, blue lakes, pink flamingos, and coiled pythons with people-heads, all of them with the texture and gleam of something beyond the disappointing reality of paper.

You can cover the paper one color, and layer yourself on it as you please. When it dries, you can close your eyes and smell the chemical in your nose, and put your fingers over it softly and feel a strange shapeless and thrilling world slowly rising off it.

I am determined that not one moment of white shall remain. Blue has its own smell. And red. And green. When green mixes with yellow, I am thrilled. Greenyellow is the juicy taste of the end of a blade of grass, soft and new to light. Or a new leaf: an unfolding surprise. School will rearrange everything. Before my school-life became linear, it was a place of shifting and formless memories. I hang on to that.

It was 1984. Or 1985.

We had gathered in a small, smelly study in a house called Old Boys, a dorm promised by the Mangu High School Alumni, but never completed. The school video sat in a cramped room, and Fat Freddy, who had contacts in America, had acquired a new videotape.

Mangu High School. Smelly toilets, cracking black-cotton-like soil, heat that dries cheap blue school-shirts in twenty minutes, meat once a week, puff adders, giant spiders, a python that was killed outside my house, lazy teachers, a fat corrupt headmaster, Mr. Kamau (Josphat), and a motto from heaven, in Kiswahili—not Latin like the wannabe schools—"*Jishinde Ush-*

inde" ("Exceed yourself"). And lice. Our exam results defied the tenets of educational psychology. We were always one of the top three schools in the country.

Life was going to be a stepladder. Now, any evidence that Kenya ever offered this trajectory has been carefully wiped away. I would write long letters on onionskin or Basildon Bond, to soft-faced yellow-skinned convent schoolgirls with dimples, letters which I would never post. The exclamation mark was a big feature of these letters; they would jig about my sentences suggestively, like my erection under the counterpane.

There were maybe ten of us in the video room that day. It smelled of socks and bread, cheap margarine and cocoa.

Freddie put the tape on. We heard the heartbeat; saw the gravestone. *Smooth Criminal*. Then, dead silence. The neo-ancient-Egyptian-woman turns her head, fingers crack, a cat purrs, hats are poised, and then, like the past about to come to life, clothes rustle—and Michael Jackson appears. He tosses a coin in slow motion, and it falls into place in the jukebox.

I can't remember the effect of the song as such. It was more how he moved in that bar, as if he had taken himself away from the instruments and given in to his body. That body. He jerked, slowed time, wheeled; jerked again when sounds swung; marked time and moved like a needle, ducked head first into the stiff fabric of the world we knew, tucked that whole sepia-colored world, now more funky and flexible than physics, into his eye-tail, and had it follow him.

This is the Voice of Kenya Television.

The Six Million Dollar Man is brought to you by K. J. Office Supplies.

NASA ONE (FLIGHT CONTROL): "It looks good at NASA One."

B-52 PILOT: "Roger. BCS Arm switch is on."

NASA ONE (FLIGHT CONTROL): "Okay, Victor."

B-52 PILOT: "Lining Rocket Arm switch is on."

B-52 PILOT: "Here comes the throttle. Circuit breakers in."

STEVE AUSTIN: "We have separation."

CHASE PLANE: "Roger."

B-52 PILOT: "Inboard and outboards are on."

B-52 PILOT: "I'm coming forward with the sidestick."

NASA ONE (FLIGHT CONTROL): "Looks good."

B-52 PILOT: "Ah, Roger."

STEVE AUSTIN: "I've got a blowout—Damper Three!"

CHASE PLANE: "Get your pitch to zero."

STEVE AUSTIN: "Pitch is out! I can't hold altitude!"

B-52 PILOT: "Correction, Alpha Hold is off, turn selectors—emergency!"

STEVE AUSTIN: "Flight Com! I can't hold it! She's breaking up, she's break—"

There is an old word I still carry from when I was a child. *Kimay*.

Kimay is a long, flapping lower jaw, which gives me anxiety. People with long lower jaws that swing, which could drop. *Kimay* is swinging my lower jaw from side to side, and is sometimes a man sawing a toy harmonica, yellow and shaped like a maize cob, from side to side.

Kimay is a very specific feeling that is hard to re-create: the feeling of disorder in the stomach that comes when a swing wobbles and stops flying up and down and instead begins shaking from side to side. It is the feeling in the stomach in a dream in which I am falling. It is the collapse of decision, when the stomach becomes a shapeless accordion, and no limb or movement can be trusted.

It is spending time in a pattern, clambering and dancing happily, then looking beyond yourself and seeing the bigger pattern of everybody, and being hypnotized by it, as your limbs are now unable to negotiate their way back.

When *Kimay* comes, I have rules: hang on tight. Do not move.

Kimay is being stuck on the roof and refusing to come down as my brother and sister, Jim and Ciru, laugh. *Kimay* is a type of person too: a person with a long, cash-register jaw and a wheezing voice, like something out of a string instrument. Or it is a wheezing-harmonica voice: people speaking through their noses, like a lot of white people do. *Kimay* is all the characters who populate all my nightmares.

Laurel in Laurel and Hardy is a perfect *Kimay*. I loathe him. His antics make my stomach churn. *Kimay* is also a man with a mustache that covers his upper lip, since I cannot make out how his lips arrange themselves to produce words.

Kimay is pleasant when mild, when it is just starting out. But unbearable when intense, or when it runs long enough for me to anticipate the imminent intensity.

Kimay is watching Kikuyu/Scottish music and dance: partners waltzing, accordion playing. Or it is the rubbery taste of chargrilled goat stomach that I hate.

It is Michael Jackson's meltdown—the wrong path can turn you into a plastic person without your realizing it.

It is the fear that the whole spread of your possibilities—with no God in sight—has no limits, and that, therefore, you need to pretend that there are limits, because if you grow out of your shell enough to look back at yourself, beyond your usual parameters, you will see a monster you cannot handle and simply break up.

Poor Michael Jackson.

Writing Kenya: Short Stories

"If you are to ask me what are the greatest issues in Africa, I would say they are that people love, people fuck, people kiss, people speak."

—Binyavanga Wainaina on the *Guardian*
books podcast, 2011

You will not find a single noble person in Binyavanga Wainaina's fiction. Not one. Instead, you will find fully formed humans, making their way in the world with every human contradiction possible. You don't have to feel sorry for them, you are not required to admire them, and you will definitely not be inspired to donate to a charity after having read about them.

And this can be a little confusing.

In his own words, even when describing his fiction, Binyavanga is never anything less than strident. It can be tempting, therefore, to think of his fiction as a fuck-you to the reigning currents of literature: a kind of revenge for the ridiculous tropical caricatures of human beings that he had to endure all his life.

But to read him this way would be a mistake. Binyavanga's

motives are purer than we might imagine from his rhetoric—though also entirely consistent with it. His achievement is not to swim against the tide, but to sidestep the tide altogether. There's an integrity to his imagination, a fundamental respect for art and humanity, and an impossible equanimity when it comes to the unsaid part of his fiction: that there is, indeed, anything remotely remarkable about investing his characters with the full spectrum of humanity they deserve.

Ironically, it may just be that, for exactly these reasons, his fiction is the sweetest revenge of them all.

14

All Things Remaining Equal

Milka sits in the boot of the Toyota Land Cruiser next to the coolers, spread out on cushions, mouth sticky with dried watermelon; sweat, thick and salty, drips into her eyes; her book lies face down next to her. Her body, suddenly jagged and long, has not yet figured out new ways to arrange itself; two new bumps under her pink T-shirt have become a perpetual reminder that everything has changed.

It is too bumpy to read her book. She will play *Cominatcha*, her favorite thing to do on her new computer: she always puts on some Kleptomaniax on Windows Media Player. They rap, loud, in her earphones, and she watches the *Cominatcha* visualization on her screen.

She has learned over the past few road-trip months to play *Cominatcha* with landscapes, rather than with digital galaxies. She faces the back window and blurs her eyes, and dust and road and trees rush to hit her, and whizz past her.

They are driving through Pokot District: brown, loose, dry earth, stones, rocks, and skeletons of trees that Gordon had told her will spring to lush and useless life when it rains.

Prosopis juliflora.

They were introduced, he said to the occupants of the car, as a donor-funded NGO project—by the Food Aid Organization. A life-saving plant, he said, a plant that could grow anywhere, and provide fuel for when the world's oil reserves started to run dry.

It spread, thorny and impassable, and turned out to be poisonous to cattle—and no international market seemed interested in it for their fuel tanks. "Fucking dictators, aid organizations. They say they care. Bullshit. Doing anything they want is all the fuckers care about. This plant is why the Pokot are starving. We are going to sue."

She had a nightmare last night: soft squealing shapes of fear, a dripping tap, lips of a fridge slap open solemnly, and a solid slippery sound rises. It ripples under her feet, and she slips and slides on it; now it is a gelatinous mouth-organ of laughter. Soft corkscrews of fear and pleasure coil in her stomach, and hard rural faces nudge at her ankles, with cold noses and warm welcoming breaths. They are laughing, like phlegm and donkeys.

Like the village: a traditional Kikuyu accordion, and squirming, squealing, dying night-insects in her ancestral home in Nyeri.

Like poverty and the smell of boiling sweet potatoes. She wants to stop leaping up in fear, wants to let go. And she does, and slides into the sound, which strums and rolls over her body, then the ripples of laughter and the Kikuyu accordion whorl thickly into her breathing, and she jerks awake, choking.

Mum is pregnant. With Gordon's baby.

Mum sits at the front, with Gordon. Her face is moist, dripping, but she looks soft these days, smug, her stomach stretched taut and hard. Three months to go. A girl. This is what Milka wants. With long, curly doll hair and skin like milky coffee, pink full lips, green eyes.

Gordon is teaching her physics, now that she is in a British-system school, in an advanced class, her physics and math honed but naked of context, coming, as she did, from a strict Kenyan boarding school, X-ellents Academy, where failure was unacceptable, and frills frowned upon, and physics was numbers, never anything else: numbers and exams.

She has always easily topped her class, and is anxious to do the same in this strange new school, where learning is friendly, and classes chaotic. For the first few weeks she sat in class, watching people laugh rudely at their teachers and waiting for something to fall, or explode.

All other things remaining equal, he said: *Ceteris paribus*.

She struggled to understand this, but now she has made it a swing. If the poles of the swing are not there, the swing will flop to the ground. Something has to stay still. Control things.

Since Gordon married Mum a year ago, things seem consistent somehow: routines, possibilities, money, school fees.

The flowers outside the car are making her nauseous. At first the bright pink-and-white flowers of the desert rose, a plant shaped like a tiny baobab tree, were fun to watch, but now she is tired of them; they go on and on, saying, Hey, hey, we have flowers in this dry place too, and she is tired of listening. In this dusty, stony place, they seem clean, as if people washed them in the morning, in anticipation of visitors.

The desert rose has the false cheer of the plastic flowers and the framed print photograph of "Dubai! Shopping City in the Sun" on their former living-room wall. Dubai at night seemed a wondrous place—strings and swishes and eyes of light.

Dubai at night was like Mum in perfume and makeup, going for a date in the far-off, so-near, shiny city, Nairobi, which, from far enough away, could be like Dubai at night.

Milka and her mother have lived in almost every part of Nairobi: for a year, they lived in an aspirational semi-detached house in South B, when Mum had a perm and a business-suit job at Barclays bank; then they moved to a strange giant concrete house in Githurai, which they shared with a fat woman, who had a carefully even-toned face with shiny eyebrows shaped like sulking slivers of quartered moon, and a fondness for Cinzano Bianco.

The woman kicked them out one day, left all their things outside the metal gate, screaming, "*Malaya, malaya*" at her mother, her eyebrows unmoved by her anger.

They have lived in the servants' quarters in one of the gated rich houses of Lavington, where Mum worked as a maid for some expatriate people from Sweden who trained people in HIV awareness. They smiled a lot.

They have lived in a slum, Kibera, just after Mum lost her job at Joska (Josphat Kamau) Investments, where she was a receptionist.

Before Gordon arrived, they lived in a one-room house near Second Avenue, Eastleigh, only a few meters away from the open markets and book-exchange stalls. Milka loved Eastleigh.

Now they are back in Lavington, in the main house.

Gordon walked into their one-room home late one night, a year ago, with Mum.

Milka had spent the day in some anxiety. Mum hadn't been home in the morning, or when she had come back from school. As the sun set, lights and shadows fidgeted, and she retreated into her "room"—a bed, with a cloth screen closing it off—and she lost herself in her happiest book: *The Darling Buds of May* ("A Love Gift from the People of Liberty, Mississippi").

Then there was the scratchy squiggle of a key in the lock. Rain and wind and laughter burst into the room like a loudspeaker. Gordon's voice was deep and nasal, and it slid off the walls with static, as sure as television. Mum sounded drunk and erratic, her voice mewing and laughing, and Milka knew to be cautious. The light came on, and brought with it giant shards of shadow. Glasses clunked on the coffee table, and liquid gurgled loudly. She felt naked—knew that she was a moving, shadowed lump in their eyes. All her movements were too loud, her bed a stage, facing the sofa.

"Milka?" Mum's voice was soft and toned to comfort, scary. Milka wrapped a kanga around her nightie, from the chest, and, for the first time in her life, not from the waist. She slipped out of her room.

He sat on the sofa, leaning back, hands behind his head, leather-shod foot over knee, his skin angry and red, and she wondered for a moment if it hurt. He smiled and called her "Young Lady," which she liked, and she took her finger out of her mouth quickly, and clasped both hands in front of her, which seemed grown up. Mum's eyes were bright, and she kept trying to pat her weave back to life. It hung limply, wet from the rain, shining from hair spray.

The car jumps over a rocky bump. It is too hot to read; too hot to think; too hot. There is a song her granny used to sing to her . . . "*Maua mazuri yapendeza*" ("Beautiful flowers are pleasing") . . . and it would climb into the chorus, then slide downhill so sweetly, "*Zoom, zoom, zoom, nyuki lia wee*" ("Hey, bee, make some noise").

Milka fought with Mum this morning, for the first time since she was a child.

Over the sheer, torso-shaping, frilled-at-waist pink T-shirt, bought for her by Auntie Linda. She had planned, for weeks, to wear it somewhere: her birthday, Parents' Day at school, their weekend's shopping trips to Sarit Center. She was always losing nerve at the last minute, always somewhat despondent after failing to put it on. So, this morning, the T-shirt stood between them: her mother pulling it one way, Milka pulling it toward her. And before her fear of her mother could overwhelm her, Milka let out an urgent breath of words, from her stomach, in Kikuyu: "I'll tell Gordon." Her mother gasped, let go, and turned away. They have not spoken since.

Gordon is driving the car, and Mum is sitting next to him. The two TV people, and Linda, a friend of Gordon, sit behind them.

Earlier, she could hear them whispering, the CNN woman saying, "Look at his head . . . shaped just like gravitas, isn't it?" And they both laughed, and Milka could see the top of Gordon's large and square head bobbing in front of the car seat, waves of gray and black running down his head. CNN has, over the years, called Gordon a "Maverick American Missionary," a hero to "The Forgotten Peoples of Africa."

There is a race. Milka is now aware of something she has felt under her skin for weeks now: that Mum will crack before the baby is born, and Gordon will leave her. Them.

Mum has said it already.

"We will move to a bigger house after the baby is born" and "Don't worry, baby, Cūcū will come to visit us when the baby is born."

The baby will allow Mum to snap at Gordon, make him take off his shoes in the house, allow her to ban smelly people and remove the eyeless Nigerian masks from the living room wall, and the beaded Maasai leather tunic that smelled of old age and smoke and fear.

Milka has often wanted to touch his hair. Those waves are the same every day: each wave precisely in the same place, yet the hair is blowing in the wind! How does it fall back in place so reliably? Does his barber know the shape of each wave to keep it this way? That hair is too flimsy to be so reliable.

Gordon has two types of friends: those she often hears laughing and drinking whisky on the veranda, dressed in bush jackets, or T-shirts distended by overuse, and dirty jeans, talking about places like Rwanda and Congo and Propaganda and Iraq, and choppy verbs: "grabbed," "shot," "burst," "hit," "gripped."

Guerrillas, Milishia—which she thought would make a nice name, Milishia. Aisha. Maybe a Somali name. They sit by the swimming pool for hours, and she sinks into sleep upstairs, her head dizzy with the overheard detail. The stories always rush from location to location: ". . . left window, across the street, swung his cameras over—Bunia, Kigali, Club Tropicana, RPF, SWAPO Janjaweed . . . and then we got on a lorry and dropped off in Kisangani."

She cannot yet understand the connection between these people and those places, has not yet grasped the idea that people make the worlds they occupy, and cannot see anything clearly outside of what they have made. All worlds belong utterly to whoever is talking about them. What were they doing in Bunia? Why didn't they go to Zanzibar, or the Ruwenzori, or the Serengeti, where beautiful things were?

Sometimes she sat around them, answering only when directly asked a question. She hoped one day to test out the jumble of language and thought and books that she kept simmering inside her.

One day, over dinner, one of them mentioned Kibera, where she and her mother had lived for one year—and it seemed not like a place she knew, mundane and full of small neighborly entanglements, smelly, cozier than Lavington. It became a place they had built themselves, in that wondrous, Swishy-Light-in-Dubai way that white people built things. This Kibera had choppy verbs: Flying Toilets, Death by Machete, AIDS, a whirlpool. Slumlords. A thriller.

What a possibility! That Kibera was all those things! "You lived there," Gordon said.

"Yes," she said, and sentences rose and fell and crashed into each other in her head. "Near the Sub-chief."

There was brief awkward silence as she retreated.

"Solemn": a word she associates with the way lips that are sealed by silence part flesh visibly when quiet people speak.

François the Canal France guy broke into the thick air: "Catherine Peale was fucking the SPLA commander. She always knew what they were up to before anybody?"

"Didn't they send her to Iraq?"

"David Clarke married his Mombasa prostitute."

"Noooo!"

"Yep. Some American Marines came with their women and started a fight. Wigs flying. Dave and his wife spent their wedding night in Mombasa police station." There is Linda, another friend of Gordon, another type, who sits with the two CNN people in the car, and who always says things like, "He didn't understand that I needed some me-time," "People are dying," "You'd think they care," or "It's such an empowering book."

"Empowering": a word Milka associates with the rising steam and bitter smell of njahi beans, which Mum cooks with coconut when Linda comes to visit. Linda is a vegetarian, the only friend of Gordon that Mum likes. Linda hates the "System"—a word that is swirling around Milka, a slow tornado collecting samples everywhere, which will turn in on itself and solidify to one idea, in one startling moment.

Linda works with AIDS orphans, for an NGO called It Takes a Village. She used to work for the UN. She has introduced new words to Milka's vocabulary.

DIFFID, DANDIDA, MSF, USAID, SUSTAINABILITY, and EDUCATING THE GIRL CHILD.

Sometimes she comes to write funding proposals for Gordon in his study.

Gordon always sounds irritated when talking to her, and Milka does not understand why they are so close.

He hates "DevelopmentSpeak."

Gordon's other friends are all Black Kenyans, "Indigenous peoples," Linda calls them: Maasais, Pokots, Turkanas, all men. They come home with him from his dusty field trips; all of them are bewildered and shy, none of them speak English, and Milka's mother loathes them all.

They all smell the same: like blankets left too long in the sun; like smoke and paraffin and sweat; and sometimes there is, steaming around them, the sweet, intolerable, seductive, fermenting smell of *busaa*.

They never spend the night. Mum cooks a large pot of ugali, fries up sukuma wiki with onions and tomatoes and crushed peanuts, cursing all the time: these people, these people in her home. Gordon unloads a crate of warm beer and they drink from the bottles for hours. Mum bangs things in the kitchen. Gordon barks in his nasal, slippery Kiswahili, struggling to harden his consonants, and presenting this hardening as clipped instructions—a ubiquitous way the language is presented when spoken by white people and Kikuyu tycoons: when not full of gentle negotiations, it becomes a way for a man to issue directives "in an African way."

One day, Gordon issued an especially crisp instruction, in English, but sounding deliberately African: vowels rounded, standing straight, not slanting, consonants hitting hard against the walls of his mouth, when Mum had been sharp with Ole Tomanga, over the toilet: "Stop it! Do Not Make Him Lose Face!"

Ole Tomanga, one of the regular Maasais, always speaks slowly, an old man, taking soft, chesty paths to his point. He has an accordion laugh: it wheezes in and saws out in one gentle windy movement, and she always waits for it.

Lose Face. Lose Your Face. Three days ago, in her new school, Milka pushed a pencil deep into Lisa Macharia (of the Funeral Parlor Macharias)—just to see her smug face break. Why couldn't she make them stop laughing at her?

She knows Ole Tomanga's fragility—the wrong words will quickly cut him to violence or departure. There is no way for his behavior to adjust to insult. He has nothing to negotiate in this leafy suburb.

Face. Face. Face. Television: woman laughs, pulling on tights, saying: "WAIT! I haven't put on my face yet!"

Faces have spun in her mind for weeks. Face off! Drums blare, trumpets promise drama on FM Radio Current Affairs, and government ministers compete to insult each other, the whole country riveted. Let's Face it, says a woman on TV, bouncing energetically in tights, with a KISS FM accent, with lips cut clean and symmetrical and ruby colored, never wobbling; pads are boring.

Matt, gloss, lined lips, new eyebrows, so many possible faces!

"You look like a prostitute," said her mother, when she was caught playing with lipstick.

Gordon is telling them all about his conversion to this place.

"The church did not understand, sending fucking lurve gifts, talking about bringing people to the heart of Jesus! Jesus! Do you know what Jesus means to the Pokot? During the colonial era, there was a great wave of conversion here. A Kalenjin woman, I forget her name, told people that Jesus was coming. She was going to lead people to the Promised Land. They were all carried by the ecstasy; and the Pokot converted en masse, and a huge mass of people set off to gather and meet Jesus. Coming over a hill, they were seen by a British district officer, who shot at the crowd, and some died. The Pokot struck back—the British brought reinforcements to crush them, and the Pokot went home and never stepped into a church again."

Linda: "Aren't they just beautiful? So sleek and lean and sexy?"

Gordon's voice is grave. "Man has lived here maybe longer than anywhere else. The Turkana who live not far from here have been found to be the oldest society of humans so far to be traced by DNA tests. It is here that man evolved; we know these landscapes in our bones."

Milka sees a group of young Pokot standing by the road, staring at the car without guile, as startlingly improbable as the desert rose. The men are more spectacularly dressed than the women: one has cut his hair into a small disc at the top of his skull; blue beads decorate this circle. His torso is taut and ridged, and around his neck is a little blue-and-red choker. Milka avoids the naked breasts of the young woman, who is smiling shyly at the car.

Gordon has opened up his library to her, a whole wall of books in his study. It took a while before she let herself in—it seemed impertinent to spend time in his room. She has managed to restrain herself from being too familiar in the house. She no longer has a source of books. She used to exchange books with street traders for thirty shillings on the street wherever they lived. Mum was free with money for this, never minding how many books Milka found. She is still trying to steel herself to broach the school library, which sits behind a jagged bottleneck of American-accented girls, stopping to chatter where four corridors meet.

She does not understand Gordon's taste in books; she was sure, is still now convinced, that he must have, somewhere, solid, reliable books (like *Oliver Twist* or Mark Twain or Wilbur Smith or Robert Ludlum or *Black Beauty* or *To Kill a Mockingbird,* her favorite book). Steady books, like him—not books so slippery and difficult to escape to. *The Electric Kool-Aid Acid Test* had jumpy sentences that she could not train her eyes to.

Slippery. Like her mother. The thought stood up suddenly in her mind, and turned. There is a certain elegant upside-downness about this idea: Mum, slippery and unreliable, life seesawing, reading Reliable American Romance Novels; and Gordon, so steady, so finicky about the smallest things (packing the car!), so strange in his tastes for books.

One day, she carried one of Gordon's Africa books to her room. After rubbing her toes against the duvet to make it warm, she opened the Africa book and saw the pictures: dead bodies, some skeletons with clothes on—Rwanda. She dropped the book and said her prayers fiercely, frowning and trying to close off her mind, as her mother's voice rose up the stairs, drunk: laughing, music playing. Gordon's voice spooled in the background, almost inaudible; all she could hear were the regular, comforting waves of bass, which touched her. And that night, she wished with all her heart, promised God that she would be good, would make Gordon like her; would read his books and talk to him about places like Propaganda and Bunia.

Would be good to Ole Tomanga. Would not be shy and stiff, would be bendable and laughing, comfortably rude even, like the children of his white friends.

Late, late that night, unable to sleep after the Rwanda pictures, she heard Mum squealing, like the wet wheels of a fast car, and Gordon growled in regular wheezing breaths, as if he was the grainy road that kept the car from slipping out of control, and the desperate regularity of his gasps seemed to suggest that one day Mum would slip off the curb, beyond him.

The car rolls past flat lands covered in small rocks; the road is bumpy now, and fine dust has squeezed through the seams of the doors and windows; everybody's hair takes on brown highlights.

Mum sits in the front-passenger seat, reading a Zebra Historical Romance and sipping a cold light beer. She hasn't spoken to Milka since they left, and Milka misses her already. She uses less foundation these days; it barely covers the skin-lightener scars and patches. No perm anymore. Gordon does not like it— now Mum always has braids, with African beads (made in Taiwan) woven in. "You okay, sweetheart?" Gordon's eyes crinkled in the rearview mirror.

"Yes, yeah. Yeah, am fine?"

"What do you think of Pokot?"

The faces in the backseat in front of her turned to face her, all smiling, and she could not release the solemn. Her pink T-shirt seemed wrong now, the wrong thing to wear here.

"I like it. It's nice."

"They're so real, aren't they?" Linda winked at her.

"Yes."

Mum used to have a thick, transforming night mask: new eyebrows, mouth smiling carefully, top lip tapping bottom lip gently and regularly expelling a soft whispered pout, face expressionless and blemish-free. Or no makeup when she was at home: dressed in a kanga, ruthlessly cleaning. Scrubbing that one room. Perm under a headscarf. Rollers on. Scrubbing. Often moody from the night before, sometimes singing from the night before, soft and happy.

Milka brought another Africa book for this trip. She had browsed through it, and the prose read like Gordon sounds. There is, in this collection, something by a writer called Kapu . . . Kapu-scin-ski . . .

She sort of hoped that Gordon would see her reading it, and

say something warming. He loves Kapuscinski. He hadn't yet. After the city's starts and stops, and the startling fogs, came the climb, so high they could see clouds below them, and it was cold. Then they spiraled down the Great Rift Valley Escarpment, a giant view spread out before them: Mount Longonot and two lakes. When they got to the dry flats past Naivasha, she opens the book and reads, and was caught by a shocking paragraph. She gasps.

"Good book?" Gordon had said, smiling at the mirror for her.

"Yes, he sounds like you." And everybody in the car except Mum had laughed, and the CNN camera guy had taken the book to look at it.

"Ah! Kapuscinski. Fucking amazing. Did you read *The Emperor?*"

She tries to speak, but her mouth is stuck in solemn again, and Gordon feeds the car with anecdotes about people he knows who know Kapuscinski. And that Kapuscinski paragraph, from *The Shadow of the Sun,* rings in her head, like a choice.

"The European mind recognizes that it has limitations, accepts its imperfections, is skeptical, doubtful, questioning. Other cultures do not have this critical spirit. More—they are inclined to pride, to thinking that all that belongs to them is perfect; they are, in short, uncritical in relation to themselves."

Mum has hardly spoken since they left Nairobi. This is not her scene. As is usual when Gordon is with his people, they spoke only to negotiate tasks—Is there enough water? Did you switch off the geyser? Pass the watermelon, baby.

"Here it is!" Gordon booms. "The museum."

He stops the car, and they open the doors, which shrug off brown earth. They unpack themselves. All groaning and stretching, and Milka makes her ears pop, her back crack, and one lip two lips, breaking the solemn.

Spread out all around them is a flat, stony plain, soft dry earth under her shoes.

Museum?

Gordon looks happy, blocky, and bronze; wrinkles in him are not a loosening of skin—they are cuts and crevices.

"You good?" he asks Milka, and she smiles shyly. He winks and whispers, "I like the T-shirt."

The CNN man fiddles with the camera and then hoists it over his shoulder. The woman looks around her, irritated for a moment. "What museum?"

"The Pokot Museum. See these stones over there?"

They all turned, and on the ground was an enormous circle of small rocks. "Imagine this"—Gordon is magisterial, and the cameraman scrambles to get a shot—"stones piled on each other in a perfect circle, a wall, an immaculate and simple camp. Thorn bushes surround this wall to keep wild animals away from thousands of cattle."

"That's great," says the cameraman. "Could you move a little forward? Yeah, yeah . . . that's it . . ."

"Can I go on?"

"Yeah."

"Imagine—a young moran sits that night on that tree to the left as the lookout. Imagine the Maasai defeated. This great empire of warriors has had to retreat—they have been pushed out by the Pokot. Years of drought and rinderpest and civil war had brought them to this. This is their last camp before the migration to Laikipia and the Mau Hills. Soon the British will—"

"Hold on, hold on. Could you walk around it as you speak, keeping your eyes on the camera?"

Gordon frowns, and waits for the cameraman to move around him as he turns and circles the stones. Everybody follows behind.

"The British will soon completely remove any threat they offer, then immediately adore them. Imagine the recently circumcised warriors, bellies swollen from stuffing themselves with meat, eyes ready for war, some wounded from the weeks of battle. Sullen that the elders have said they must give in and move on. Young boys and girls restless and excited; cattle bicker in the corral, unfamiliar with being in such a large gathering. Did the elders have any trouble restraining the moran? Did the Pokot warriors follow them or line alongside jeering?"

They all stand. Quiet. Moved, but not quite able to assign so much drama to this bleak landscape. And Milka thinks of Ole Tomanga, and turns to look at her mother, who is uncapping a bottle of water, disinterested.

The CNN woman breaks the silence. "So what about now? Aren't they getting Food Aid?"

Gordon turned to them again. "You see. Now the Maasai, and the Pokot, are cursed by the greatness of their past. Accepting what they need to change in order to thrive makes the past irrelevant. Those that had weak cultures, like the Kikuyu, gave it all up for modernity."

Mum turns to Gordon, mouth turned down to a sneer, and the cameraman swings to her direction. "Ai! Ngai! What did you say? When the Maasai were crying for help in Narok, we were fighting the British in the forests. It is us Kikuyu who are building this country—while these people sit here and beg. And all of you get happy because they suck your breasts and say nothing. Why didn't you marry a fucking Pokot if Kikuyus are weak?"

Milka sees Gordon's jaw swelling and receding. She can't bring herself to move. Gordon does not say anything, and Mum turns back into the car and switches on the radio.

The CNN people ask Mum to turn the radio down. Mum is sulking on the front seat, and Linda has snapped at Gordon: "Fuck you, Gordon! You're such a fucking Patriarch!" Linda goes to the car to comfort Mum.

Gordon is rescued from awkwardness by the arrival of a lean, ropy young man in a crisp white shirt and trousers. "This is Simon—the Sub-chief of this area!" The TV people pounce on him, and they walk with Simon around the museum. Gordon and Milka follow.

Simon is telling them, "These stones are not touched by anybody . . . they are our memory of a great time . . . even children know not to touch anything . . . We Pokots do better than most tribes at school, but most of us leave all that to come back here. When I finished at university, they sent me to Maasailand to be Chief there, but I couldn't live there. Then they sent me to Kericho, but eventually I came back home . . ."

Gordon swells up again, and soon is summoning majesty for the camera, eyes gazing out to the distance, framed by crisp lines. "Is it that we see our way of living as life itself? Is this man's greatest gift? His curse? That we will not relinquish our way, whatever our intelligence tells us?"

He spreads his arms wide, to the landscape. "We will live our way, and walk free across fenced land with our herds of cattle; or build ever-larger buildings, and guns. Not even a wall of fate in front of us will make us give up our way. We will crash into it at full pace, convinced our way will push us through. And often it does, and sometimes it does not."

A few minutes later, Gordon slaps Simon's back, and grabs Milka's neck into a soft hug, while the cameraman takes shots of the landscape. Mum had turned the radio loud, and was asked to switch it off by the TV woman. They board the car and head for the borehole and tanks—Gordon's World Bank–funded water project.

Milka knows her sister will speak like television, like International School of Kenya, like "We are the world, we are the children." Like "Make it a better place." This baby will not share Mum, as she had—she inside Mum, layers of shared secrets and lies separating them, tying them together; she aloof from Mum, Mum open to her—both of them silently agreeing not to acknowledge this situation. And Milka knows herself, already, as Mum's assistant in this endeavor: less a daughter, more a partner. For the past year, she and Mum have been uncertain around each other. Mum has been afraid of her, has alternated between over-affection and sharp, hot, threatening whispers, far from Gordon's hearing.

One night, some months ago, Gordon and Mum went to a

party at the UN headquarters and came home early, catching her in front of the mirror in the living room, dressed in his draw-string pajama trousers and in Mum's loose and baggy cardigan, dancing hip-hop to some angry South African Kwaito music, which was blaring out of the music channel on television. She turned to find them standing at the door, and was ashamed. In the moments it took to tune down the television, the living room stood still: the masks; the creaking and crackling rattan furni-ture; the framed prints of various tribal peoples Gordon had met in his work in Kenya and Papua New Guinea and Malawi; the collection of manly oddities on the mantelpiece: old Congolese beer bottles, black-and-white photos of naked Nuba men, a little goatskin tobacco-pouch, a grimy old pair of binoculars; the bright and beaded collection of pygmy knives, spread out in a fan—and Gordon, weather-beaten in khakis, diminished in force by the bright television colors, by the rat-a-tat rap, by the wide mouths and pointing fingers, so close to the screen, they seemed to be addressing each person in the room.

Mum groaned and covered her ears. Gordon muttered, "Rub-bish," and his eyes remained on the screen, until the volume button on the remote control rendered the musician's move-ments ridiculous.

Cominatcha is not working for Milka on the trip back to Nairobi, there are too many small frictions in the car.

Simon is squashed between Linda and the CNN woman, legs angling sharply, thighs as taut as forearms under his trousers. Linda is speaking animatedly, her voice less prickly than usual, asking Simon about the Sustainability of Local Institutions.

Linda's hand is on Simon's thigh, and the cameraman keeps glancing at them, and smiling to himself.

Simon turns to Milka, asks her name, and which school she goes to.

"International School," and she is ashamed to say this; can hear how much her accent has changed, as she speaks to him.

Two young women step out of the brush in front of them, in leather tunics, with short mud-colored mops of dreadlocks on their heads. They stare the car down fiercely and turn back into the bush. Simon points at them. "Those are initiates. They were circumcised last month. They have to live in the bush now until the next ceremonies. No men can cross the line on that road. They will kill any man that approaches them." Linda gasps. "You support this? That's terrible! How can you support mutilation?" Simon laughs, and Milka squirms. She has found herself, so many times, hearing some comment from some member of a group of girls that cuts her deeply, and she laughs, and her whole body loses instinct for a moment, everything is heavy and awkward, as she tries to arrange her face not to care.

Milka's voice bursts out, louder and shriller than she would like. "They look like warriors. I want dreads like that!"

Mum laughs, an edge behind it. "No Mau Maus in my house, girl!"

Gordon is grave. "Some women run away to be circumcised. We try to stop it."

Linda is facing the window, tears running down her cheeks. The CNN people want to stop and film. Simon says no, sharply, his body suddenly concerned with its seating—he closes his knees and places two hands awkwardly on them, like an uncertain schoolboy. A hard nut swells and thins on his jaw. Linda vows to nobody in particular that she will come here and have a gender-mainstreaming workshop, if she can find the funding. The car dips into a suddenly verdant strip, trees above them, and Milka's skin is bombarded by thousands of leaves of cooling shadow.

They cross a stream, and are out again on stone and dust, and goose bumps prize her thoughts out of the group; they spread warmly through her body. Her T-shirt is dusty, and she is uncomfortable in it. Pink dirties badly.

Milka leans closer to Simon's back. He smells of sharp, clean sweat, a charcoal iron, Lifebuoy soap, and sunlight. She wants to touch the bones that run down his white shirt.

"Uncle Gordon?" she asks. "Will Simon come and visit us at home?"

Mum slaps her tongue loudly against the roof of her mouth, and Gordon turns to look at her sharply. "Simon is a busy man. You must ask him."

A group of young men walk in front of them, and the TV woman sighs. "They are so beautiful. I wish I could take one home."

Gordon growls, "Don't be silly."

Linda peers out of the window, squinting at the afternoon glare. "They don't seem to be malnourished and they don't have ringworms like the people in Ukambani."

Gordon responds, "That's because they haven't yet met enough tourists and the fucking Church and modern life. Just you watch and see how they will be when the World Food Program is done with them. Already people here have adjusted their habits to Food Aid. The young men refuse to take the cattle to the mountains to graze when there is no rain. The old men drink busaa all day in Loruk, and the women wait for food packages. They are finished."

Simon's face has not changed. Milka sees his back tighten; a train of bones reels down his back; his hands become string instruments, tight cords climbing sharply to knobbly cliffs. She is prickly and hot and soft. Her hand reaches out, and she fists it and curls it back into herself. He smells of ironing and charcoal and sweat and truth.

"If you drop me off here, I will be fine," he says. Gordon drops him off, and says goodbye in Pokot. Simon ignores him, and Milka shouts, "Bye!"

Milka turns to watch him walk away; he swerves off the road and into the bush, his walk springy and alien. His shirt and trousers flap in the wind, suddenly ugly and fragile as brown dust and thorns threaten.

And soon they are on the tarmac—built by Gordon's physics, Linda's donors, and Kapuscinki's mind—straight and clean and making equal rock faces, and escarpments and geology and hundreds of unknowable hominid fossils, and ten or twenty tribes and five or ten towns and five lakes, and rain and sun and grimy city suburbs and leafy city suburbs and the tensions Milka knows will make the house unbearable this evening. This once Great Rift Valley, which held First Man prisoner for tens of thousands of years, will be comfortably digested by cushions, power steering, and a two-hour session of mental *Cominatcha*.

15

Hell Is in Bed with Mrs. Peprah

1979, Nakuru, Kenya

For the first time in a week, a feeble sun reveals itself. Two weeks ago, Nakuru District was all dust. Everywhere there were fires, and boys collected burnt chameleons to scare their sisters. As far as a person could see, trees, plants, and grass were all frozen into thorny, blackened sculptures, waiting to be watered to life. Eight days ago, the rain came, and drew a curtain over everything. Today, the veil has peeled away, leaving wobbly, silvery dew and a revolution of green.

Milka woke up this morning with a carpet in her mouth and a film of leftovers all over her body, feeling far away from herself. Rain, moist air weaving itself into nostrils, dreams, and sleep after four months of dry heat; the surround of nothing but rain; all other usual sounds muffled: the midnight train leaving the station, dog choirs rehearsing, a rat scurrying across the ceiling. Rain will wrap you in a consistent noise and close off the rest of the world.

Her skin is covered with goose bumps: nice-feeling, and teetering on the edge beyond which they will itch. She is only slightly chilly, as she sits by the window of the car, waiting for the shadow of trees to pass and squirming with pleasure, as mobile tattoos of sunlight caress her legs and arms and face. She shivers. The big fever tree next to the hospital is coated with a spider-webby gloss. Its bark is usually an avocado color. Today, the green is gold. The flowers of the fever tree are dots of yellow light on the dark umbrella canopy, shedding flashes of powder on the grass. As if irresistibly driven by the stinging urgings of impatient bees, all kinds of flowers have burst open from their buds. The bees drink and shoot off, weaving around in a drunken celebration.

Milka thinks that if she was to roll on the grass and rub herself with the yellow dust from the fever tree, and nibble the green shoots now, while they were still unworldly, her goose bumps would burst into bloom.

She remembers only that Mum is sitting next to her in the driver's seat when they get into town. Mainly because town today is a hooting, muddy intrusion into her bliss.

"Milka! I don't know what's bothering you today! You've been daydreaming the whole morning. I hope you are not sulking again because I told you that you have to go to the salon first! You can't go to Liza's without doing your hair! That Liza is always so pretty and well groomed. Heh! Sweet-milk! I worry about you sometimes!"

"I like how I look, Mum. I'm not Liza!"

Mum parks the car outside the hair salon. "I'll come back for you at twelve. You be good, Sweet-milk! We can stop for ice cream later."

Milka walks into the salon and sits down. They are used to her solemn silences, and spend only a moment in greeting before resuming today's domestic editorials. She sits down on the swinging seat and twirls it around for a bit, noticing that her feet are now almost long enough to touch the ground. There was a time when she had to be carried onto the chair. There is a new picture on the wall, between two mirrors: a Black man, dressed in a creaseless suit, with immaculately cut and parted hair. There is a caption: ONE OF MOTOWN'S BEST DRESSED MEN. The whole thing baffles her. He wears no sequins, no fur-lined jacket, he has no Afro. He isn't even wearing satin bell-bottoms like the Jacksons. He is dressed just like her father. How can "One of Motown's Best Dressed Men" be wearing something her father wears?

She can hear music from the record shop next door: Superfly!—the come-do-dirty voice moaning, "Gat to get over, gat to get over now, got to gerrover . . ."

A lady sits next to her; she has skin as brown and matte as Cadbury Cocoa. Long, long hair, and wide, mobile lips, varnished with red lipstick. Milka flinches at the sight of the lips. They look like the turgid tumors of naked pink buttock she's seen on baboons in Lake Nakuru National Park, inviting a thorn to burst them open.

Mavis, one of the hairdressers, lights the gas flame and lets the comb sit on it for a while. The smell of burning hair and oil fills the room. Nobody notices the smell.

The hot comb glides through the Cocoa lady's hair, like those push-push lawn-mowers they use in school. This is why Milka refuses to let her mother have her hair straightened—how do you compete with hair like that lady's? Milka's hair is like the scenery on the drive to Gilgil: scattered and stunted bush.

The baboon-bottom lady has a lot of makeup on, and is carrying on like her parents do when they have visitors. When Baba opens the drinks cabinet, lights his pipe, and then plays slurring saxy jazz on the record player, and a few hours later, sitting in her room, she can hear adults burst into noise, like the kids in school do when the bell rings.

The Cocoa lady is talking loudly now, as if she is talking to the whole room, "He! So they left Oyster Shell, and went to Amigos. I met them there; five minutes didn't pass, and they were fighting again. Some American guy stopped them. He! The guy could box like Muhammad Ali. Muhammad, Muhammad Ali, he floats like a butterfly and stings like a bee! So, me, I decided to go with one of the Americans: bwana, he was light, like an Arab! Even his eyes were green like a mzungu's: he had an Afro just like Shaft's. Haa! Bwana, and the muscles! I was just thinking, *haki,* me, I can let him *toboa* me wide open—shaft me—just for a baby that looks like him. But, si, you know Kenyans? The way they talk nice-nicely when you are there, meanwhile, they are cut-cutting your blouse behind your back? Smiling at you, saying, You look so nice in your new blouse, sist-ay? Eh! Anyway, there was this ka-silly Nigerian woman, that new professor at the university. She kept talking with the American. Ma-intellectual things, as if those can catch a man, eh? And anywaaay, who wants a woman so black? So, me, I started to rhumba, you know, like a Ugandan, shaking iiiiit! Ai! Him he forgot that Black professor. So we went. The Americans had comboa-ed a room upstairs. The man, he funua-ed a bottle of Johnnie Walker. Ha! Then he started! You haven't heard *siasa* like that! Ati 'Black Power,' ati 'Black is beautiful'; ati 'We are in a revalooshen!' Me, I just wanted to tell him Mau Mau is over, and, anywaaay, who is he to talk about Black Power, the way he looks just like a half-caste? So I washa-ed some Lingala music, you know, so we could groove a little. He starts to say this African music is beautiful, ba-aby. Ati Lingala! Ati beautiful! It's like he wanted to be us, the way we always just dream of being an Afro-American!"

Milka is getting impatient. The Cadbury Cocoa–skinned lady's last sentence lies undigested in her mind. She is too wired with waiting to give it enough attention, but it has that ah-so-that's-it truth about it—the sort of truth that your forgotten mind swallows immediately; the sort of truth that the normal, day-to-day mind struggles to find use for.

Sometimes, Milka thinks, your normal mind throws away the truth in irritation. Maybe this truth sits on a highway in my mind, and just gets tossed right out by fast-moving thoughts, like a soccer player's thoughts, which must be very fast and busy but hardly deep.

She giggles to herself: she has been thinking about thoughts, and the thought she tried to think about has escaped from her memory. She can't retrieve it, but she lets her mind wander.

One day, some soccer player, breathing hard and covered in a sheen of muscle-gloss (that she would just die to touch). He'll trot up to the sidelines and ask the open air around him, "But why is such-and-such the way it is?" And Milka's smug, deep-inside mind will take over. She'll breathe in, and smell the man in him without her legs becoming porridge. She'll turn to him, a smile on her face, a sort-of I-can-take-you-or-leave-you smile; and, with not a stammer or a doubt in her, she will tell him the answer, then think, "Hey! When did I get so clever?"

The Cocoa lady is still talking, as they put rollers into her hair. "Argh! But to be Black! Then I pay all this money for curls, and it rains, and I have to come back. Bwana, I wish I had hair like Donna Summer . . . do you think it is a wig? He! Gold, and brown, and you can throw it back so men can start to shake-shake! And then when I'm dancing rhumba, I don't have to worry that curls will just stick to my head, and the oil will drip. Ahh! I wish I had hair like Donna Summer!"

Mavis laughs and says, "*Lakini* you! So you buy a wig and shut up! There are young people here—eh?"

Milka is getting irritated. Argh! Where are they? They haven't even started undoing her raffia plaits! If they keep this up, her mum will say there isn't time for ice cream before going to Liza's, or the shops will have closed. The music from the shop next door is not helping things. Superfly has been replaced by loud, loud Lingala music. Lingala scares her: no tranquility, just this arrangement of sounds that seems to have no direction. Demands! Like reggae, asking things in fresh, raw places in her that she doesn't like. So she holds guard over her self, the same way she does when she feels a fluttering in her stomach and a wet rush in her panties.

People who listen to that kind of music always seem to belong to a place with no simple tune to hang on to, embracing their frailties: babies with strange men, exam failures; and letting themselves grow in wild, unmannerly directions, like a Kei apple hedge that is never trimmed.

Ah! But they can dance. They dance so she sees them in shapes and stretches that move as if held by the same fabric, but fluent in endless individual possibilities: boundaries that sometimes seem to be tailor-made for everybody.

Sometimes she gets caught unawares. A song like "Sitaki Uni-ambie" begins so beautifully. It so gently slides her into a field of butterflies, then it becomes too much, sinking her into somewhere with an agitation that leaves her queasy with rancid pleasure. But that first part of the song, oh! It always makes her want to fly away to a dance-space that would shock even people who go to Amigo's Discotheque.

She and Liza often laugh, watching people dancing to Lingala on television.

— Look at that chic, she has such a biiig bum!

— The guy is drooling! Yuk! That's disgusting!

A sharp inhale, and a blush of delight/shock.

— She hasn't got a bra!

The Cocoa powder-face lady looks at herself in the mirror; her hair is now being twisted into the rollers, and she sighs loudly, squirming on her seat, seeking a stretching pleasure.

"He is coming to take me to Lake Nakuru today. Wait till he sees my hair! Heh! And those fools at the lodge will not stare at me like I'm a prostitute—eh? Not with an American. Ai! Those waiters—new from the rural areas—they think ati-lipstick is the mark of Jezebel—eh? In nineteen seventy-nine? Bwana—those Americans, also, they are just mad. Ati—noow he was telling me on the phone that they are going to see Idi Amin—they want to move to 'the Motherland.' Noooow—how did The Motherland become Uganda—me, I thought they came from ma-Nigeria or akina-Ghana, those places? Sooo, ati now Amin will give them passports because he is their African brother—Amin! Ai—they are silly!"

Nancy finishes unwinding the raffia on her head. Milka looks again in the mirror. She prefers *matuta* braids to anything. It seems to her that her hair looks best with those little plaits of scrub all over her head. But her mother would not approve.

"It just isn't ladylike! Matutas are for maids, dear!"

Cornrows, running to the back of her head, are the next best option, but her hair is too short to hold them for a week. The black-wool hair-twists are okay, but they pull her scalp too much, so, as usual she has to settle for a raffia-weave. Last week's twists are spread all over the floor, and her naked hair is all grungy, coiled into the shape the raffia had held, which resembles a furry caterpillar.

She peers at her face: she likes to see it before the shampoo. The large, rebellious lips that she likes to keep pursed seem to look right with her hair simple and scruffy. It is as if she doesn't have to look for cuteness in the mirror. She looks at her face, all of it this time, not the bits Mavis has been working on. She releases her lips, and for a moment she sees beauty: lips as lush and soft as the base of a blade of new grass—a meadow of the thickest kikuyu grass resting between two imposing cheekbones. A frisson of sheer, cat-stroking pleasure climbs all over her. Then it is gone, and her lips seem clumsy and rubbery again, and a regular taunt from school rises to the surface of her mind.

Ugly.

She purses them.

She knows that after a few hours, when the raffia has been twisted into plaits, and her scalp has been oiled; and the plaits shaped into steeples, turrets, and verandas; after the final balcony looms over her forehead, her face will disappear, as if it has been sucked up into her hair. If she peers hard at it, it will reveal itself as foreign, pulled into a surprised blandness that everybody calls "cute"—if she purses her lips.

Her mother adores her like this; and is always at her most friendly when Milka is in fresh, new raffia twists. Often they share Mum's dressing table, flirting with the mirror, in a cloud of giggles and possibilities: surrounded by pots and colors and smells, and wigs and masks of so many possible people. People who belong just to her and Mum. Always, as if it is a new idea, Mum discovers the ribbons that will look just right on her hair: yellow and pink, which she ties into a bloom. Then, later, when

Milka is alone, she finds she can't stop the surging, burning demon that, she is sure, will vomit out of her in church one Sunday.

Something must be wrong with her, she thinks. Life the way Mummy advertises it is so simple, everything is so smooth, perfumed and lubricated. What makes me want the other things?

"Milka! You sweet gel!"

For Professor Peprah, Milka smiles without restraint, the smile that looks like a quartered watermelon. She likes Professor Peprah, who seems to have swum herself, against the tide, into a beauty: glittery gold stars dot her black, black skin, making it seem as smooth and bottomless as night. Oh, and the purple lipstick! And the psychedelic kaftans! Even her hair is eccentric, with strands as thick as wire, streaked with lightning bolts of gray.

Auntie Peprah doesn't squeeze Milka into a tube, like toothpaste-makers must do; or like Auntie Wambui, who balances a cup of tea on one knee, while sitting upright, knees together, with her big bum clenching to hold on to the chair while her mouth snaps up and down, like garden shears that prune a many-tendriled hedge into one square and obedient truth.

According to Milka, there are two types of truth: feel-right truth and I'm-telling-you-truth. Auntie Wambui is full of I'm-telling-you-truth.

Everybody laughs when Auntie Peprah sings in church; her voice is a loud, mirror-threatening echo. When it hits bottom, it can be a quite un-Catholic scraping of gravel. She likes to write letters to people when she is unhappy with some aspect of the sermon; or like when she wanted the blond Jesus picture removed from the church! People were so annoyed! They looked at each other, eyes appalled to wideness at the idea of a Peprah-Black Jesus with dreadlocks. Jesus a Mau Mau! Or a Rasta! Auntie Peprah just laughed and called them "neo-somethings," and said that Jesus was a . . . that turning upside-down word . . . rev-olu-tionary!

Milka's dad hates Auntie Peprah: women must be demure,

decent—not loud, and Oh! Bwana, she is ugleeee! Once she overheard him say, "Ai! Hell is a man in bed with Professor Peprah." But Aunt Peprah talks to Milka about another Mum. Mum who has a master's degree but won't get a job. Dad doesn't like this.

So Mum and Auntie Peprah meet in the hair salon. Mum's fair skin and dimpled face always seems indistinct next to Auntie Peprah. But Mum is the most beautiful woman in Nakuru? Everybody says that she looks like that woman in *Shaft in Africa*.

Whenever she is with Auntie Peprah, Mum peels away, and wakes up another person. They talk about poems and books and dreams. It is as if she is now out of the world where she is spun into a sum of everybody else's needs.

Auntie Peprah starts, "Where is dat silly gel! How long have you waited, sweetheart? Can't you people start wid da chile first—eh? Hmm! It smells here, too much burnt hair! Where is Ciku? I want lines! Now you don't go be pullin' my hair! Ha! I should go to Accra every week to do my hair. You Kenyans, you jus' like white tings. Mzungu, mzungu. Don't you worry, gel. If you miss ice cream at Zoom Zoom, I'll take you in my VW Kombi to Tipsy!"

The Cocoa-face lady looks sullen, and stares at this stand-alone woman she cannot understand, "But you, Mama, why can't you get a husband. Eh? Always angry. Always this, always that. Ah! Even trying to steal my man in Amigos. Do you think he can take you just because you talk ati sistah, ati brother? Ati ma-oppression, ati ma slavery. Ai, those things are gone!"

Professor Peprah laughs. "My gel, my sweet woman. Who are you outside your short skirts, and buttocks dat shake up and down, never sitting, always callin' a man? If you need a man to make you feel beautiful, dat is your problem. Me, I just need a mirror."

The whole salon cracks up, and the Cocoa lady stands, shaking so much that two rollers fall from her hair, "Ai! Ai! My dear—what mirror, and your face, which sucks up all light! You need Ambi skin cream, and then you can talk to me. Where is your PhD when your breasts are aching for a man? All men they become so stupid when I rhumba that I need no PhD!"

Professor Peprah's eyes gleam. "Sweet little gel, I need no PhD to see you live your life like an itch dat is needin' to be scratched. Us Ga women, our men like us strong, and intelligent, en' we fight in bed, en' we love in bed. How are you different from a cat? Being called pussy, pussy—and saying nothing but porrrr."

Milka is all hot and bothered. This explosion of grown-up things is disturbing, and the Cocoa lady is now wielding the hot comb, and her curls are unraveling in her anger. Mavis comes between them, and Mama chooses just now to come in.

On their way out, Milka laughs and tells Aunt Peprah, "He! You really got her, Auntie!"

Mama looks fireworks at her.

In a few minutes they are in Aunt Peprah's Kombi going to buy ice cream, and Milka is silent, and Auntie huffs and puffs, and Mum calms her down.

"But, Professor, why do you bother to talk to these low-class girls—eh? She is beneath you! Why did you go to Amigos alone anyway? Dr. Kamau really wanted to take you. He called, and called. He loved your poems—even the one about—you know *those* things."

Professor Peprah laughs. "Ha! Maybe that is why he wanted to meet me in Amigos? To find out about my grasping mouth / between my legs / ruling me?"

Mum gasps. "Davinia Efua Peprah!"

Auntie Peprah just laughs, turns to Milka and says, "Ha! You gels should not see such things, but you are now a woman, eh? I can see those breasts. Ha! Women, we just fight and fight."

Milka does not reply. She is thinking, thank God we've left with my hair like this, so Mum can plait me matutas tonight, and I'll look just like I want this week. And Mum now doesn't know what to say to me, so she'll do what I say. And Mrs. Peprah, maybe she was just like me when she was young? Not one of the pretty ones . . . maybe that's why she got so angry. Maybe she made herself beautiful, you know, for *herself*. Is she really called *Davinia*?

Lately, it is as if she has been sliding in oil. That's it! Sliding in a smooth cylindrical tunnel coated with oil. Other tunnels branch out of it, other options that she often stumbles into and has to hold the edge tightly, or she'll slide down the chute into a person she cannot control. The Cocoa lady is one tunnel, free to purr and question nothing. Then there is Mrs. Peprah, bristling at every touch, using her mind to blast all opposition.

As they are about to take the turn into the supermarket, Milka looks at her mother in the front seat, laughing like tinkling glasses in a film. A thought freezes her mind, as shocking as glass breaking. She would never choose to be her mother, so lost in other people's aspirations, so determined to be beautiful.

16

An Affair to Dismember

There is this game I play, a game Mrs. Green, my late adopted mother, taught me. She would fold a piece of paper, while I watched her hands, watched the piano tendons ripple, the strange blue veins. Then she would ask me to draw what pattern the paper folded into. I never failed to get it right.

Last night, dizzy with head-fuck after reading Wole Soyinka's play *The Road*, I lay in bed and closed my eyes, and conjured an enormous piece of paper and folded it this way and that, folded it in ways I have never attempted. Then I sprayed it with something to make it brittle. I opened my eyes and put on some music: Moses Molelekwa on piano, the piece he played at the North Sea Jazz festival in Amsterdam, where he got sucked into a hurricane of his brilliance, then burst out crying after waking to find himself surrounded by a standing ovation.

I closed my eyes again, and breathed in, and let the paper open slowly. The pattern unraveled in my mind's eye: angles and triangles shining and shadowed. I laughed, and let it break in every brittle seam, and the shards of patterns flying high like the first crescendos of the piano. Then, with ease, I made them fall into place again. I threw them high again, and lost the pattern as they came tumbling down, as Moses crouched over his piano working through something intricate, caught in the most fragile of places, trying to juggle things at the far reaches of his ability. I could almost feel his relief as he passed the threshold and mastered himself. I joined him in his giddiness, throwing the jumble of patterns up again, and marveling at how my mind so effortlessly put the brittle paper together again. Then that crushing, tearing sound of tape getting caught in the cheap recorder, and the song whining to a halt. I swear I heard glass break as the shards came tumbling down, tearing into me as I tumbled. I slept with Mrs. Green in my mind.

I was eight years old before she came to my school in Murang'a, Kenya. I lived in a tranquil bubble, with hungers, agreed communal rumblings of belly, as normal as the surround of unripe maize plants. Coffee beans bought schoolbooks and fertilizer. I had never worn shoes.

Then she arrived, and asked me to come and live with her. My parents let me go, awed by what she offered; awed by me, now that they had discovered I played with numbers and words no primary schoolteacher in the village could understand.

The magic Mrs. Green brought was powerful. As we drove off, I saw the maize plants around us take off in a stomach-curling whirl, blending into the porridge I was drowning in. Dust, wind scraping against the Land Rover, my first car ride. Speeding as we did, through the dusty road and onto the tarmac, it seemed like this car was something that defied time and space. How else to explain how, in an hour, I was farther from anything I knew than I had ever been? Safe, in a science-built place, with bricks and a microwave.

She smelled like an angel, not the slightest pungency about her, as if the person had been scrubbed away and only something flowery remained. When she spoke it sounded like her words whistled through her nose before coming out of her mouth. When we Kikuyu people make words, we keep our nasal cavities out of the process.

She noticed my confusion and smiled, and her mouth opened

wide and scared me, it was so red inside, like a wound. Against her pale skin, her teeth seemed yellow, but she had television gentleness about her, like the mother in *Little House on the Prairie*, which we used to watch at the headmaster's house every Saturday.

"Do you want supper?

"Haven't you ever seen a fridge?"

A mouth from heaven: jellies, cakes, doughnuts, preserves, milk, and jams, all lit like an altar. I dived into the jaws of the fridge and ate. Oh, you'll be my son now, she said.

She had rented a house in a white suburb in Nairobi called Karen. For the first month she coached me at home, then arranged for me to attend a private school in the mornings, and to have special music and mathematics classes in the afternoons.

I learned to read her face: first with some fear, and later with a hidden disdain. I noticed that smiling in this new world was a limited thing. One doesn't smile to one's extremities while one speaks of serious things, because just talking to people is supposed to be a happy thing. One uses the word "one" a lot.

Mrs. Green was very different from my mother, who, when displeased, would think nothing of throwing her slipper past my ear as I made off giggling. Mrs. Green's method of punishment was guilt. Her smile would slip, ever so slightly, and her voice would shoot up to the maximum shrillness decorum allowed. Once or twice, the most disciplined tear in the world would swell gently in her eye, and I would wonder what it would take for it to roll down her cheek.

I became alert to everything in that house: to the whisper of her silk slippers on the stairs, allowing me to relax in sleep; to her voice ringing like merry glass when visitors came, rubbing her fingers on my head when I came to say hello, and calling me her "son," while the visitors looked baffled.

I found her smell after a while, in the mornings before she washed, or when she was upset. It was a peculiar smell, lacking a connection to earthy things, almost the smell of clothes that have soaked for too long. It often bothered my nose in an about-to-sneeze way.

Every two weeks or so, her husband and daughter would phone. I never spoke to them, but she would always pass on my love. Her husband was a vicar. "Sort of a sleepy priest," she explained. To my surprise she giggled as she said this. Reverend Kipkemoi, from the local Anglican Church, came to visit her sometimes, and she always turned coy when he was around, laughing too loudly and hugging me, something which she did not normally do.

Her daughter, Jemima, started to write, telling me she wanted to be pen pals.

The grant that Mama Green had organized to pay my fees was cut back. She went back to England—for a visit, she said—and left me behind in a government boarding school, where my accent was the source of much mirth. My skill with numbers infuriated everybody. My parents came to visit for the first time, after worrying that they hadn't received any letters from me for a while. They assumed I was still under Mama Green's wing, and I did not try to tell them otherwise. I was cold with my mother. I spoke to her in English and kept a distance, terrified I would smell like Mrs. Green, and suddenly aware that my parents smelled of soil and smoke and sweat. I spent my holidays living in the Anglican mission attached to the school.

The letters from Mrs. Green came every month, with photographs and vague promises.

We'll see you soon.

Waiting for the grant.

Things are so busy here.

Three years later, a week before I would be the youngest student ever to sit for the Kenyan Ordinary Level exams, Reverend Green wrote me his first letter, telling me Mrs. Green had died in a road accident.

Jemima continued to write, lots of hi-how-are-you saying-nothing letters. I replied, always attempting to mimic her cheer, always failing to be fluent in it. We lost touch after I left school.

I never wake up in a sweat. Not unless I have a hangover, or malaria. Generally, when I have one of those Mrs. Green dreams,

I wake up feeling like a rock has fallen down my gullet and ripped right through my insides. In the morning, weaverbirds make their way down the chute and flutter about—rebuilding.

The shack is my home and business, in Mwea, on the flatlands not far from Nairobi, Kenya. I sell meat, and carcasses hang above my head when I wake up. There are five minutes of beauty in my shack every morning: light swells slowly through the many gaps in my walls; even the carcasses hanging by the windows acquire a benign gleam, as if a life-light has come to claim them. Between 6:36 and 6:45 the glow dominates every crevice. For these minutes, I feel paradise trying to squeeze itself in and carry me away, a Jesus picture from *Bible Stories*.

Then, suddenly, morning is here and I lie on my bed, surrounded by peeled, headless goats. The smell of meat is unyielding, and brings me home with relief. The donkeys start screeching at ten to seven in the morning. It is already 86°F outside, and I long for water. There is no tap water in Mwea, though there are irrigation canals everywhere, for the rice paddies.

Ndirangu brings the water at seven. I am his last delivery. He has a new tank top, MUSCLE BEACH, CALIFORNIA. He bought it at the secondhand market in Embu Town. It has added to his Nikes to give him a more finished cool. If his donkey survives the month, he will have locked away his vulnerability behind this American arsenal. He tells me he has agents as far as Nairobi looking for "Tommy Hiro-figaa."

Ndirangu likes me. Correction: Ndirangu likes my biceps and abs. I get a prod, followed by a full examination whenever he comes round. I don't mind. Those whom he doesn't like get water that has fluffy brown flakes doing languid somersaults just below the surface. I make sure to give him a daily exercise tip; this way I get to drink the better river water. I haven't the guts to tell him that occasional sit-ups do it for me: the muscles I am interested in are in my shoulders and chest.

I linger after coffee. I hate to leave the butchery. Reading *Just William* poses a risk after one of the dreams, and Stephen Fry's

Paperweight (a delightful series of rants against all things "twee") is reserved for my lunch break. I settle for the much-thumbed first pages of Mongo Beti's *Mission to Kala*. I stop when Medza, bubbling with superiority, is poised to enter the village like a triumphant conquistador. I am now able to leave home feeling I can paint all the shit around me with good humor.

On my way to the post office, I bump into Maina at the bus rank.

"Sasa Einstein! How is the butchery business?"

I grunt in reply. He wears a double-breasted waistcoat and his polyester tie matches his breast-pocket hankie. Yuppie: *made in China*. I was at school with Maina. He was the resident brain till I came along and yawned past everybody. His bad suit, his home, with an apple-green velvet (*deluxe*) sofa set, was supposed to be my certificate to success.

I see him in the bar sometimes. He has acquired a pompous guffaw: Ho, ho! Another round, steward! Hot-air ho! My car has sixteen valves! Look at my mobile: hollow ho ho ho ho.

The three Hippos are already seated under the tree in the middle of the bus rank. They are county councilors, waiting for prey. Their gray matter devotes considerable resources to the subject of kickbacks, roast meat, and beer.

Mornings for kickbacks. Afternoons for meat. Any time for beer.

This is why we have no tap water. Mwea is a boomtown sharing a border with three districts: sometimes mud and sewage; sometimes dust and plastic bags; always the slap of cement on a new, rickety, unregulated building; always talk of cash-money. It is the place hungry young people who cannot make it in their home districts come to seek their fortunes. They are everywhere, lean and eagle-eyed, standing where they can see newcomers, coiled to chase after any cent. They will make money out of lifting, carrying, ferrying, providing information, acting as middlemen for anything. If you stop one and say you crave a banana, they will fetch one for you, and get a commission for doing so.

The town sits next to the highway to Nairobi. Every evening, cyclists bring boxes and boxes of French beans, headed for Europe.

Somebody is calling me.

"Dooolf!"

I hate that nickname, and the action hero that inspired it. I feel like a hulk that thinks with his muscles. Still, it grates less than "Einstein." Karanja is calling me. He is eighteen years old, and I am sure he will be a millionaire by the time he is twenty. I generally avoid him. He talks of nothing but French-bean prices and Aristotle Onassis.

"Hey, Dooooolf! Some hot white woman is looking for you!" I turn. A frail, dark-haired young woman is standing beside Karanja.

"Hello. You're Geoff? Geoff Mwangi? My name is Jemima, Jemima Green."

I am surprisingly calm. Here she is, the girl who took my adopted mother away, Mama Green's real daughter.

All I can think is: *It works!* All these years I've used home-made concrete weights that have turned me into a rock, an immovable object. *I will not care!*

I see a brief submission in her eyes, deference. She didn't expect me like this. She would have remembered the stilted boy who wrote letters straight out of *Better English*. I carefully take her hand and look at her the way I was trained to do with white people, straight in the eye. Her eyes are shaped exactly like her mother's but possess a different energy—not fluttering about to ensure invisible boundaries are never breached. They are curious, with the naive confidence the younger white people seem to have: "*Nothing can possibly happen to me.*"

What breaches my objectivity is the smell, that white girl smell, like cobwebs in the nostrils. That smell is like a mosquito in my nose after last night's dream.

"Hello, Jemima, it's a pleasure to meet you finally. How is your father?"

"Oh, hello! Dad's the same, being a busybody—writing long

letters to everybody about the homeless. He's become quite a socialist—absolutely despises Blair."

I don't know what to say about this. I have never met her father.

"Are you just passing by? Can I offer you a Coke, or some tea?"

"No. I came to see you. I'm staying at the hotel—could you walk me back? Now that I've found you, I need to confirm my booking."

Karanja is just standing there, overwhelmed by a sheepishness I didn't know was possible from him. God! He is actually doodling in the dust with his foot! Standing before me, the reason why Onassis married that Kennedy woman. My eyebrows chase him away, and we head off to Jemima's hotel.

She talks the whole way there; filling up the nervous gaps with questions she answers herself. I am often tempted to leak like this but can't: even now my impassiveness is pushed to the limit by a brimming of things to say.

She stops.

"I'm talking too much, aren't I? I do this when I am nervous."

I am angry. My restraint is eternal; I cannot breach it, and it nags like a hard-on that never ends. How could she survive being bubbly having lived with Mother Don't-talk-if-you-have-nothing-to-say Green? Was I so pliable?

Her chatter resumes.

"Oh, my friend Dora, she's from the West Indies, she says that in Trinidad everybody talks like this! From the heart! Oh, wow, look at those gorgeous tomatoes? They're never this red in England!"

She dances, and dances around the core, never once dipping her toe in to test the heat: "Oh! Ah! Bugger that! Shit! Bollocks! Really? Wow!"

Shut up!

I tune out. Last month my dad wrote me a letter: he is happy in Murang'a, making good money from horticulture. He misses his first-born. His new wife is not like my real mother, who died a year after I finished high school. She is flighty, wants to return to school or some such nonsense. He is getting old, and curses the day he allowed that white woman to take me away.

"Come grow carnations," Dad says. "Let's make money! Come be with us again!"

Jemima is staying at the White Lion, an old colonial hotel that smells of stale polish and decaying upholstery. There is a group of Nairobi salespeople sitting in one corner, laughing loudly, huddled around their wit as if it is the only thing that will keep them alive in this place. Mr. Henderson, the old man who lives here, is in his usual seat at the corner of the bar, the skin on his face cracking, as if death is about to burst out of it. Every few years, a member of his family comes to beg him to leave and go back to England, but he refuses. He is still waiting for the Ministry of Lands to return his farm, which was taken by a well-known politician's family twenty years ago.

We sit at the other side of the bar. She disarms me, persuading me to have a beer, then another. Her smell fades by default, and I am able to see her with a friendlier eye. Her face in repose droops downward, with an almost Jewish melancholy. The far ends of her eyes slide down, like a welling tear. Below them, twin lines etch a continuing descent; and, below that, her mouth, a thin line, faces downward like eyes averted.

But her repose is rare. The lines find endless arrangements of expression, giving her face a rubbery mobility and lending a comic element to her melancholy. Her hair is nondescript brown. Yet somehow her face and her body language are lifted to vitality by a pale, gleaming skin, like porcelain with a dim light behind it.

"It's so bloody hot. I never thought it would be. I really can't picture Mother in a place this hot."

"Karen is milder; that's where we lived mostly."

She inhales deeply and exhales into someone different, somebody with an eggshell of a voice.

"Look, I came here because we have issues to deal with. I've hated you too long; I can't shake it off. I'm getting married next month, so I need to get clear of this shit."

I am surprised. When we were pen pals, she was full of sunshine and bubble. I imagined her to be a terribly happy person, glowing behind the rounded script and prancing around in a country garden like the jolly cartoon animals did on her writing paper.

"Why did you hate me?"

"Because you were the one who made her good. She drove us crazy! Dad and I were relieved when she went to Kee-nya—sorry, you call it Ke-nya, don't you? Then she became another person: a mother who wrote letters asking me how I felt. How I felt! Then there were the endless letters about you. What a genius you were! Reading at age two! Writing at three! Prizes, awards—and Black too, so I couldn't even *really* hate you! Oh, shit—now I'm crying!"

I laugh. I was in such awe of her, it never occurred to me at the time to be jealous.

"Your mother was never a nice person. I was simply the lever on her pedestal: *Missionary Adopts Destitute Prodigy!* That so-called genius was never mine; she discovered it, owned it, and managed it. Sometimes I think she left with it too. If anything made her a better mother, it was the fact that she was an angel from a distance. You should read the letters she wrote from the Vicarage! 'Darling' this, 'angel' that! I only heard that from her when there were guests."

The barman is staring at me. I realize my accent has changed: it mirrors hers, down to the intonation. This unconscious betrayal irritates me, but I can't seem to find entry to my usual accent.

"Why did she run off?"

"Don't you know? She was having a fling with Reverend Kipkemoi. Then she lost her grant so the plans to open a school for 'gifted' children fell through."

"Really? Mother? An affair? Not that old—"

"I caught them once. He had parked his car in Ngong Forest. I used to go there to collect butterflies."

Jemima bursts out laughing. "You should have seen Dad's face fall when the taxi came through the gate! Did you go back to your family?"

"No."

"Didn't they want you back?"

"They did, but I didn't want to go back. How could I? I went to boarding school and rented a room in the holidays. I thought she would come back, if only to visit."

"So do you see your parents?"

"I visit sometimes. I haven't seen my father since my mum died."

"I'm sorry. You must regret ever tangling with Mum."

My laugh is stones rattling on a corrugated-iron roof.

"Education the way I got it doesn't leave much room for that kind of regret. Where I come from, there isn't a single person who doesn't consider me lucky."

"So why did you become a butcher, live in this dump?"

My voice is surprisingly calm. "I became a butcher because there is money in it, and because I can't bear to work for anyone. I'm not good with people."

A mosquito coil ignites in my stomach and begins its slow burn, fueled by the panic inside me. Conscious of the ambiguous place I am in without my usual accent, I feel queasy, wide open. She is in charge now. She can afford to display herself without fear, and lend me a face full of pity.

"Silly bitch! She lied to me! She said you refused to come with her, that you . . . Oh, never mind."

I am going to fuck her. I will watch those eyes flutter in a drowning panic below me. I will watch them shrink away from the hanging goatskin, wrinkle at the smell of old burnt meat. I will not have her come here, and leave sneer marks like snail trails where I live.

My hand reaches for her cheek, my voice falls to a murmur,

and I notice my accent again with surprise. "I lied. She didn't leave because of the affair. She left because she realized that her life was you, the Vicarage and English gooseberries; she never stopped talking about bloody English gooseberries!"

We laugh, and her talk slips into intimacy. My voice simply glides alongside—gravelly soft, whereas hers is whisper soft. I say nothing that makes me feel. She opens up completely and starts to give her words to me before testing them out. I can't believe how easy it is.

I am on my third beer when the migraine attacks like a poisonous wart on my temple. I visualize it oozing a toxic green sap into my head. I can't help but be Black next to Jemima; I can't just be Geoff Mbiyu, on a Biggles adventure. I can't even be Jean-Marie Medza, a nerdy conquistador.

"Are you okay? You've gone a bit gray."

"I'm sorry. It's my head. I've got to go to the butchery. I'll catch up with you in the afternoon."

On my way out, Mr. Henderson turns to me and says hello, an expression of distaste in his face.

"One of the Oxfam people, is she?" he asks.

"No, she's my sister."

I don't wait to see his face change.

The kitten that adopted me is waiting at the door. I call her Karen Blixen, and frequently wish she would get out of Africa. While I gather charcoal and light the stove, she maintains a persistent plea: "Feed me! Feed me!" I mix tripe and buttermilk in a bowl. The damn thing still can't trust me enough for me to come near her. I head to the bathroom with my bucket of water. I can hear her, her meows charged with question marks:

"Miaw? Miaw? Aw? Raaaouw?" ("Are you far enough away? Can I eat now?")

The first touch of hot water on my head multiplies the throb. I lie down on a mat under the flame tree in the courtyard. I want to dry slowly, savor the cool. In the pause between throbs, I set out beacons. I mark a new territory with slow deliberation:

Cool, Highland cool . . .

No faceless hordes of mindless darkies. *No Conrad? said Mrs. Green. You must read Conrad, he really was on your side.* I let numbers run through me. I am still digesting *A Brief History of Time,* a book I memorized in two sittings. Ideas turn in my brain, until cascades of number-songs calm my mind. I still can't get myself to doubt what Hawking says, or to try to challenge it. I don't have the confidence. I just accept them and dance with the ideas from time to time.

Is this an African thing? To worship understanding? To put our education on the mantelpiece, and spend our lives admiring the fact that we managed to understand, because to challenge these things is to risk failing?

Do Not Deface Your Passport.

Whenever I turn on the mat, the throbbing accelerates. I include the throbs in the waterfall of numbers, where they become a potentiality with no mass, no time. Each throb is now a synapse, asking to blow into existence.

I sleep, staccato with the subsiding knock-knocks. Sleep spits and hisses—my selves mixing like hot fat and water.

Jemima comes at dusk and announces herself by rubbing her face feathers on my cheeks. I wake abruptly, and pull her down next to me. At first I seek submission, but the pounding nearly splits my head open. She is crying. I slow myself down and follow her flavors, from crotch to armpit. My senses are closed to all; her breathing seems very loud. I follow the rhythm of her breath, and soon it is as if I am her, white and writhing on a mat under a flame tree. My headache oozes away, diluting its sap in our pleasures.

We part and lie on our backs, and discover that all this time a whole motion picture is above us. We watch the sun-glowing clouds battle the dark. The clouds seem unreal, moving slowly across the sky, unoiled and effortless. All this was happening while we ground each other to submission.

We open up.

"You know, people keep talking about green. How beautiful it is to sit in a field of green. I hate green, the strong chlorophyll smell of it. When I was a kid, the hungriest time was when the maize was taller than me and we were surrounded by *that smell;* it would coil into our stomachs, and they would churn it like a meal and fill us with the taste of bile. I much prefer the color of dry stalks tied together, and mounds and mounds of golden maize-cobs heaped by the side. Now *that* is bounty."

"I feel that if I lived here, I would be strong. England is so *tame.* Everything has been so *done!* I can be what I want to be here. I hated it when Mother came here—I thought Africa was *mine.* I loved Karen Blixen! Wasn't she just divine?"

"I've been saving up to travel in the UK. I hope they give me a visa this time. I would love to attend the Edinburgh Arts Festival, and buy books and books in London."

She giggles. "You could put on a play at the festival, you, a conductor, playing your symphony to an audience of headless goats."

We trade images, each revealing more, each disappointing more. Night drops like a hot damp towel, and clouds block the stars. I hit bottom: my head starts to throb, and I feel raw and bruised. We smell stale, and grit-laden drafts are making their way through the gates.

We start to collect the bits of ourselves hanging loose, then, gathered together, we notice our goose bumps: vulnerable! Yikes!

Fortifications are built; our joint gears dislodge, and start to grate on each other.

"So what does your fiancé do?" I ask.

"We . . . eell, since you asked, your sweat is pungent, more sharp than musky—like Dettol, only sort of muskier," she says.

"Will you tell your fiancé?"

"Of course I like your smell—it's just, different somehow. Oh, don't sulk! On second thought, I do like the smell. I feel like you're human now, not just a tight-arsed paragon. Your letters could have been written by R2-D2. By the way, do you say Kee-nya? I thought Kenyans call it Ke-nya?"

My eyebrows rise, then drop like an eagle after prey.

"What anthropological expertise! Are you ready to write a travel book yet? Or did you read that in *The Rough Guide*? Did they also tell you how to teach me to be a Kenyan? How to pronounce my country? You could start an NGO, you know, use that expertise."

"Fuck you."

She wants to leave, and has summoned enough ire to send a rocket to the moon. She is back in a few seconds. I laugh. She heard bullets from the video next door: *Universal Soldier*. I laugh, and tell her this. She gets angry, starts to cry, then gets angrier.

I laugh to myself. There's nothing as scary as being beyond the *Lonely Planet*. I escort her to the hotel. She sulks and sniffles all the way back. I leave her simmering over a warm beer at the bar. As I walk out, I see Mr. Henderson making a creaky beeline for her.

I see in my mind the old man patting her hand, his enormous hanky floating around her face, held by his Old Africa Hand, with shuddering fingers, and blue veins that will clench to attention when talking about bleeding hearts, and left-wing newspapers, and London perverted. She will tell him about her mother, and he will say sadly, "She couldn't know."

Jemima will come to tears when he tells her about his dogs, whose progeny appear in dustbins nearby, bearing bits of the familiar, sometimes just the eyes. They are wild now, wounded and malnourished, sometimes their teats hang, naked and sagging.

In this dark bar, with shadows dancing, he will talk of the dark outside, scrambling to get in, looking for a crack of light to take your last shoe, your last cent, your daughter, your property. You will wake up to hear donkeys screaming, whips slapping. Can't leave clothes on the wash line. Twenty years on, this town can't dig a bloody borehole.

She will huff, as he speaks, puff as he speaks, each huff, each puff, blowing me darker among the shadows.

What was: he will start paint-brushing the air again, this time drawing lions in bathtubs and leopards as pets. Eyes will open wide as she hears of dalliances with the Delameres, and lounging with Lord Erroll, hunting with Hemingway, getting bombed with Blixen. By the time he fades into a long monologue about the war, she will be thinking, "Poor Mum."

I walk back, mumbling shadows following me everywhere, an embarrassing new respect. I hear Karanja shout out "O-He! Van Damme *mwenyewe*!" *Van Damme Himself.*

A new name. I'm sure I will be the first to get clean water in the morning.

No matter, there is a song in my mind:

She says Ke-nya, and I say Kee-nya,
Kee-nya, Ke-nya; Ke-nya, Kee-nya,
Let's call the whole thing off . . .

I feel good. I will go to bed: untangle the Moses Molelekwa tape, close my eyes, and let shards of brittle paper fall into place. There is always a new way to fold the paper, and it always falls into place.

17

According to Mwangi

Once upon a time there was a man called Mwananchi. Now this guy had one talent. As a youngster, he would stand on a street corner of Booroo housing estate and tell stories. Booroo estate was the newest and largest estate in Nairobi, built to house the new generation of forward-moving Kenyans.

Kids from Phases 1 to 4 of the housing estate would pass by his "joint" when sent to the shops by their parents. His joint was an abandoned old car that sat next to a certain lampshade he had decorated himself in Manchester United football team's colors. He told his stories sometimes in Sheng, the version of Kiswahili that all the cool people spoke, or sometimes in that hip Nairobi English teachers laughed at.

Parents hated him. They wanted him to be exiled to some small village somewhere: whatever it took to get him away from their children, who would come home with all sorts of crazy ideas, funny new slang. Some tried to get hold of his parents to complain about him, but his parents seemed elusive—promising to come for meetings and never showing up, or sometimes simply not picking up the telephone.

What made his stories special is how they managed to capture the place the kids lived in. Their parents, still with one foot in their home villages, still with colonial hangovers, busy building the nation, had no real idea how their children's world worked. This was the first generation of kids in independent Kenya, the first generation to be born in a city. There were no books about them, films about them. They didn't even see themselves on television.

There were many kids in Booroo who were funny, or witty, or who came up with better slang, but Mwananchi was democratic—he didn't slag off one group of people to entertain the rest. He saved all his venom for adults, those alien people who did things differently from what they said at home. There are few secrets among kids, and fewer secrets among kids in Booroo. He had the tact, though, not to name names.

Mwananchi would weave a story out of Big Ben and Leonard Mambo Mbotela and James Bond and *Kivunja Mbavu* and the Flintstones and Kelly Brown and Mama Milka, who sold vegetables from door to door.

He could turn a mandazi into a character—John Mandazi the goalie, who thought the goal was a frying pan and was always jumping about, and who would swell up when the ball came near him. One day, before the finals, some kids were on their way to the match when they met their parents, who asked them, "What are you doing dragging that giant mandazi around?"

And the kids said, "Aiee! Mammee! But he's our goalie—we can't play the match without him!" The parents looked at each other and dragged off John Mandazi and fed him to the *chubana ndebe* guy, who was always hungry.

Then there was John Mandazi's brother, Canaan Banana Mandazi, who was a fat city council official with brown teeth and four wives . . .

Once Mwananchi told a story about a mean old schoolteacher called Pingiling who used to make his children bend to his will—and would beat them up until they did. Pingiling was a widower. In the end, Pingiling found that his family had grown tough, like Muhammad Ali. Untouched and worshipped, he had frozen into glass. So one time he whipped his daughter with the stick from a caterpillar tree and she screamed and struck back, and his eyes opened wide as he felt himself starting to shake, and his last words were "Pingiling!"

Then they swept him into the dustbin.

One girl, Sheena Patel, started to cry when she heard that story. Years later, she refused to go back home from England after she had done her A-Levels. Her father had arranged a marriage for her. He died alone a few years later.

Pingiling.

Achieng was in love with Mwananchi. She was one of the youngest of his regulars. She would follow him around everywhere—thumb in her mouth, dragging a skipping rope behind her and staring at him without blinking.

Years later some would recall that they first learned about sex from his famous story "*Muguu Wazi* and the Bouncing Baby." For weeks kids in Booroo would say in one of Mwananchi's falsettos, "It's a bouncing baby booy!" Then they would crack up laughing. That night, after they heard the story, they released themselves and started to talk about sticky dreams, and pimples as loud as police sirens, laughing all the time. Some discovered that day that they weren't suffering from a strange illness.

Booroo is situated on the edge of the Athi Plains; and on a clear night stars jump at you. Shooting stars, blinking stars, stars that are planets; stars that turn out to be somebody's headlights. The day after the first *Star Wars* film was shown at a Nairobi cinema, the kids gathered at the lamppost. Mwananchi was ignored, and the kids all stared at the sky, and talked about Obi and Princess Leia, and laughed at the Aliens who were speaking Kikuyu. Why would Aliens speak in Kikuyu?

Mwananchi was angry that day. It was the first time he had been ignored in the joint. It was also clear to everybody that he hadn't seen the film. He sat listening to them for a while, then left angrily, saying, "That all dead *maneno*. Dead. A story is *now*, bwana—now. I make a story, and watch you, and change it as I watch you, and you add some of your own taste, and that's a story, bwana. How can it be given to you, eh? Now, how is that your story, bwana . . . argh."

He left, and they paused for a minute before exploding into chatter about the film. They all got home really late that night, and a few of them got beatings.

The next day Mwananchi bounced back. He told them about the rocket launch at Patel Brotherhood Hall in Nairobi, the rocket that was being powered by curry powder and njahi-bean farts. This didn't capture their interest at first. Then he drew the characters. The Space Ahoi, he called them. Who are Ahoi, he was asked? Ai! Don't you know—the warriors of the new frontier: Matatu touts, the Mau Mau, Rastas. All those hungry, angry people. They are being taken by the Patel Brotherhood to farm tomatoes on a new planet called M'babylon. Ahoi!

Ahoi!

They all laughed.

Mwananchi made them lie down on the asphalt and look up at the stars. Then he told them about the interstellar football matches that God plays with his angels. Against the red devils. His God had dreadlocks and listened to Bob Marley music. Some of the kids looked at each other. One or two slipped away after hearing this blasphemy.

The red devils liked Jim Reeves and Skeeter Davis. He told them how the crew of the curry-powder-powered ship had seen this football match. One of them, Sarit Patel, drew the lines from star to star, following some hidden message in his mind—and the football match lit up for the whole ship. Mwananchi imitated Leonard Mambo Mbotela's football commentary.

"Star people! *Na mpria,* star defender—*anachenga,* star striker, staar . . . GOOOOOOAAAAL!"

Then people went off to boarding school and started thinking about sex and Michael Jackson, and keeping their curls wet, and those streetlamp sessions became uncool. Everybody migrated to the Saturday holiday fashion show by the supermarket, where boys stood at one corner pretending not to see the girls, and girls walked in giggling groups pretending to buy sugar. Sometimes they bumped into Mwananchi at his joint—talking to younger kids, but after a while he disappeared.

He was remembered in odd ways, though, over the years.

Maillu, one regular but shy member of his audience, found that the flavor of Mwananchi's wit had touched him; and, sitting in the students' bar at the university, years later, he needed only to think of those carefree nights by the lamppost to lose his stutter and make people around him laugh. Some forgot Mwananchi, but the magic stayed in them in nameless ways.

Two people remembered him in literary ways. One, Njoki, in a great haste to submit oral literature stories for her Sixth Form project, wrote five of his stories from memory, in Sheng, translated them into "posh English," and submitted them. Her teacher tore them up in horror and threw them into the bin, where cigarette butts, chewing gum, and dirty magazines went.

"Dat is not oral litera-chuwa. Read Okot p'Bitek! Oh, where are ta rappits and ta hyenas, and ta grantmatter's knee? Eh! Did you go and listen to your grantmatter in ta village? When I was in Makerere University . . ."

Njoki went to Kenyatta University library, copied stories from oral litera-chuwa books, changed them a little, and got an A in litera-chuwa. She now lectures in literary criticism. Her paper "The Role of the Rabbit in African Mythology" was a hit at the Bonn Symposium.

Mwangi was a man desperate to be interesting, but the place in his mind where charm should reside was full of cotton wool. Mwangi burned with passion for Mwananchi's words. He started his literary career listening to Mwananchi's stories, then read story-books, and novels—not so much finding laid-back pleasure, or empathy, or validation even. He was looking for ways to break them down, to understand.

Why? Why does this work, and that doesn't? After many years, he got his PhD in litera-chuwa somewhere really prestigious in the UK. Then he wrote his novel, a beautiful thing, like stained glass, shining with prose so stark it seemed naked; some characters were gritty, some were magical but real; some decon-

structed; some stood in existentialist angst; others spoke in de-
colonized English. Oh! The publishers went bananas—a Kenyan
voice at last! Many bought the book, which sat next to the set of
Encyclopædia Britannica, a trophy. Students of literature around
the world pounced upon it, and libraries groaned with the weight
of literary papers. The plot coiled and struck like a snake in
places; then balmed like a mother's kiss; then built coils in the
stomach—then uncoiled them—all this by page ten. From page
eleven, to prove he wasn't just after giving mindless entertain-
ment, the plot deconstructed, and the next fifty pages were one
vast and profound interior monologue.

And the prizes! Li-te-ra-ry this, and Li-te-ra-chuwa that! Wri-
tahs this! Ai! It was all so exciting that nobody asked if anybody's belly caught fire when they read the book. Or if anybody
read it and cried in themselves, saying, "Oh, but that's me, he's
just spoken to my soul!"

His grammar! Oooh! Irritated by contradicting rules and de-
funct spellings and neo-colonial biases, Mwangi reinvented
grammar, made it efficient, polished it, and it stood like clean
bones in the *bundu:* a new set book for the world. Some schools
in Scotland and Ireland, looking for an English they could make
theirs, chose his grammar as their standard. The African Union
unanimously passed the proposal to set up a committee to investigate the committee they had set up in London to investigate the
subcommittee charged with decolonization of language. Twelve
EU committees met around the same subject and declared that,
for purposes of harmonious paperwork, they would adopt
Mwangics as the new English.

The Mwangics campaign had adverts running around the
world saying, WE HAVE HAD ENAFF!

The euphoria faded after a while. Mwangi took off to pro-
mote his book in America. Kenyans abroad stood straighter
with their African compatriots. "Have you read Mwangi?" they
would ask some Nigerian or Zimbabwean. In Kenya, people
with visitors from abroad finally stopped giving their guests
Karen Blixen to read. Our Voice, they would think, as the guests

would unwrap the gift and smile with pleasure and say, awed, "He's Kenyan? I thought he was from South Africa!"

For years, it was:

Mwangi says
According to Mwangi
In Mwangi's opinion

By this time, maybe about twenty-five people around the world had read Mwangi. The rest feasted on the many guidebooks there were, memorizing the synopses. In fact, some of the guidebooks became set books.

Only one person was brave enough to say something against Mwangi, a well-known journalist, famous for his boozy ways and unapologetic opinions. He said, "Arh! They say Kenyans don't read! Well, I say Kenyans don't read because all the great stories are not in books. Great stories sit in bars and burp and come out after a few brown ones. Mwangi will sell books because big books fill bookshelves, but who wants to take it out? The bookshelf will collapse if you take that book out."

He suggested that the English Kenyans spoke in bars become the standard. *Mwang–hics,* he called it.

The year 2000 was a wistful year for many in Kenya. Things were bad: roads falling apart; no money; retrenchments; AIDS everywhere; beer expensive; school fees consuming everybody's entire salary. Being Born Again started to be flashy, churches demanding this and that—they called them "lurve gifts." So many people sat at home, and held their children close, and reminisced. They started to phone friends they hadn't seen in years, seeking validation, wanting a connection to freer days. And so the question was being asked, "But what happened to Mwananchi?"

— Oh, he went to Bulgaria, he is a doctor . . .
— Ai! Didn't you hear! AIDS!

— Apana! Can you believe—he is a receptionist at the *Week-end* newspaper. He failed Form Four—got a third class coz he failed English.

— Nooo—he is married in Ukambani. Was he a Kamba?

— Ai? What tribe was he?

The rumors failed to endure. People were surprised to find that he had vanished without trace.

People who knew him started to ask in bars and churches and at the many funerals. It became clear that nobody really knew where he lived, or who his parents were, or even his surname. Some now started to think, "Ai! Was he ever there?"

Maillu came closest to Mwananchi's legacy. When he was promoted, he became the Director of School Sports in his province. Traveling to sports events around the country, he started to hear this song all the schoolkids sang while cheering their team: "Mama Milka." It would always leave him in tears, and he remembered how Mwananchi came up with that song one day, and how people would add rhyming couplets to it. He remembered how they would always celebrate the beginning of school holidays with new additions to the song. It was a song with a bit of everything, a bit of every language the kids spoke, a bit of what films they watched, what comics they read, what new football slang had arrived from the surburb of Eastlands—the place where all slang came from. Then, a few years later, listening to this new Nairobi FM station, he heard a group of strange young youths, Warufagaa, singing the latest hit: "Mama Milka." It was the first time a Kenyan song was ahead of the American crooners in the Kenyan charts.

Some of the old gang, frustrated that Mwananchi had left no memory of himself, wished they had kept his corduroy jacket; or taped him, just to hear that voice. Some said, "Argh! Why didn't he write the stories?"

Some wondered whether his stories would be as magical now, but found they couldn't remember a single story, just odd words like "Pingiling," followed by a happy warm feeling in their stomachs.

Achieng met Njoki at a wedding one day and asked her, "Do you remember that day, after watching *Star Wars,* when Mwananchi told us about those curry-powder spaceships?"

Njoki looked at her in surprise. "Are you still thinking about that clown? Ai! But you! There was nowhere he was going, you know. He was so gender-biased and he was always affirming Eurocentric values! What happened to African culture?"

It was at this wedding that I met and fell in love with Achieng.

And it seemed that, as Mwananchi faded, things in many people's memories began to lose reality too. They started to ask themselves those questions that libraries don't have answers to; those questions that seem meaningless and whose answers are simply a validation that they lived, and that their lives mattered.

— But did the old Big G chewing gum really taste like that?

— Do you remember that ka-time so-and-so's parents came back from Shags early? He! The party!

— And the rocket that was fueled by curry powder?

— Was there really a tree full of caterpillars at Jane Rono's house?

— What did we taste like?

Some resigned themselves and bought small plots of land in their parents' home villages. Like their parents, they started to pretend to be farmers; like their parents, they pretended confusion about things national and retreated to a tribal space. Every weekend they would head off to the village to pretend to enjoy themselves, while their children met at lampposts and listened to "Mama Milka" on Kiss FM.

So one day, in Westlands, Mwangi bumped into an old Booroo neighbor as he was heading for his weekly interview with the BBC *Mwangics* show. Achieng was in a terrible mood for no particular reason, just feeling rudderless, and she asked him brashly, "Have you ever wondered what things would have been like if Mwananchi had written down his stories and sent them to a publisher?"

Mwangi laughed and laughed and laughed. "Ai! Are you crazy? He couldn't put together a sentence in English, that guy!

They would have just stamped it 'substandard.' Publishers are looking for litera-chuwa, you know. Such a book would never be on any reading list that matters!"

Achieng snapped back at him, "How is it, that among those of us who knew him, he matters so much more than you do?"

At that very moment, a waiter at a nearby café tripped, and his entire tray dropped on the floor. *Pingiling!*

Achieng laughed.

18

Ships in High Transit

Stupid Japanese tourist. During breakfast, on the open-air patio that faced the plains of Lake Nakuru National Park, he saw the gang of baboons, saw the two large males fulfilling with every grunt and chest bang every human cliché about male brutality. Here is an aspect of reality as consensus: the man has spent his entire life watching nature documentaries. He said this to Matano, with much excitement, over and over again, in the van to Nakuru last week. How can he remind his adrenaline that these beasts can kill, when he knows them only as television actors?

So he hid a crust of bread and, when everybody was done with breakfast, threw it at the group of baboons outside and aimed his camera at them. The larger male went for the bread, and then attacked the man, leaving with a chunk of his finger, and decapitating the green crocodile on his shirt. The baboon was shot that afternoon. A second green crocodile replaced the first.

That was last month.

Then there is Matano's boss/business partner, Armitage Shanks, of the Ceramic Toilet Shanks, or maybe the Water Closet

Shanks, or the Flush Unit Shanks. Or maybe a Faux Shanks: it is possible he borrowed the name. Matano had never asked. He knew that Shanks carried a sort of hushed-whisper weight in Karen and Nyali and Laikipia, together with names like Kuki and Blixen. Matano also knew that somewhere in the Commonwealth some civil servant shat regularly in an Armitage Shanks toilet.

Shanks lives in Kenya, running a small tour firm, hardly heroic for a man whose family managed to ship heavy ceramic water closets around the world. But he hit on a winning idea.

Some dizzy photographer woman, Diana Tilten-Hamilton, had been telling him about the astrological history of the Maa people, told him about her theory that they were the true ancient Egyptians, showed him her collection of photographs, just days before they were shipped to the publisher of coffee-table books: photos packed with pictures of semi-naked Maa astrologers, gazing at the night sky, pointing at the stars, loincloths lifted to reveal lean, scooped-out, copper-colored buttocks.

He found his great idea.

Heirlooms.

So he hired ten of the best woodcarvers from the Mombasa Akamba Cooperative, hid them out in a small farm in Laikipia, and started a cottage industry. Maasai heirlooms.

The spin:

Thousands of years ago, in the great Maa Empire, Maa-saa-i-a, a great carver, lived. It was said he could carve the spirit of a moran warrior from olivewood. At night he occupied the spirit of the bull. During the day, he spun winds that carve totem spirits out of stray olivewood.

When the Maa-saa-i-a Empire fell apart, after a great war with the Phoenicians over trade in frankincense and myrrh, the remaining Maa scattered to the winds. Some left for the south and formed the great Zulu Nation; others remained in East Africa, impoverished but noble. Others fought with Prester John, and others became gladiators in Rome.

The great carver Um-Shambalaa vanished one night in the

Ngong Hills, betrayed by evil spirits who had overwhelmed the ancestors. He waits for the Maa to rise again.

Until last year, nobody knew the secret of Maa-saa-i-a, until Armitage Shanks went to live among the (rare) Highland Samburu. He killed his first lion at seventeen, with his bare hands (witnessed by his circumcision brother, Ole Lenana), and saved the Highland Samburu with his MTV song "Feed the Maa" (sung with his former rock band, the Fecal Martyrs). Shanks was asked by the Shamanic Elder of the Greater Maa to be an elder. His name was changed. He is now called Ole um-Shambalaa—"The Brother Not Born Among Us." The elders pleaded with Ole um-Shambalaa to help them recover their lost glory. They gave him all three hundred of their ancient olivewood heirlooms to auction. To raise money to make the Maa rise again . . .

This was how Matano came to manage WylDe AFreaKa tours. Shanks was now a noble savage, and could not be bothered with tax forms . . .

Or airport welcoming procedures:

Dancing girls in grass skirts singing: "A wimbowe, a wimbowe."

Dancing men singing: "A wimbowe, a wimbowe."

Giant warrior with lion whiskers and shiny black makeup walks on all fours toward clapping German tourists, flexing his muscles and growling: "A wimbowe, a wimbowe."

In the jungle . . .

Actually, Shanks lost interest in WylDe AFreaKa right from the start. Apart from an annual six-month trip to wherever Eurotrash were camping out, to "market" (where he avoided all the Scandinavian snowplow drivers and Belgian paper-clip-packers and Swiss-cheese-hole-pokers who were his real clientele, and spent time in Provence and Tuscany and the South of France), he generally worked on other projects. First, there were the constructed wetland toilets (it is hard for a Shanks to keep off the subject), then the Fecal Martyrs, who got to No. 8 in the charts on the Isle of Man and toured Vladivostok ("Feed the Maaa-aaa-aah, let them know it's Easter Time . . ."); then the

Nuba Tattoo Bar he started in London, opened by a cousin of Leni Riefenstahl. The tattoo bar had naked Nuba refugees operating the tills, before the Sudan People's Liberation Army threatened to bomb him (Shanks claimed in a BBC interview). Then there was the spectacular failure, Foreign Correspondent, the Nairobi coffee shop that closed because people complained that they kept losing their appetites in a place decorated with grainy black-and-white pictures of whichever Africans happened to be starving at the time. In between all these ventures, Shanks was learning tantric sex, polishing off a bottle of Stoli every night, and keeping away from Mr. Kamau Delivery, his coke dealer, to whom he always owed money. Lately, though, he has been more scarce than usual. Somber. Matano knows this is a phase, a new project, which always means a short season when more money will not be available. He paid out salaries three days early, before Shanks could get to the account.

The van leans forward to the ramp, as Matano prepares to board the ferry. He looks at the rearview mirror. The couple he has just picked up at the airport stop gesticulating excitedly; their faces freeze for a second, they look at each other, the man's eyes catch Matano's. Jean-Paul turns away guiltily, and says to his wife/lover/colleague: "Isn't this great? What a tub! Wonder when they built it—must be before the war."

"Is it safe, do you think?"

Matano smiles to himself. He looks out at the ferry, and allows himself to see it through their eyes.

Stomach plummets: fear, thrill. Trippy. So *real*. Smell of old oil, sweat, and spices. So exotic.

Color: women in their robes, eyes covered, rimmed with kohl; other women dark and dressed in skirts and blouses looking drab; other women sort of in-between cultures, a chiffon blouse, and a wraparound sarong with bright yellow, green, and blue designs. Many people are barefoot. An old Arab man, with an emaciated face and a hooked nose, in a white robe, sitting on a platform above, one deformed toenail sweeping up like an Ali Baba shoe. A foot like varnished old wood, full of cracks. He is stripping some stems and chewing the flesh inside. There is a bulge on one cheek, and he spits and spits and spits all the way to the mainland. Brownish spit lands on some rusty metal, pools and trickles, slips off the side on to some rope that lies coiled on the floor.

The tourists' eyes are transfixed: somewhere between horror and excitement. How *real*! Must send a piece to *Granta*.

Same scene through Matano's eyes:

Abdullahi is chewing miraa again. The banished son of one of the coast's oldest Swahili families, he abandoned the trucking business for the excitement of sex, drugs, and Europop (had a band that did ABBA covers in hotels, in Kiswahili, dressed in kanzus: "Waterloo, *niliamua kukupenda milele . . .* "). Now he is too old to appeal to the German blondes looking for excitement in a hooked nose and cruel desert eyes. To the Euro-wielding market, there are no savage (yet tender) Arab sheiks in Mills and Boon romance books anymore; Arabs are now gun-toting losers, or compilers of mezze platters, or servers of hummus, or soft-palmed mummy's boys in European private schools. There are no ABBA fans under sixty, now that everyone listens to Eminem and Tupac. Now Abdullahi has become a backdrop, hardly visible in the decay and moldy walls of Old Town, where he has gone back to live . . .

Matano's mobile phone rings, jerks him out of his daze.

"Ndugu!"

It is Abdullahi, and he turns to look at him. Abdullahi smiles, the edges of his mouth crusted with curd from the khat. He lifts his hand in an ironic salute. Matano smiles.

"Ah," says Abdullahi. "Your eyes are lost in the middle of white thighs again, bro. You're lost, bwana."

"It's work, bwana, work. Si you know how it is when the mzungu is on his missions?"

"So did you think about the idea? I have everything ready. The guy can come into Shanks's house tonight."

"Ah, brother, when are you going to see that I am never going to play that game?"

"*Sawa*. Don't say I didn't warn you when you see my Porsche, and my house in Nyali, and my collection of Plump Giriama sweetmeats. You swim too much in their waters, brother. I swam too, and look what happened. Get your insurance now, bro. They will spit you out. Dooo do . . . brother! This deal is sweeeet, and the marines are arriving tonight, bwana."

Abdullahi sends a projectile of brown spit out into the sea, and laughs.

Matano shakes his head, laughing to himself.

Poor Abdullahi. Ethnic hip-hop rules the beaches: black abdominal muscles and anger. The darkest boys work the beaches, in three European languages, flaunting thick, charcoal-colored lips, cheekbones that stand like a mountain denuded of all except peaks, dreadlocks, and gleaming, sweaty muscles.

Abdullahi makes a living on the ferry, selling grass and khat, chewing the whole day, till his eyes look watery. These days he isn't fussy about how he disposes of his saliva. They used to hunt white women together. Once in a while, Abdullahi comes to Matano with some wild idea—first it was the porn-video plan, then the credit-card scam, always something proposed by his new Nigerian friends.

Abdullahi forgot the cardinal rule: this is a game, for money, not to seek an edge. Never let the edge control you. The players from the other team may be frivolous; they may be able to afford to leave the anchor of Earth, to explore places where parachutes are needed. This is why they are in Mombasa. The Nigerians would discard him as soon as he became useless, as they do everybody else.

Matano once got a thrill out of helping Abdullahi, giving him money, directing some Scandinavian women to him, the occasional man. Being Giriama, Matano resents the Swahili, especially those from families like Abdullahi's, who held vast lands on the mainland and treated Giriama squatters like slaves. But Abdullahi was a victim of his own cultural success. How are you able to pole-vault your way to the top of the global village if you come from three thousand years of Muslim refinement? You are held prisoner by your own historical success, by the weight of nostalgia, by the very National Monumenting of Old Town, freezing the narrow streets and turning a once-evolving place into a pedestal upon which the past rests.

Matano, the young boy in a mission school, from a Giriama squatter family, has not got this sort of baggage (the our-civilization-has-better-buildings, more-conquests-than-yours baggage). Every way directs him upward.

Matano hates the ferry. As a child, on his way to school, sitting on his father's bike, he would get a thrill whenever they climbed aboard. These days, he hates it: hates the deference people show him, their eyes veiling, showing him nothing. They know he carries walking, breathing dollars in the backseat. Once, a schoolboy, barefoot like he used to be, sat on one of the railings the whole way and stared at him—stared at him without blinking. He could taste the kid's hunger for what he was. Sometimes he sees shame in people's eyes, people carrying cardboard briefcases and shiny nylon suits, shoes worn to nothing. They look at him and look away; he makes their attempt to look modern humiliating.

Then there is the accent business. Speaking with the white people with so many people watching, he always feels self-conscious about the way he adjusts his syllables, whistles words through his nose, and speaks in steady, modulated stills. He knows that, though their faces are uncertain here, on this floating thing carrying people to work for people who despise them he will be the source of mirth back in the narrow muddy streets of the suburbs, where his people live. They will whistle his fake mzungu accent through their noses, and laugh.

In a town like Mombasa, his tour-guide uniform is power. He has two options when dealing with people. One: to imagine this gap does not exist, and be embarrassed by the affection people will return. Behind his back they will say: such a nice man, so generous, so good. It shames him, to meet wide smiles on the ferry every day, to receive a sort of worship for simply being himself. The other way is to stone-face. Away from his home and his neighbors, to reveal nothing: to greet with absence, to assist impersonally, to remain aloof. This is what is expected. This is what he does most of the time, in public places, where everybody has to translate themselves into an agenda that is set far away, with rules that favor the fluent.

Of course, he can be different at home, in Bamburi Village, where people find themselves again, after a day working for some Kikuyu tycoon or Gujarati businessman or Swahili gem dealer or German dhow operator. Here, people shed uncertainty like a skin; his cynicism causes mirth. He is awkward and clumsy in his ways; his fluency falters. His peers, uneducated and poor, are cannier than him in ways that matter more here: drumming, finding the best palm wine at any time of night, sourcing the freshest fish, playing Bao or drafts with bottle-tops, or simply filling the voided nights with talk, following the sound of drums when the imam is asleep and paying homage to ancestors that refuse to disappear after a thousand years of Muslim influence.

What talk!

Populated with characters that defy time, Portuguese sailors and randy German women and witches resident in black cats, and penises that are able to tap-tap a clitoris to frenzy, and a padlocked Mombasa City Council telephone tweaked to call Germany, and tell your SugarOhHoneyHoneyMummy, oh, baby, I come from the totem of the Nine Villages. Warriors (growl) no women can resist us, how can I leave you, baby, so weak and frail and pale you are, my muscles will crush you, my cock will tear you open, we cannot be together, you cannot handle me in bed (sorrowfully), I am a savage who understands only blood and strength, will you save me with your tenderness? Send me money to keep my totem alive; if my totem dies, my sex-power dies, baby, did you send the invitation letter to immigration, I am hard, baby, so hard I will dance and dance all night,

and fuck the air until I come in the ground and make my ancestors strong. My magic is real, baby. Have you heard about the
Tingisha dance, baby, taught by my grandmother? It teaches my
hips to grind around and around to please you? Will you manage me? A whole night, baby? I worry you may be sore.

You must be entertained. Material is mined from everywhere,
to entertain millions of residents in whitewashed houses and
coconut-thatch roofs, who will sit under coconut trees, under
baobab trees, under Coca-Cola umbrellas in corrugated-iron
bars. Every crusted sperm is gathered into this narrative by
chambermaids, every betrayed promise, every rude madam
whose husband is screwing prostitutes at Mamba Village, every
leather breast, curing on the beach, every sexcapade of every
dark village boy who spends his day fuck-seeking, and holding
his breath to keep away the smell of suntan lotion and sunscreen
and roll-on deodorant and stale flesh stuck for twelve months of
the year in some air-conditioned industrial plant.

The village is twelve huts living in a vanishing idyll. From the
top of the murram road, where Bamburi Cement Factory is situated, there is a different territory: the future. Beyond the cement
factory, an enormous constructed ecology, Haller Park, incredible to all, but not yet larger than the sum of its parts—it still
needs a team of experts to tweak its rhythms. There are also
enormous ice-cream-cake hotels, crammed rooms in hundreds
of five-shilling video halls, showing ONE MAN, ONE MAN, who
can demolish an entire thatched village in NAAM, with a mastery
over machinery full of clips and attachments and ammo and ab-
dominals. Even the movements are mastered and brought home,
the military-fatigue muscle tops bought in secondhand markets,
the bandana, the macho strut, the lean-back, missile launcher
carved from wood, lean back and spray; the sound of the gun
spitting out of your mouth.

"*Mi ni* Rambo, bwana."

"Eddy Maafi."

Video parlors rule. With Chinese subtitles.

The couple at the back of the van are still talking. He is lean and wiry and tanned and blond and has a sort of intense, compassionate Swedish face, a Nordic nature-lover. He has the upright American accent Continental Europeans like to adopt. He is wearing glasses. She is definitely an American and looks like she presents something on TV, something hard-hitting, like *60 Minutes*. She has a face so crisp it seems to have been cut and planed and sanded by a carpenter, and her hair is glossy and short and black. She is also wearing glasses. They are the producers of some American TV program . . . Shanks told him to give them the fat Sultan treatment, which he defines as: "Grapes, recliners over a sunset, hard-but-honest barbarian boys, or voluptuous barbarian girls, and Anusol suppositories always in the glove compartment."

"The place is a bit cheesy, but the food's great, and anyway we'll be roughing it in Somalia for a while. Jan said he hasn't found anywhere with running water yet. We mustn't forget to buy booze—Mogadishu is dry, apparently."

"Shit. How many bottles can we take in?"

"Oh, no restrictions—there's no customs and they never bother foreigners."

"Do you think we'll get to meet Shanks? He sounded great on the phone—"

"He'll come across great on camera. He does actually look Maasai, you know, lean and intense sort of . . ."

"The red shawl won't work, though. It's too strong for white skin."

"It's amazing, isn't it, how real he is? I could tell, over the telephone, he has heart."

"Do you think he's a fraud?"

"A sexy fraud if he is one. He hangs out with Peter Beard at his ranch in Nairobi. I saw it in *Vogue*. He drinks with Kapuscinski."

There was a brief and reverential silence as they digested this miracle.

"Should we call him Shanks, or Um-Shambalaa?"

They both giggle.

When they met Matano at the airport, they said they were thinking about doing a film here, although wildlife wasn't their thing. They say they like Human Interest Stories—but this is all sooo gorgeous. So empowering. We must meet Um-Shambalaa, isn't he positively shamanic?

There is something about them that Matano dislikes. A closed-in completeness he has noticed in many liberals. So sure they are right, that they have the moral force. So ignorant of their power, how their angst-ridden treatments and exposés are always such clear pictures of the badness of other men, bold, ugly colors on their silent white background. Neutral. They never see this, that they have turned themselves into the world's *ceteris paribus,* the invisible objectivity.

He puts on a tape. Tina Turner: Burn, baby burn . . .

"Looking for something real," they keep saying.

Twenty years he has been in this job, ever since he took it on as a young philosophy graduate, dreaming of earning enough to do a master's and teaching somewhere where people fly on the wings of ideas. But it proved impossible: he was seduced by the tips, by the endless ways that dollars found their way into his pockets, and out again.

He has seen them all. He has driven Feminist Female Genital Mutilation crusaders, cow-eyed Nature freaks, Cutting-edge Correspondents, Root-Seeking African Americans, Peace Corps workers, and hordes of NGO-folk: foreigners who speak African languages and wear hemp or khaki. Dadaab chic.

Not one of them has ever been able to see him for what he presents before them. He is, to them, a symbol of something. One or two have even made it to his house and eaten everything before them politely—then turned and started to probe: so is this a cultural thing or what? What do you think about democracy? And homosexual rights? And equal rights?

Trying to Understand Your Culture, as if your culture was a

thing hidden beneath your skin, and what you are, what you present, is not authentic. Often he has felt such a force from them to separate and break him apart—to move away the ordinary things that make him human—and then they zero in on the exotic, the things that make him separate from them. Then they are free to like him: he is no longer a threat. They can say, "Oh, I envy you having such a strong culture" or "We in the West, we aren't grounded like you . . . such good energy . . . This is so real."

Da-ra-ra-ra.

Ai!

All those years, the one person who saw through him was a fat Texan accountant in a Stetson hat, who came to Kenya because he had sworn to stop huntin' and start takin' pictures. After the game drive they had a beer together and the guy laughed at him and said, "I reckon me and you we're like the same, huh? Me, I'm jus' this accountant, with a Dooplex in Hooston and two ex-wives and three brats and I don' say boo to no one. I come to Africa, an' I'm Ernest Hemingway—huh? I wouldn't be seen dead in a JR hat back home. Now you, what kinda guy are you behind all that hoss-sheet?"

The van lurches out of the ferry and drives into Likoni. What is a town in Kenya these days? Not buildings: a town like this is nothing but ten thousand moving shops, people milling around the streets, carrying all they can sell on their person. The ingredients of your supper will make their way to your car window, to your bicycle, to your arms, if you are on foot. If you need it, it will materialize in front of you: your suit and tie for the interview tomorrow; your secondhand designer swimsuit; your bra; your nail clippers; your cocaine; your Dubai clock radio; your heroin; your Bible; your pre-fried peri-peri prawns; your pirated gospel-music cassette; your stand-up-comedy video; your little piece of Taiwan; your Big Apple, complete with snow falling, and streets so pure that Giuliani himself must have installed them in the glass bubble.

The hawker's new sensation is videotapes. Reality TV Nigerian-style has hit the streets of Mombasa. Every fortnight a new tape is released countrywide. Secret cameras are set up, for days sometimes, in different places. The first video showed a well-known counselor visiting a brothel; the next one showed clerks in the Ministry of Lands sharing their spoils after a busy day at the deed market (title for the highest bidder, cashier resident in a dark staircase). Matano hasn't watched any of them yet. He hasn't had the time this tourist season.

The Swedish Nature lover, Jean-Paul, looks out at produce knocking on the van window. His face seals shut, and he takes a book out of his bag. *Jambalaya, the Water Hungry Sprite.* Matano has read about it in a *New Yorker* magazine that one of his clients left behind. A book written by a voodoo priestess (and former talk show host) who lives in Louisiana, which had the critics in raptures. *The Next Big Thing.* The movie will star Angelina Jolie.

Matano's blind spot—

Extract of a conversation that Matano had with one of his annual Swedish lovers, Brida, who adores Márquez:

"What is it with you white people and magic realism?"

Brida runs her nails down his chest, and turns the page in her book. Matano jerks away.

"Don't you find it a bit too convenient? Too guilt-free? So you can mine the ashrams of India, or the manyattas of Upper Matasia, or Dreamland Down Under, with a didgeridoo playing in the background, without having to bump into memories of imperialism, mad doctors measuring the Bantu threshold of pain, Mau Mau concentration camps, expatriates milking donors for funding for annual trips to the coast to test, personally, how pristine the beaches aren't anymore—"

"Don't be so oppressed, darlink! I'm Swedish! Can we talk about this in the morning? I promise to be very guilty. I'll be a German aid worker, or maybe an English settler's daughter. And you can be the angry African. I will let your tear off my clothes and—"

"Why should it bother you? You come every December, get your multicultural orgasms, and leave me behind churning out magic realism for all those fools. Don't you see there is no difference between your interest in Márquez, and those thick red-faced plumbers who beg for stories about cats that turn into jinns, flesh-eating ghost dogs that patrol the streets at night, the flesh-eating Zimba reincarnated? I mean, every fucking curio-dealer in Mombasa sells that bullshit: 'It is my totem, ma'am, the magic of my family. I am to be selling this antique for food for family. She is for to bring many children, many love. She is buried with herbs of love for ancestors to bring money. She was gift for great-grandmother, who was stolen by the ghosts of Shimo La Tewa . . . '"

Brida laughs and puts her book down for a moment.

"It is life, eh? Much better way to make money than saying: 'Oh, I be sell here because I be poor, my land she taken by colonizer/multinational beach-buying corporation/German dog catcher investing his pension/ex-backpacker who works for aid agency—'"

Brida runs her fingers across his forehead, clearing the frown.

"Don't spoil my book, darlink. I'm in a good part. In the morning we talk, no?"

"Why should I make it easy for you? Why don't you read your own magic realism? At least you are able to see it in context. You nice, liberal, overeducated Europeans will look down on trolls and green-eyed witches and pixies, though these represent your pre-Christian realities, but you will have literary orgasms when presented with a Jamaican spirit-child, or a talking water closet in Zululand."

"You think too much, Matanuuu. I shall roll you a joint, eh?

Maybe we fuck, and then you can present your paper at the Pan-African Literature Conference, while I finish my book in peace."

Matano laughs.

Jean-Paul turns to the *60 Minutes* woman, and says, "God, her prose sings. Such a hallucinogenic quality to it."

She looks dismissive. "I prefer Allende."

She leans forward toward Matano, and slows her drawl down, presenting her words in baby-bite-sized syllables: "So, which Kenyan writers do you recommend, Matanuuu?"

"Karen Blixen," he says, his face deadpan. "And Kuki Gallman . . ."

Ngũgĩ is recommended only to those who come to Kenya to self-flagellate; those who would embrace your cause with more enthusiasm than you could, because their cause and their self-esteem are one creature. They also tend to tip well, especially after reading *Petals of Blood*.

When he is alone, he reads Dambudzo Marechera, who understood the chaos, understood how no narrative gets this continent, who ends one: "And the mirror reveals me, a naked and vulnerable fact."

He remembers the name of the *60 Minutes* woman: Prescott Sinclair.

There is nowhere Prescott has been where the sea smells so strong, and she opens the in-flight magazine one more time just to look at the piles of tiger prawns being grilled on the beach and the fruit cut into fancy shapes.

She is irritated at Jean-Paul again. She likes to work with him outside America; he makes a good and harmless chaperone. But she finds his matter-of-factness annoying. He motors through everywhere and everything at the same pace, disinterested in difference. He reads the right books, is perfectly accommodating to her moods, is never macho, bossy, or self-serving. He is apologetic about his fastidiousness. She has tried, many times, to goad him to reveal himself, to crack. She is starting to think the person he presents is all he is.

Brynt, her boss: the work maniac, sex maniac, and ulcer-ridden, seeker-of-mother-figure (who must come) wrapped in pert breasts, fat free. He is exactly the man she has constructed and told herself not to have to want. She cannot resist him. He wears her out, demanding that she leaves her skin behind with every new job, become somebody else, able to do what she never would. In bed, she must be the tigress, the woman able to walk away purring while he lies in bed, decimated. Sex for him is release: he carries electricity with him wherever he goes, but can't convert it into a memorable experience. She has in her mind, whenever she thinks of him, the image of a loose electric cable, writhing around aimlessly on concrete, throwing sparks everywhere. She can't leave him alone—his electricity continues to promise but always fails to deliver, and often it feels as if it is her fault: she isn't being for him what he needs to convert his electricity into light.

She broke up with him a month ago. Has avoided his calls. Taken her work home. Volunteered for jobs abroad. Jean-Paul must know, but hasn't even said a word. Why is he such a coward?

The driver who has been quiet since she tried to make conversation with him turns to them, smiles, and says, "Welcome to Diani! We are now turning into Makuti Beach Resort. *Karibu!*"

Does the person define their face or does one's face define the person? Matano often wonders why it is that people so often become what their faces promise. Shifty-eyed people will defy Sartre, become subject to a fate designed carelessly. How many billions of sperm inhabit gay bars and spill on dark streets in Mombasa? How does it happen that the shifty-eyed one finds its way to an egg?

Trust can have wide eyes, deep-set; mistrust is shifty, eyes too close together. Or is it? Among the Swahili on the coast, it is rude to look at someone directly in the eye; one must always be hospitable, hide one's true feelings for the sake of lubricated relationships, communal harmony. "Smarmy," an English person might call this, especially when it is accompanied by the smell of coconut oil and incense.

Armitage Shanks, by the born-with-a-face personality theory, is a martyr. Eyes that hold you: sea-green, with mobile flecks that keep your eyes on them whenever he says anything. Spiritual eyes: installed deeper in the sockets than usual, with little wings on the edges of the eyelids that lift them to humor, and lines of character. He would be a spiritual leader, a man whose peers would come to seek quiet advice from. If he was a Muslim, he would be interrogated at every airport in the West.

What sort of mechanics define these tiny things that mean so much to us? What is done to the surface of the eye to make light gleam on it in such a liquid manner? Are there muscles that are shorter than most people's, attaching the eye to the face, sinking the eyeball deeper into the face? What child was born, a million years ago, with the eyes of an old and humorous man? What words were whispered around the village? About this child's wisdom, his power to invoke ancestors, so women threw themselves into his bed as soon as his penis woke up and said hello to the world?

Ole um-Shambalaa's face is lean, ascetic, lined, and dark, nearly as dark as Abdullahi's. The hair is blond, closely cropped. Ole um-Shambalaa is not supposed to be frivolous. Anymore.

He leans forward to open the door of the van, and smiles. Prescott and Jean-Paul make their way out, both flustered by the heat and by the fact that they are not sure what rules he plays by. Will he bow down to greet them? Or kiss their noses? Would shaking hands seem terribly imperialist? Shanks does not guide them; he stands there, still, in a way only Eastern religious people in films or certain animals can be: muscles held tense, smiling with enough benevolence to awaken the belly. Wings of warmth will flutter in the stomachs of these two guests.

A millisecond before Prescott blurts out her learned Maasai greeting, he reaches both his hands to her, and takes her hand. He does the same with Jean-Paul, looking shyly at the ground, as if humbled by their spiritual energy.

He turns, without greeting Matano, and heads for the lobby, tight lean buttocks clenching as he walks. Prescott is shocked at her thoughts. It seems sacrilegious to think of sex with this man; but she wonders, despite herself, whether he practices tantra or some exotic Maasai form of spiritual Orgasmism. Oh, shit, don't they practice FGM?

Matano makes his way to the staff quarters. He always has a room at the hotel, but he uses this only for what Shanks calls Vagina Dialogues.

The staff houses are all one-roomed: cheap concrete and corrugated-iron structures, arranged in an unbroken square. Matano finds his colleagues seated on three-legged stools in the inner courtyard, playing Bao.

"Dooo . . . do. *Matano mwenyewe amefika. Umepotea ndugu*" ("You've been scarce, brother").

Outside this courtyard, Otieno is known as Ole Lenana. Every day, shining like a bronze statue, dressed in a red loin-cloth, with red shoulder-length hair braids, he heads off to the beaches to get his picture taken by tourists, a pretend Maasai. He used to be a clerk at Mombasa County Council. He receives a small pension from Frau Hoss, a fifty-year-old German lady who comes to Mombasa for two weeks every year, to paint her wrinkles tan, and to sleep with a darker tan.

Otieno swears by *vunja kitanda*: "Break The Bed." A combination of herbs he insists gives him stamina, even with old, gunny bag breasts. Matano has something to tell him, about Frau Hoss.

Matano says his hellos, then goes into Otieno's room. Inside, it is partitioned with various kangas. The bedroom is a curtain stretched across the side of the bed; the living room a money plant in a cowboy cooking-fat tin, three cramped chairs, covered in crocheted doilies, and a small black-and-white TV. There are photo albums on the coffee table. In a trunk under the table are Matano's books, most given to him by tourists, maybe half of them in German. He picks out one that he received a week ago. He has been waiting since to see Otieno, to show him Frau Hoss's book.

He strips, puts on his black swimming trunks, wraps his waist in a blue kikoi. He joins the rest, sits on a stool, legs left higher than his shoulders, kikoi curled into his groin for modesty. He can smell coconut milk and spices. Women are cooking at the other end of the courtyard, chatting away, as they peel, crush, grind, and plait each other's hair.

"So, did you see Um-Shambalaaaa?"

The group of four burst out singing: "Um-Shambalaa, let's go dancing. Ole um-Shambalaa, disco dancing . . ."

Matano laughs. "He has lasted till lunch without coke? He is serious about this maneno?"

Otieno turns to Matano. "He is paying me, bwana, to be Ole Kaputo, the Maa Chief's son."

"Nooo! Ai! This deal must be of much money! That is why he was afraid to talk to me. There'll be bumper harvests this time. I think these ones are television people. From America."

There is silence as the rest digest the implications of this. America. The Bao game proceeds, and conversation weaves languidly around them.

Matano passes the book around. Kamande, the chef, takes one look at the cover and hoots with laughter. Otieno is on the cover, body silvery, courtesy of Photoshop, kneeling naked facing the mud wall of a manyatta. Everything in the shot is a variation of this silvery black, his red Maasai shawl, the only color, spread on the ground. Two old white hands run along his buttocks, their owner invisible. It must be near sunset: his shadow is long and watery, a long wobbly shadow of cock reaches out to touch his red *shuka*.

Otieno looks bewildered, then grabs the book. His eyes frown, confused: who is this person? Recognition. Gasp. The books changes hands, all round the circle, and everybody falls over themselves laughing. The women come to investigate. Fatima, Kamande's wife, looks at it, looks at Otieno, looks back at the book.

"Ai! Why didn't you tell me you had a beer bottle in your pants? I will find somebody for you if you learn to use it properly! Not on these white men—what can they show you?"

The women laugh and carry the book away to pore over it.

Otieno turns to Matano: "Where did you get it?"

"A tourist left it in the van last week. Frau Hoss said she taught you—tantric love."

"I will sue!"

"Don't be stupid," says Matano. "Write your own book. Let's write it, bwana! The publishers will eat it up! African sex is hot in Germany . . . you will make a killing! Call it *My Body Defiled*. Then make sure you sit without your shirt on the cover, looking sad and oppressed."

They laugh.

Prescott sits with Jean-Paul at the pool bar next to the beach, watching the sunset, having a drink, and waiting for Shanks.

There is no barrier from here to India. There are scores of short muscular boys silhouetted against the dusk, covered in and surrounded by curios, doing headstands and high jumps and high-fives and gathering together every few minutes to confer. Sometimes they look at Prescott; one winks, another bounces his eyebrows up and down. Then she is relieved as they spot a tourist, gather up their wares, and go to harass someone else. There is music playing at the bar: some sort of World Music for Europop fans. "*Jambo, jambo, bwana, habari gani? Mmzuri sana . . .*" ("Hello, hello, mister, how are you? Very well . . .")

From a well-known guidebook: "The Kenyan's smile is the friendliest in the world. He will tell you 'Jambo' and serve you *dawa* cocktails."

The beach boys cannot come to the hotel, but Prescott has been told that they will be all over her in six international languages if she crosses the line of the coconut trees.

One of the boys walks toward her, managing to bounce off the balls of his feet with every stride, even in the sand. He has a brief chat with the security guard and walks up to their table. She looks at his lean face, eyes like a startled giraffe, with thick, stiff strands of eyelash.

"Jambo!"

"Jambo. I'm afraid I'm not buying anything today. No money."

Jean-Paul is shut away, among characters that talk like blackened fish and look like Bayous, and make love like jambalaya. Somebody with a banjo is searching for the lost gris-gris bag.

Beach Boy frowns, and slaps at his chest, puffed up. "Us, you know, BEACH BWUOYS, it is only money! We want to sell you Bootiful Hand-U-craft of the Finest T-u-raditional Africa. Eh! A man like me, how it feels to run and chase mzungus every day: buy this, buy this? I dig to get cool job, any cool job: garden, office, or bouncer in Mamba Village Disco, even Navy Offisaa. I have diploma, Marine Engineering, but Kenya? Ai! So now t'fuzz, the pow-lice, they chase homebwuoys. And the hotel, they chase homebwuoys. But this beach—this is our hood. Dig? So you want special elephant-hair bracelet? Is phat! Very phat!"

He isn't smiling. He is looking out to sea, tapping his foot on the ground like a glass vase of testosterone, just waiting to be shattered. In Philadelphia, she would have been terrified of him. She would walk past, her tongue cotton wool, a non-racial smile tearing her reluctant face open. Now she wants to pinch his cheeks and watch him squirm as his friends look on.

"I want a necklace, a Maasai necklace. Can you get me one?"

He looks at her with seamless cool and raises one eyebrow, then frowns. "Tsk, tsk," he seems to say, "that is a hard one." The silence lasts a while, then he looks at her and says, "For you, Mama, because you so bootiful. I will try." And he bounces back to his mates, one arm swinging with rhythm around his back like a rap artist walking to his Jeep.

She laughs.

Jean-Paul says, "God, look at that sunset . . ."

Prescott says, "It's never as good as the postcards, is it? Fuck, poets have a lot to account for. They've killed the idea of sunsets, made meadows boring, and completely exterminated starry nights. Sometimes I think they're just as bad as Polluting Industrial Conglomerates Run by Men."

Jean-Paul smiles patiently and looks across at her, compassion in his eyes. She wants to slap him. Brynt hasn't phoned. Though she isn't taking his calls, it's important that he calls, so she can get the satisfaction of not taking his calls.

Shanks appears from the glass doors on the other side of the pool. He has tucked his red Maasai cloth into his shorts; his torso is bare, and his arms are draped over an ivory walking-stick that lies on the back of his neck. His silhouette is framed by the last vague rays of the sun, the postcard silhouette of the Maasai man whom the Discovery Channel will introduce, deep voiced, as "an ancient noble, thriving in a vast, wild universe, the color of shadow."

He squats on his haunches next to them and glides his eyes around them both. Smiles.

"Peace."

Prescott smiles vaguely. Jean-Paul has cracked already: his mouth is wide open.

"You have eaten?"

They nod.

"Come . . ."

They follow him. His walk is not graceful, like Prescott expected. Rather, it is springy: he bounces to one side on one leg, then does the same on the other. It is a distantly familiar movement, again something from Discovery. Some walk some ethnic peoples do somewhere in the world, and they are noble.

They leave the residents' area of the hotel, and cross through a gate; before them, sitting under a huge baobab tree, is a huge whitewashed mud-and-wattle hut, with a beach-facing patio constructed of rugged acacia branches, stained pine-colored. There is an enormous apple-green couch shaped like a toilet, with large sewn lettering that reads ARMITAGE SHANKS.

Shanks points to it. "My great-grandfather had a great sense of humor. He furnished his drawing rooms with seats that looked like toilets."

They sit on the cushions on the floor. Shanks crosses his legs as he stands, and lowers himself straight down into a cross-legged sitting position.

A very tall man walks out of the hut, carrying a tray. He is introduced as Ole Lenana. It is Otieno.

"My circumcision brother."

Shanks and Ole Lenana chat away in a strange language, then Ole Lenana joins them, unplugs the beaded tobacco pouch hanging from his neck, and starts to roll a cigarette.

"Did you know . . ." His voice startles them, suddenly the voice of Shanks, not um-Shambalaa. "In the sixteenth and seventeenth centuries, before commercial fertilizer was invented, manure was transported by ship, dry bundles of manure. Once at sea, it started to get heavy, started to ferment, and methane would build up below deck. Any spark could blow up a ship—many ships were lost that way. Eventually, people began stamping the bundles SHIPS IN HIGH TRANSIT, so the sailors would know to treat the cargo with respect. This is where the term 'shit' comes from. Ships in High Transit. Many of those around these days . . ."

Prescott is wondering whether this is how the Shanks family sanitizes their history. Fecal anecdotes that have acquired the dignity of a bygone age, presented in a dry, ironical tone.

"The Maasai build their houses out of shit. This is a house built from the shit of cattle, mixed with dung and wattle, and whitewashed with lime. You know, forget the bullshit in the brochure. That was for *Vogue*. I can see you two are not from the fluff press. I don't really believe this Maa-saaia mythology stuff, because it makes no sense to me. I make myself believe it because I need to. Maybe, being a Shanks, it is the shit that attracted me. Maybe it was to do something that would give me a name and a life different from something branded in toilets around the world. Maybe I was tired of being a name that flushes itself clean with money every new generation. Maybe I like the idea of having the power to save an entire nation. Or maybe it was just for the money. All I can tell you is that I want to help save these people, that these heirlooms you will see tomorrow are the most exquisite creations I have ever seen. The world must see them."

Prescott says, "But don't you think there's something wrong with that? Isn't it like taking ownership of something that isn't ours?"

She is thinking, "Houses of bullshit, my God . . ."

Shanks says, "I earned my membership, like any Maa. They trust me. I am one of them." He was um-Shambalaa again, and stood and he and Ole Lenana gripped forehands and looked deep into each other's eyes, and Ole Lenana fell to his knees and muttered something guttural, emotional, and grateful.

The cigarette is being passed around: Jean-Paul, Prescott, um-Shambalaa. Dope. She looks up, startled by a shadow. It is the tour guide, Matano, his torso bare, muscles gleaming. He is drinking beer.

"The sisters are here to sing."

They walk in, women shrouded in red cloaks, singing. Voices, mined from a gurgly place deep down in the throat, oddly like percussion instruments. This is a society that lives laterally, Prescott thinks, not seeking to climb up octaves, find a crescendo, no peaks and troughs: ecstasy sought from repetition; and, as the music grabs hold of all atmosphere, the women begin to bleat, doing a jump every few moments, a jump that thumps a beat to the music and lifts their piles of necklaces up and down. Up and down. Ole um-Shambalaa stands up; Ole Lenana joins him. They head out to the garden and start to jump with every bleat. Prescott has an image in her mind of the stomach as a musical instrument, bagpipes squeezed to produce the most visceral sounds the body can. She finds herself jerking her neck forward and backward, to the beat. The tide must have risen, for the waves seem to be crashing on the beach with more fervor than she can remember. Damn him, damn Brynt. She will not cry.

The women have gathered around Jean-Paul's cushion. There is an expression of mild panic on his face, which he can't shut out. They grab his arms, stand him up. He starts to jog himself up and down, a tight smile on his face, his eyes wild, looking for a way to bolt.

None of the women singing know a word of what they are singing. Not three hours ago, they were chattering away in Kiswahili, while cooking supper. After dark, they don beads and kangas and practice in the servant's courtyard, heaving and gurgling and making all kinds of pretend Maa sounds. This is why the hotel allows them to stay in the servants' quarters with their husbands.

Matano is watching Prescott. She is just about to allow herself to be reckless. He slowly makes his way toward her and stands behind her chair, allowing his presence to occupy her space.

At the airport he caught her standing alone, looking bewildered about this new place. Those eyes, her skin so white, made him shiver. He has in his mind the constant idea that white women are naked, people with skin peeled like baby rabbits, squirming with pain and pleasure in the heat. It is always profoundly disturbing to him that they are rarely like this in reality, so forward and insistent, interrupting his seduction with demands. THERE! THERE! Grabbing his face, holding on to it, making his tongue work until they are satisfied. Many of them have no faith in his abilities, feel they need to manage all his activities.

Was it Anaïs Nin who wrote the erotic story of a wild, giant beast of a man, an artist, and a brash and demanding woman who came on to him, and he rejected her, and she chased and chased him, learning to be demure. One day, long after she had submitted and become who he wanted, he jumped on her and they molested the bed for the whole night.

Jean-Paul has succumbed. It started with the women laughing at him, as they watched his body awkwardly trying to find a way into the rhythm. He burst out laughing at himself, and his movements became immediately more frenzied. Now he howls and jerks faster, a string puppet out of control.

An hour later, Prescott sits with Matano at the edge of the camp. Ole um-Shambalaa is sitting cross-legged in the garden, absolutely still. Matano has wrapped his hand around her waist and is singing a Maasai song in her ear, ever so softly. Behind him, the women's self-help group are still singing. Their eyes have become glazed: they look like they could go on forever.

She can't seem to stop shaking. It must be the dope. And the music.

She jerks out of his embrace and says, "I'm sorry, I'm just wiped out. I've got to go and lie down."

He shrugs and turns her to him and smiles, looking at her. Then his large hand reaches and pushes her hair behind her ear, his wrist leaving a smear of sweat on her cheek. She is singed by it, and immediately afraid.

She can't sleep. Her heart is thudding in her chest, and when she lies on her back, an enormous weight seems to force her down, pushing her into her bed, and she has to struggle to breathe. It must be the dope. She stands. It is quiet outside; they've all gone to sleep. She stumbles out of the tent, her legs numb, stinging like pins and needles. The feeling spreads over her body, and she goes to the bathroom and looks at her face in the mirror. It looks the same, a bit wild, but not much different. She sees the Maasai necklace hanging out of her toilet bag and takes it and puts it around her neck. She looks in the mirror: on her it looks tacky. The strong colors suck up her face.

There is a message from Brynt on her mobile phone. "Did you find Shanks? Call me."

What reins you back in, she wonders, what makes you want to be what you were again? After this mind-bending magic, how can Chicago compete with this primal music, with bodies rubbing themselves against thick moist air?

Maybe truth is always a consensus. Maybe it doesn't matter what kind of proof backs up your submission; maybe your submission has no power without being subscribed to by a critical mass of people? What is the truth here?

Back home: there is fear so far inside fear you don't feel it. Mortgages, a lifeline that cannot escape upward mobility: you have to be sealed shut from those who live laterally to thrive. If you cannot maintain openness to this, you can always control it. Packaging. Sell it, as a pill, a television program, a nightclub, a bonding retreat, a book, jambalaya prose. Control it. Make the magic real. Allow it to occupy only a certain time. This is the human way—the rest is animal. But, tonight, it will be real, it is real, Brynt is a faraway myth. It will be different in the morning. Now she heads back to um-Shambalaa's.

Matano finds himself thinking about Abdullahi's proposal. A week ago, Abdullahi took him to meet the Nigerians, who intimidated him, strutting like nothing could govern them, buy them. Noticing his skepticism about the deal, one of them laughed at him.

"You Kenyans! You let these *oyinbos* fock you around, man. Eh! Can't you see your advantage, man? You know them; they know shit about you. So here you are, still a boy, still running around running a business for a white guy. So stoopid! I saw him in the in-flight magazine when I was coming from Lagos with new stock. Ha! Um-Shambalaa!"

The group of Nigerians broke into the Kool and the Gang song on cue: "Let's go dancing. Um-Shambalaa, disco dancing . . ."

"So do you dance for um-Shambalaa? For dollars? We're offering you real money, man. Four hours, you let our guy in, and you have enough money to fuck off and buy a whole disco, where you can dance for German women the whole night, brother."

Matano wonders for a moment why this deal is worth so much, then remembers the numbers. The thousands who gather under baobabs to listen to stories of the strange hotel tribes. The closed-loop system the Nigerians have devised to reduce piracy. All the videos are released to the video parlors on the same day. At the same time. FM stations who have taken to advertising in the videos. Politicians who pay to feature in the urinal breaks. NGOs which pay to send "Wear Condom" messages between sex scenes.

Matano looks at the group on the grass now. Jean-Paul is slow dancing with (Ole Lenana) Otieno, who will argue in one of the afternoon sessions in the courtyard that the best way to get his revenge is to fuck them.

"There is nothing more satisfying than making a white man your pussy!"

The rest will laugh and call him *shoga*.

They will all make sure Fatima does not hear them speak. They value their lives. Kamande will look back nervously to see that she is otherwise engaged.

For what, Matano thinks: fifty dollars? Maybe a watch? Why should Jean-Paul give a shit how he is judged in the laugh sessions under baobab trees? Who, in his circle of peers, in his magic-made-real characters, will care?

He calls Abdullahi, and says, "Send them in, bro. Bring in the guy—the back door is open."

He sees Prescott walking toward him. He will perform on the sofa of um-Shambalaa's house. The drinks are laid out, the dope. Servants wander in and out and are soon invisible in the revelry.

Morning is another part of the lottery. The sun will rise. Somebody will receive a call, Chicago will roar back into her life, down a telephone line. She will wash Matano's smell off her, sit on the toilet and cry, still stuck to chasing the spewing electric cable. Jean-Paul will see a pile of tacky plastic beads on the floor, red hair-dye on his pillow, will smell stale nakedness on his sheets. That Lenana is no other reality in the morning. He wants money, is listening to Kiss FM, has splashed himself with Jean-Paul's cologne, before examining the shadow of his penis with some satisfaction. He must spend the next few weeks practicing his German. He will be on German TV soon, if all goes according to plan. Jean-Paul is itching for him to leave, for the chambermaid to come in and clean last night away. He will sit on the beach and escape to the Bayous. Tonight, he will only see um-Shambalaa's reality through a camera, for their program *A World of Cultures*.

Fatima and her troop of women share the spoils in the morning. Ole um-Shambalaa paid them an extra bonus, just to make sure there was no mischief. Fatima cannot stand um-Shambalaa, and is not afraid to hide it: he cannot do without her. She is the most plausible gurgler, and Kamande is the best chef this side of the island, and, because he has the same name as Blixen's badly spelled "Kamanti," is worth more in drinks-before-dinner anecdotes. Fatima managed to get thirty dollars from Jean-Paul by threatening to take his shirt off while they danced last night. About three dollars of this money will be officially declared to husbands; the rest will go to their communal slush fund. Things will appear in the household, conveniences explained away. School fees are mysteriously paid.

"Ai! Don't you remember? It was a gift from Mama so-and-so, after I helped her cooking when her relatives went away."

The nest egg is growing. Every three months, each gets a lump sum. Khadija is planning to leave her husband soon. She works as a chambermaid, and will return, after the morning shift, with a collection of forensic stories: red hair-dye on a pillow, how Otieno smells just like Jean-Paul's bathroom, and Matano, when will he leave those white women alone? It is definitely time they found him a wife . . .

Abdullahi is thirsty. The ferry smells of old oil. Last night, after the operation in um-Shambalaa's house, he took an old lover to bed and performed like never before, surrounded by ABBA, incense, and cocaine. Today, he will buy himself a car.

The practiced will thrive in the morning: both made their transitions before dawn. Matano left um-Shambalaa's room, after carefully pulling strands of her hair from his short dread-locks. He made his way back to the courtyard, and lay out on his kikoi watching dawn and counting the stars, the way he used to with his mother as she cooked in another courtyard, not five miles away. He reads Marechera.

Ole um-Shambalaa is in his small plane. He woke up at four in the morning. He sat on the Art Deco Shanks toilet and ex-pelled. Sunrise will find him in Laikipia, talking to the elders, tracking an elephant, chatting to the young morans, learning new tricks. He will visit his factory, explain to the greediest of the elders how they can benefit from it, dish out wads of cash, enough to buy a goat or two. He will call his new enterprise a "conservancy." The Maa Conservancy. He will return at dusk, when his color is hidden by shadow, ready to play for Prescott's cameras. Tonight, he will show them the heirlooms.

Abdullahi brings Matano the tape and his cut in the after-noon. Two hundred thousand shillings. Not enough to buy the disco, but just fine, thank you. They sit in the TV room of the hotel with some of the staff, and laugh and laugh and laugh at the lateral gurgles and drunken sex talk. For the next few months, this will be the main feature in every video hall at the coast. Sold to them, one time, and in a closed loop to limit piracy (as if anybody would risk pirating the Nigerians), for five hun-dred shillings per tape. Ten-bob entry, sex, imitation Maasai women, and "Um-Shambalaa, let's go dancing."

Fock the copyright, we're Nigerian.

Someone is shouting loudly in the lobby, drunk. The first Marines are checking in: ship landed today, exercises for Iraq. Matano smiles to himself and catches Abdullahi's eye. Which one of them will call the Nigerians?

"Hey, bud, did you see them honkin' hooters hanging at the pool bar?"

"I wanna beach-view room, you stoopid fuck. Fucking Third World country. Fucking Ay-rabs everywhere."

Out in Africa: Essays

A few years ago, Binyavanga Wainaina was stranded at the Addis Ababa Bole International Airport in Ethiopia. As he settled into a long wait, he watched flight destinations flip on a giant screen in front of him like some fantasy of Pan-Africanism come to life. From Abidjan, Lagos, and Brazzaville to Johannesburg, Maputo, and Kampala, and on to Mombasa, Mogadishu, and more, the cities emerged to form the perfect map of his desire.

As the child of a mother who belonged both to Uganda and to Rwanda, as a Kenyan who came of age in South Africa, Binyavanga had an instinctive understanding that he belonged to more places than his passport allowed. He came to Pan-Africanism early, and naturally, and kept with it.

But Binyavanga's ability to relate to diverse parts of the African continent often caused trouble. Twenty years ago, the European Union sponsored him for a trip to Yei, a remote county in the then unified nation of Sudan (now South Sudan), to get him to write about the malaise of sleeping sickness there. They expected to get a straightforward account of devastation and death. Naturally, they got nothing like it, and quietly abandoned the project, leaving Binyavanga free to publish his account of the journey independently—an account which won over the European field organizations working in the area, if not their principal funder.

A happier match was made in South Africa a few years later, when Ferial Haffajee, then the editor of a weekly newspaper called the *Mail & Guardian,* signed up Binyavanga for a fortnightly column on continental affairs. It quickly developed a cult following, and for the years it ran there was nothing quite like it anywhere else: a whimsical, freewheeling space to write about the African continent for continental Africans.

There may be no finer example of this freewheeling style than an essay he wrote on a 2006 trip to Togo, in which he covered the modern political state as carefully as the market for female undergarments, rendering an indelible image of a nation made by football, fabrics, and fascists.

19

The Continental Dispatch

COLUMNS FOR THE *MAIL & GUARDIAN*

The Power of Love

I was fourteen years old when "We Are the World" filled our television screens—and I discovered that we are loved.

That was an amazing kind of love: a giant chorus of exotic-looking people coming together as one, and they pouted and gurgled and they agreed. Yeah, yeah. Once in a while one of them would bend forward as if they were retching their love for Ethiopia from a really deep place in their belly, a personal testimony, and I knew it was true the world would be a better place, for you-uu-uu, and for me-ii-ii.

And there was this guy, who looked pale and thin and bruised, with wispy brown English hair, like Jesus had, who suffered for us, abandoning Boomtown Rats and Stray Cats to reach out and touch. And he is now the King of Ethiopia.

Then Canada did the same in a weepy song called "Tears Are Not Enough." Vowels wobbled, words stretched out. Tears, tears, are not Enou-ou-ou-gh.

And the French gurgled, "L'Éthiopieeeeeeeeeeee . . . ohhh! L'Éthiopeeeeee."

In the years since then, much love has poured into my city, Nairobi. For the Girl Child, for many hundreds of Awarenesses, for Poverty Eradication, for the Angelina Jolification and Anti-Desertification of Semi-arid Regions in Sahelian Countries.

The resources poured in have been incredible: tens of thousands of 4×4s are tearing the country apart looking for a project to love. It used to be that big expensive cars were needed by the Fathers of Our Nations, so they could Develop Our Nations. Now, the Lovers of Our Nations are here to Develop Our Nations, and of course they need cars to be efficient. Standards must be maintained. Things need to be run in accordance with International Standards.

Rents in Nairobi are now on a par with Europe's, to service the tens of thousands of Kenya-loving people who run Kenya-loving projects to save Kenyans and Sudanese and others from Misery. Restaurants with names like Casablanca and Java and Lord Erroll feed these people at a very high standard, and many parts of Nairobi look like New York City. And we are very excited about this! We have a German school, a French school, a Swedish school, and an international school. This means Nairobi is developing very fast. You can get cappuccino in Loki—a giant refugee camp in northern Kenya.

I have learned that I, we, are a dollar-a-day people (which is terrible, they say, because a cow in Japan is worth nine dollars a day). This means that a Japanese cow would be a middle-class Kenyan. Now, a dollar-a-day person cannot know what is good for him—which means that a nine-dollars-a-day cow from Japan could very well head a humanitarian NGO in Kenya. Massages are very cheap in Nairobi, so the cow will be comfortable.

Nairobi is crawling with five-dollars-a-day, twenty-five-year-old backpackers who came and loved and compassioned and are now the beneficiaries of five thousand dollars a month consulting for the United Nations (CV: "After working in bars in London, I was involved in a tobacco-harvesting project near the gorilla sanctuary in Uganda when the overland truck was stranded for five days, and I taught schoolchildren to sing 'Born in the USA' "), while master's students from Kenya are selling fruit by the side of the road for a dollar a day, and live in Kibera slum, the only place where rent is cheap, but this may change, since Ralph Fiennes went and loved Kibera in *The Constant Gardener*.

(Am I the only person who thought Fiennes's wife in the film was sleeping with the Black doctor, only to discover that the Black doctor was gay? The doctor was a placebo to political correctness, to authenticate the movie, just like an ineffectual Steve Biko authenticated *Cry Freedom*, showing how Donald Woods rescued South Africa from apartheid. The doctor cannot affect the narrative—the true saviors of his country are Fiennes and Rachel Weisz. But they love him. They really, really love the good gay doctor. They would never sleep with him on screen, though.)

Last year I met a lovely young woman from England, all of nineteen, who had come all the way to Naivasha, to a specific location very near a lovely lake, next to several beautiful game sanctuaries and a lodge run by her boyfriend's father. But these were not her concern. She was in Kenya to teach the people of some peri-urban location how to use a condom. She told me that she talks to groups of men and shows them how a condom can save their lives. I asked her whether there were no nurses or teachers who could do this at maybe a tenth or one hundred thousandth of the cost it would take to keep her in this lovely and rather expensive location, and her eyes melted and she said, "But I care about people. Can't you see people are dying? Something must be done."

"In my gap year."

She did not add.

I was very moved.

Various royal princes have been here in their gap years, and we have seen them cutting a tree or hugging a baby. One famous actress will adopt all the babies of Africa. And the Strategic Development Goal of that is that in fifteen years' time the Hollywood Bratpack will be Ethiopian and they will sing a song to save Ethiopia in a more authentic manner.

Many of our schoolchildren have been raised to Awareness, and this is thrilling news, that they are now aware. And, every so often, on television, we are treated to schools' music-festival poems by six-year-olds, which go something like this:

> The Girl Child! Let us all educate
> The Girl Child!
> The Girl Child!
> For our Millennium Development
> Goals
> The Girl Child! The Girl Child!

In 1995 I got a part-time job with a cotton ginnery in Mwea District that my father had invested in. My job was to meet with farmers in the dry areas and encourage them to grow cotton. It was not difficult to do—farmers wanted to grow cotton but lacked a market. Throughout those few months I heard talk of a legendary African king called PlanInternationo. People said that PlanInternationo gave them water and tanks and school fees, and every chief and government official I met went all moist talking about this king.

One day we went to the Thika District Agricultural Office to talk to the extension officers, whose *paid* job it is to advise farmers on their options. They asked us if we had been to see the people at PlanInternationo. We said no. They looked rather sad. We asked them if they could give us a person to take us around to meet farmers. They said yes, for some unaffordable number of dollars a day, many more than nine, or ninety, they would. We can't afford that, I said. Oh, but that's what PlanInternationo pays, they said. They love us very much!

Then I met a senior guy at one of the big Humanitarian Agencies in Kenya, who said he wanted to bring Bono to perform a concert in Mogadishu. To raise awareness.

Late last year we heard that people were starving to death in many places all over Kenya. Immediately, the government urged the donor community to help. And the donor community urged the world community to help. And we saw the large, sad eyes of many nameless people on the very verge of death; and caring spokespeople, all white and tanned, told the world: people are dying!

Meanwhile, our government had broken all tax-collection records, and in other parts of Kenya we were having huge bumper harvests. People died.

The most-loved people in Africa are the tall, thin, noble people who were once, or are still, nomads and who live near Wild Animals. The Pokot, the Samburu, the Maasai have received more love than anybody in the world.

I met a woman at a dinner in New York who resembles and speaks like Scarlett O'Hara (My dadee this, my dadee that), who said she was a friend of Rafe (Fiennes). Scarlett is about to start producing handbags from the tails of Mongolian horses and she Just Luuurves Kenya and she is building a clinic for the Maasai people and sending a group to London to sing about manhood ceremonies to raise money. Nobody, really, has seen how the Maasai have become wealthy or even healthy out of all the thousands and thousands of projects. But the Maasai, they can be certain that they are loved.

What you can be sure about in all these love projects is that it is easier for a thirtysomething Scarlett O'Hara—or a Boomtown Rat—than it is for a PhD-wielding, Maasai-speaking, Maasai person to decide who the Maasai will be to the world.

Because that is the Power of Love.

Brand the Beloved Continent

The continent-watchers among you may have heard of Christoph Blocher, a historian who specializes in making the Swiss look hard at their Second World War past and see roses. He doubles as the Swiss Justice Minister.

Recently he said, "How one should deal with Africa, I do not know. Leaving it to itself is one possibility. Nobody knows how Africa can be industrialized. Perhaps they will manage on their own one day." And: "We pay three hundred million dollars in development aid to Africa. I don't even want to talk about the use of it. As a businessman I can't see any."

And then the light went off! It occurred to me that there are many who cannot see the investment opportunities in Africa. At university they taught us that every threat is an opportunity. So I decided to write a proposal to potential investors, and to Christoph Blocher, who has three hundred million dollars he does not know what to do with. The key points are as follows.

Branded babies. Africa has a surplus of babies. With birth rates as high as five percent in some places, this is a definite growth market. As Madonna's and Angelina Jolie's babies grow, there will be a demand for color-contrasted adopted babies from Africa. Babies could be sold for hard and useful cash in Europe and America, where fertility rates are low.

Misery. India has its gurus and Africa its misery. We suggest an approach that is not defensive. Although most Africans are not wallowing in misery, most of Europe needs to believe that we are. We propose to turn this into an economic opportunity, developing packages for volunteers needing to "find themselves" and to pay lots of money to feed starving children or "sensitize" people. Merchandising could be produced—there are many possible permutations of misery—film rights, novels, documentaries. Many photographers know that Pulitzer-winning pictures can be found only where people are too desperate to care if they are being dehumanized. This is an excellent opportunity. We propose a continent-wide licensing of all major wars, traumas, and miserable events.

Branded nations. Branding is the way to go. This may be the new form of nation-building. Madonna is a huge international brand. Malawi is not. Madonna loves Malawi. Angelina Jolie loves Namibia. If Namibia became "Angelina Jolie's Republic of Namibia," millions of tourists would come, providing vast mer-

chandising opportunities. Bottles of desert sand, Jolie images
carved into mountain ranges. The Brad Pitt National Park. We
could make a fortune.

Speaking clocks for Africa. I am truly excited by the possibilities of this venture. I recently learned, from an Africa expert,
something I have failed to discover after thirty-six years of living
in Africa! A few years ago, Andrew Natsios, then head of the
U.S. Agency for International Development, told *The Boston
Globe* that Africans "don't know what Western time is," and
that "many people in Africa have never seen a clock or a watch
in their entire lives. And if you say, one o'clock in the afternoon,
they do not know what you are talking about."

We propose manufacturing, marketing, branding, and selling
Talking Clocks for Africa. The clocks can be subsidized by
USAID, and they can come in a thousand spoken African languages, and be distributed around the continent by donkey cart
and United Nations food drops (bouncy, hardy clocks made out
of Congo rubber? Designed in Switzerland maybe?).

White elephants. Africa is the home of the elephant. Africa is
also the home of the white elephant! Did you know there is an
abandoned fish-processing plant in the middle of the Kenyan
desert? Built by the Norwegians? Imagine the opportunity represented by all the failed grand plans to save Africa over four decades. Tourists will buy little collector boxes of the rubble by the
boatload! These are very valuable mementoes: they show how
much so many have cared over the decades.

Timeless rhythm. We are a rhythmic people and, in fact, it is
this genetic rhythm that makes us dance so well, and have a
carefree attitude that is much in demand among the youth of
Europe, Japan, and China. We can patent the genes of rhythm
and sell them to Europe.

Extreme sports. This is the world's fastest-growing sports
brand. Africa has a competitive advantage: many of our long-
distance athletes start early by running ten kilometers to school,
where they will be beaten if they are late. Advanced training
begins when they flee from police, who will not let them trade in

public areas, because they are "chasing away foreign investors." Our police use guns, rubber bullets, batons, tear gas, and M3s.

This would make a thrilling sport for tourists if they came down to Nairobi, for example, and bought a hawker's permit. Instead of trying to industrialize by allowing entrepreneurial Africans to trade freely and cheaply, and "informal manufacturers" to manufacture freely, we can turn the whole thing into a kind of reality television. Our ministers will say "Clear the hawkers and the artisans!" and the police and askaris will give chase! Those caught will be kicked off the show.

This draft proposal is addressed to Mr. Christoph Blocher and any other interested investors. My colleagues and I can immediately start a company to manufacture, market, brand, and patent the above to help industrialize Africa. Please believe in us. An investment in our scheme of three hundred million dollars per annum will support sustainability, poverty reduction, and the Millennium Development Goals.

We would be happy to forward you our CVs. We can all run very fast, we cannot tell the time, and we have rhythm—all the skills necessary for a successful project. Furthermore, we are happy to work with expensive European Union consultants who can take home most of the money you give us in consultancy fees and hardship allowances.

We would be quite happy and rich if you left us with just two dollars a day! Not a bad investment, eh? This way your economy continues to benefit from helping us, and we remain grateful and pathetic. It's a Win-Win, Can-Do approach!

Yours in humility, ignorance, and misery.

African Future Inc. (B. Wainaina, potential MD)

Born-Again Sustainability

I am not a practicing Christian or a right-winger. But I'm not an ostrich either, and that is the subject of this column.

As the hordes of the World Social Forum gathered in Nairobi to "end poverty" and build "another world," two well-known televangelists announced their plans to run for President, prompting much screaming in the local media.

When I got back to Kenya from Cape Town in 2000, things in my hometown, Nakuru, were very bad. The hard-working meritocratic middle class was finished. The working class was broken. The informal sector was booming and busting. The politically connected were billionaires.

Those former headmasters and nurses who got their children out of the country came discreetly every week to collect fifty dollars from Western Union to buy food. Interest rates had hit the mid thirties, and many hard-working small-business owners had lost everything to the banks.

A woman my family knew well had lost her home and her business—the first Black-owned supermarket in Nakuru—which she had run for more than twenty years. She had lost the ability to speak, and communicated in hand signals. She was a beautiful woman, had never married, and lived what she now saw as a decadent life. She spends her days fellowshipping in an empty shop.

One day, driving down to town, I saw a familiar figure. A woman I had known since childhood was limping down the road toward town, carrying a very large bag on her back. She and her husband owned a large Bata franchise, which supplied school shoes to thousands of kids, including me, in the 1970s. I stopped to pick her up. I noticed that one side of her face had collapsed. She sat in the car and updated me: her son had disappeared while in Israel; her husband had left her for a young woman; she'd had a stroke. She'd lost all her money. She had found God. She was Born Again!

Later I found a giant new suburb just outside my hometown, built by primary-school teachers, some of the worst-paid people in Kenya. They had built a beautiful, safe place—small brick homes, a cow for each home, churches, and safety. All of them

Born Again. They had their own bank and sent their children to shiny new "academies" that guaranteed God, moral fiber, and straight As at less than two thousand rand a term.

All this was happening while Kenya was slowly tearing itself apart: the economy in freefall, ethnic clashes looming, and capital bailing out.

Safe civil space huddled around the ecstatic churches. You could build a network of people to live next to, to invest with, to play with your children—as the venomous state made it impossible for you to find safe ground anywhere. There was no written contract to trust, no government plan, institution, or program that was not gaseous; there was no ambition you could manufacture that came with stepladder possibilities for the future.

You needed two things: a belief in possibilities that was intense enough to make the chaos bearable and a mechanism to allow you to trust and build a community you could trust. And who better to trust than somebody who has shared ecstasy with you? This is a thing you know how to measure.

And you start to build a "civil society."

The Bible has been translated into 680 African languages. Three million copies are distributed in the continent every year. Though many people talk of "African culture," the truth is that the Bible has been a widely used source of ethical and practical guidance and cultural reference in Africa since the turn of the century. The safe civil structures in cities like Kinshasa and Lagos now revolve around the Born Again movement.

There are many Born Again churches started by corrupt pastors who indulge in usury, and not "development." What is forgotten is how mobile this phenomenon is. Pastors rise and fall based on trust. In the Catholic Church a priest may be venal or useless—but his institution remains solid and self-assured, whether or not parishioners are satisfied. Among the Pentecostals, a church is only as good as its ability to provide durable rapture and trust. A church can last a year. Or twenty.

If the state is a comedy and a myth, what bonds make you a good citizen? What makes you an entrepreneur with enthusiasm and hope for the future? What do you see coming for your children?

I do not see an African citizenry of good liberals coming out of this phenomenon. But I see a world being built that appears more lucid, and forward-looking, safe, and reliable, than the world outside it. And this phenomenon is the fastest-growing thing on the continent. More people have come to invest in it than in Sustainable Capacity Building and Democratization and all the plans and talk and action of the other "civil society."

So. Should we go on playing ostrich?

The Savior of Kumbayaa

Intro. Deep voice, in an English accent: "There is a beautiful valley, Kumbayaa, in a primeval forest, above the hills of Ixopo-on-Mara, where elephants, for millennia, have come to eat rich minerals on the cliffs. This was before they found the diamonds. Now greedy Black miners–poachers–mercenaries came and ruined everything."

Synopsis. The elephants of Kumbayaa are noble and timeless; they do not have petty rivalries or jealousies. The children don't play—they follow their mothers, trunk on tail in a long, noble line. They walk to face their death at the hands of the dirty, evil miners of Kumbayaa, who have been cobbled together by a dirty old mercenary, Leonardo, who lost everything when his wife left him, his heart dried out, and he got on a plane with some French adventurers to Kenya, to lead a life of debauchery and khaki and greed in Africa.

As the elephants walk toward their annual licking ground, ancient drums warn, acacias tremble, all the World Music of African indigenous deserts gathers momentum, as all the Indigenous peoples of Africa, watching the movie, are sending desperate ancient musical text messages to the elephants, saying, "Nooooo, noooo. Don't gooooooo."

But, alas, the elephants are timeless people. They trumpet

their message back to the rest of the timeless peoples: "Ancient brothers, we will face our fate with dignity. You will understand, you timeless, noble peoples, you."

The red sun sinks, the elephants stand together in a circle, performing an ancient ritual—silhouettes standing over Ixopo-at-Sunset, as the narrator (called Attenbara by the Indigenous peoples) speaks in a deep voice to the world. Crickets scream in disbelief.

In the blood-red sky of the morning, they look down from the craggy cliff upon the squealing, money-seeking mercenaries, their shanty towns and wild screaming markets, and the bad poacher–miner people—and start to descend. The bad poacher–miner people turn and start to giggle gleefully, as bloodlust and money scream.

Flashback. The miner people were once a good Indigenous people, but became bad after eating the fruit of school fees, plastic bowls, and pocket radios. In 1890 a colonial conservationist called Sir John—named by the elephants PHRUUUUUU! The Savior of Kumbayaa, a man with a deep and throbbing voice—boomed with surround-sound anger at the miner people, "Leave, fools! Leave the gardens of Kumbayaa!"

The miner people heard; they fell to the ground with fear and then ran, leaving behind their ancient artifacts, their skins and hides, their rock paintings and happy evenings dancing nobly around the fire. As they fled, they could hear him booming, "What happened? He said you were once such a noble subsistence people. I helped you!"

The miner people started farming cash crops, trading, poaching. Then, one day, Leonardo visited them and told them that their old homeland, Kumbayaa, was really King Solomon's mine. Sir John's Blood Red Diamond was found there.

In the early red dawn, the elephants descend.

Machetes and guns start to whir and pump, the elephant matriarch falls, and from the distance we hear the clip-clop sounds of a horse. It is Bob, riding cowboy-style, hair flying in the wind, shooting noble bullets, while behind him on other horses are: Bono, Angelina, Madonna; and, from cliffs and trees, all of Africa sings, "Kumbayaa" in all their languages, the chorus rises to the hills. ET stands up to dance, and all the Indigenous peoples are now in a chorus, a Ladysmith Black Mambazo chorus, as Bob Geldof, played by Daniel Day-Lewis, confuses the dirty miner people by throwing United Nations food parcels on the ground.

A giant, wild miner person (Djimon Hounsou) leaps above Bob, about to bludgeon him with his cash register, and from the hills Leonardo shouts to the world, "Oh, Lord! What have I doooooone!" and shoots the irate cash-register-bearing leader of the Kumbayaa Miners Association.

All nature is silent, as Bob stands slowly and lifts the elephant queen in his arms. She puts a loving trunk around his neck. He walks up to the brick government office at the bottom of the cliffs of Kumbayaa, and places her at the foot of the corrupt African politician who opened Kumbayaa for trade. Violins. The man stands, his head bowed down in shame, for he had forgotten that he was a timeless and throbbing and noble person.

Sorrowful and caring Leonardo brings a Canadian company to Kumbayaa, to show how sustainable mining is possible. They save three hundred elephants by investing in satellite phones, laptops, radios, and a team of trackers to save the elephants.

So as not to further corrupt the miner people, the Canadians will extract, mine, and export the blood-red diamonds of Kumbayaa, and start a small fund to help the miner people to learn how to make bags out of tourist bottle-tops and recycled tinned-food containers.

Leonardo will start a community empowerment organization, and take a wife from among them, and advise them to be true to themselves, and not deal with the nobility-polluting people who make world music records out of timeless peoples. Africa, again, has been saved from itself.

When All Else Fails ... Become a Writer

I don't drive a Toyota. I've actually never owned a car. I can't comment about its dominance of the world market. I do not read *Car* magazine, unless it is the only thing in the toilet at the time. So I was surprised to find myself reading a rather long piece about Toyota's corporate culture recently in *The New York Times Magazine*.

One thing a Toyota plant manager said stayed with me: "You actually create the conditions where things have to work to make it work."

I lived in South Africa for ten years, from 1991 to 2000. For much of this time, I was in Transkei studying for a BCompt. Now, I knew what a BCom was when I left Kenya, but when I arrived in South Africa, I quickly learned that a BCompt was the final word. Alas, the BCompt was not to be. After seven years—most of which I spent sleeping, being paranoid about daylight, and learning to piss in bottles, I failed Applied Statistics seven times.

That degree nearly killed me. It was not so much that I was failing for the first time in my life or that I could not get out of bed, sometimes for days. It was that I did not know what was wrong with me. So I kept jumping back at the degree, because it seemed that the only way to be clear about what was in front of me was to follow the dotted line: finish, get a job, buy a sixteen-valve. I did not know then, and do not know now, what a sixteen-valve is or does.

Of course, it did not help matters that I had no papers. I was terrified of being in Umtata during the day, because I expected some person in a uniform to gently tap my shoulder and ask me for my passport.

I was not aware of it at the time, but I was slowly building new skills. I read novels—emptied the Umtata Town library, spent a lot of time on the internet, and joined communities of writers, sending very bad, fantastical stories to the strange, lonely tribes I met online. They included a man called Charlie Sweet in Duckshoot, California, who was building a bunker because he was sure the world was ending in December 1999. His Japanese wife, an Amway salesperson, was not talking to him.

I learned to type with two fingers. I made student cards for half of the schools in the hills of Transkei. I faked an interview with Bantu Holomisa and sold it to a publication. Erm . . . sorry.

In this cramped life, in tiny servants' quarters—my imagination was set alight.

The millennium was a big deal—and I had concocted a theory that the world would collapse into a singularity within itself: nations would grow on the internet, and a global brain of software and a billion desires online would rule us—a clear full circle from the days when manuscripts were the property of monks and kings. Now, a fourteen-year-old had as much access to information as the CIA.

My first and favorite piece of real writing happened without a conscious effort. I had returned from a trip to see my grandparents in Kenya, and was euphoric. In my first enthusiastic week in Umtata—just before I went to bed again—I sent a long email to Charlie Sweet, a truly generous man. Years later, this piece would earn me respect. At the time, it was just correspondence.

So when the university would have no more of me, and I could not sponge off anybody else's generosity, when I could not ask my parents for any more money, when I could not afford to sleep anymore, when I failed Applied Statistics for the seventh time, when I was so unable to make any living and I lost fear that my visa situation would be found out—what had I to lose? When all these things happened, all at once, I decided to make a go of it as a freelance writer and moved to Cape Town.

At no time during this entire period was I usefully aware that I had spent years building a skill and craft that could sustain me. I chose to write because it needed no visa—for years my checks would be paid out through friends, because it was something to do that cost no money, because I loved books, because it made me feel I was worth something in a country so obsessed with itself at the time that any other place was invisible.

I used to meet people and they would ask where I came from, and I would say Kenya, and they would say, "Oh, that's nice, what do you think about us?"

On Kapuscinski's "Gonzo Orientalism"

That is precisely the subject of a conversation I have one day with A., an elderly Englishman and long-time local resident. His view: that the strength of Europe and of its culture, in contrast to other cultures, lies in its bent for criticism, above all, for self-criticism—in its art of analysis and inquiry, in its endless seeking, in its restlessness. The European mind recognizes that it has limitations, accepts its imperfections, is skeptical, doubtful, questioning. Other cultures do not have this critical spirit. More—they are inclined to pride, to thinking that all that belongs to them is perfect; they are, in short, uncritical in relation to themselves.

—Ryszard Kapuscinski, *The Shadow of the Sun,* 2001

The greatest mind to bear upon Africa since Conrad.
—*Evening Standard* on Ryszard Kapuscinski

I have tried, just once in my life, to be an Angry Black Man. I planned a picket in New York City against a man I love to hate—Ryszard Kapuscinski. He was going to speak at a conference organized by American PEN. Nobody seemed to want to join me. There were better things to do in New York, like drinking—I do not lie—a Hibiscus Juice and Chili Margarita. So I got drunk.

The next day, Chimamanda Adichie, a Nigerian writer, told me that she would help me gate-crash the chichi party being held

in the apartment of Salman Rushdie's friend Diane von Furstenberg. Google had informed me that Kapuscinski and Rushdie
were friends.

We stood in the sad corner of the Von Furstenberg cathedral,
with a mournful-looking Eastern European writer. Kapuscinski
was not there. A DJ was playing Michael Jackson. We ate raw
celery, raw carrots, and raw turnips.

Soon Chimamanda was spotted and whisked away by a warm
and fruity cloud of Important People in Publishing. I walked
around, looking for any cooked vegetable, any non-roughage.
There was nothing. I drank a Martini.

After a while, Chimamanda came out toward me and said:
"Come, now you can tell Rushdie about Kapuscinski."

I stood in front of The Rushdie, somewhat nervously. Then, I
asked him why he had invited the racist writer Kapuscinski to
come to the PEN conference.

"Not Ryszard? Oh, Ryszard is not racist! He is a beeeewuti-
ful soul!"

I quoted to him some Kapuscinski lines. Rushdie looked at
me compassionately, and said: "Those must have come from his
older works."

I was about to refute this, when he turned to his wife and
forgot about me. I headed for the bar to find another Martini.

Since he died, Kapuscinski has been called "The Master of
Modern Journalism," "Translator of the World," "The Greatest
Reporter in the World," and "Third World Chronicler."

He is also the guy who came up with my all-time classic lines
about Africa:

"Let us remember that fear of revenge is deeply rooted in the
African mentality."

"In Africa, drivers avoid traveling at night—darkness un-
nerves them, they may flatly refuse to drive after sunset."

"Africans eat only once a day, in the evening."

"In Africa, the notion of metaphysical, abstract evil—evil in
and of itself—does not exist."

"Africans believe that a mysterious energy circulates through the world."

"In Africa, a cousin on your mother's side is more important than a husband."

It was Kapuscinski, more than any other single writer, who inspired me to write the satirical essay "How to Write About Africa."

In his review of *The Shadow of the Sun* for *The Times Literary Supplement* in 2001, John Ryle pointed out that serious omissions, factual inaccuracies, obvious inventions, and lies appear with great consistency in much of Kapuscinski's writing. He concluded: "His writing about Africa is a variety of latter-day literary colonialism, a kind of gonzo orientalism . . . conducted in the name of humane concern, that sacrifices truth and accuracy, and homogenizes and misrepresents Africans even as it aspires to speak for them."

David Rieff, in a review of the same book, wrote: "One scarcely knows where to begin. The level of generality—the white man, the bush, the torment—is such that Kapuscinski's assertion not only can't be taken seriously, it can barely be discussed . . . It is the kind of thinking . . . that one associates with racist skinheads . . ."

Kapuscinski died anointed, everywhere, as a hero of Africa.

There are many fools like Kapuscinski wandering about. They don't get published. They do not become legends. The questions about him have more to do with lingering superstitions about the continent held by editors and foreign-correspondent types, who built him up, entranced by his Polish-flavored, left-leaning, Rider Haggard-world of strange, voiceless, dark peoples doing strange, voiceless, dark things.

Ecstatic fans said his distortions of reality were actually "allegories" and "metaphors." Those sharp eyes that saw deep allegory became suddenly vague about the naked social Darwinism that underlies all his work. When Kapuscinski was critical of the sloppy reporting of the facts by "Western journalists," when he repeatedly said his work was reportage, based on facts, it was assumed that he was just being a modest, Polish, authentic, left-leaning, beautiful-soul kinda guy.

Too modest to admit that his literary Africa was so amazing, it replaced the real thing in their eyes.

Knee-Jerk Nativism

Two weeks ago, two people of "Indian origin" were beaten to death by a crowd in Kampala, Uganda. The crowd rioted because the Mehta Group, a huge multinational with significant investments in Uganda, has asked to be allocated one-third of the Mabira Forest Reserve, one of the country's last remaining natural forests. Ugandan President Yoweri Museveni supports giving away this rich source of biodiversity.

When I was a kid, a documentary called *Shocking Asia* made its way into our cinemas. At the time, Kenya was into censorship. *The Six Million Dollar Man* was banned because it would make young boys jump off roofs. Kenyans could not kiss on television because it would result in instant national sexual orgies. Yet, for some mysterious reason, which wasn't so mysterious after all, *Shocking Asia* played for years on end, "due to popular demand."

I went to watch it, all of fourteen, hoping to see a nipple. I left feeling nauseous, vowing never to visit India. Here was a place of mutations and multiple arms and trunks all having twisted sex. And dirty rivers and fetuses and general horribleness. Sodom.

For the school-going Christianized population of Kenya, who loved *Reader's Digest* and watched *The Sound of Music,* India was the closest thing to a future hell. In high-school "crusades," we were told that Indians brought demons to Kenya.

The truth was that a new generation of get-rich-quick politicos wanted Kenyans of Indian origin to leave. Under the banner of "Africanization," the new rulers hijacked the economy and proceeded to disembowel it.

And, of course, their anti-Indian demagogy was not without other results. During our abortive coup in 1982, hundreds of women from Nairobi's "little India," Parklands, were raped.

Finally, it seemed the end of an old history was beginning. For our history has been intertwined with that of others for at least a millennium. When Vasco da Gama arrived in Malindi, a city-state on the coast of what is now Kenya, he hired a Gujarati captain to ferry him to India.

This is not taught in Kenyan schools.

We were going to be Black-Surrey-on-Rift-Valley.

The Kenyan upper middle class inherited disdain for the shopkeeper. As the highly subsidized nation of white settlers came to expect things they did not earn, so did this new generation of Kenyans. To send your child to India for university was "hellish"; to send your child to England was your natural right and you were furious that you could not afford it. You came back from England determined to plant bougainvillea and chase away the grubby shopkeepers. Kenya was going to leap from independence to become a country of doctors and teachers and chrome-skyscraper multinationals. But we did not want to have to make cheap goods in smelly factories.

A political class of people has created a certain expectation: that the angry masses will react predictably to their "monsters," because those monsters have already been created. In Kenya, as in Uganda, a class of people incapable of building wealth used crude knee-jerk nativisms to rob. They stole windowpanes and machines, turned viable cotton ginneries into scrap metal, stole even the raw cotton supplied by poor farmers. Stole until the factories stopped running. All the time pointing fingers at *Shocking Asia*, at a shop near you.

The new elite nearly destroyed Kenya to send their kids to school in England. The people they shook down were almost always the small-time traders. Meanwhile, many highly skilled people were kicked out to make room for the mediocre.

So look behind the mob, to the whispered meetings held by

small-time politicos the night before over meat and beer, to find motivation.

In all this steam and frenzy, people will be quick to forget that the Mehta family has built many essential industries in Uganda.

It is not in question that Museveni sees himself as a religious figure, fated to answer all questions for Uganda.

The Mehta family also has an ego problem. From the group's website, on the late founder: "Shri Nanjibhai Kalidas Mehta—a humanist whose heart was filled with immense love and affection for people . . . a contemporary of the Father of the Nation who practiced the doctrines of the Mahatma."

These two oversized egos have overreached themselves. I am sure there are the usual lazy political entrepreneurs who are playing crowds and boardrooms to make money and make political names. Is there anybody as dangerous as those who want to profit politically and financially from the "rage" of the "people"? There are enough examples, in our recent pasts—in South Africa, Tanzania, Kenya, Uganda, and elsewhere—to warn us about the danger of this sort of ethnic paranoia.

There are no easy "exploitation" stories that we can extract from the incoherence of the mob.

There is no possible benefit to this. Except more killing. Lives are at stake in these cheap jostles for power.

Beware White Men with Briefcases

Years ago I had a conversation with somebody in Cape Town who was helping to develop a tourism-marketing plan. She told me that the largest number of tourists to South Africa came from the continent and that they spent the most money. None of this was the result of a plan—at least up to that point.

This made sense to me. I had already met and known many Kenyans—mostly businesspeople, often women—who would come to South Africa to buy stock for their businesses or look for universities for their children. They would spend some days in the warehouses of Jo'burg and Durban, sell some things, buy lots of things—then maybe spend two days at Sun City and depart.

Although thousands of Kenyans do this every year, I have never seen a package advertised.

Kenya is like this too. In many unmeasured ways, Nairobi services the businesspeople, agencies, and governments of eight countries: Uganda, Tanzania, Rwanda, Burundi, Sudan, Congo, Somalia, and Ethiopia. Right now the only new routes Kenya Airways is opening up are lucrative African routes.

Traders come in from all over, looking for spare parts and socks; for new Mercedes-Benzes and toothpicks; for bales of secondhand clothes and banking services; for cement; for cost-effective private schooling; for seedlings and freelance website designers. The most vibrant parts of the city surround the bus ranks that service this massive market.

Of course, our world being what it is, there is no service to make the lives of these poor travelers easier. Kenyan police love to harass Black African foreigners because they are more afraid of authority figures than anybody, and they will cough up whatever is asked. There is no office set up by the city council to support trade and traders anywhere near Tom Mboya Street—no place to complain, no forum to discuss how to make this business grow.

Instead, there are askaris with clubs. Those billions of shillings that flow into the city every month need to be managed, and the management plan is clubs and tear gas and the efficient collection of fines and fees.

These neighboring countries may be Kenya's largest source of income, but then we must consider definitions. Take "investor." An investor is a white man with a briefcase; a brown man with a briefcase is here to "bribe"; a Black man with a briefcase is an "illegal immigrant."

There are signs, though, that the thinking is slowly changing.

A Senegalese company that makes innovative customs software has just won a huge contract from Kenya. The donors were shocked. Who thought technology could be bought and sold within the continent?

Now. The blunt truth of all of this is that there is little meaningful investment that can come from a white man with a briefcase. This is because he lives in a different solar system. What he refers to as a low-cost life for him and his family is beyond the means of Kenya to provide.

There is a lovely story that circulates in Nairobi about the coffee-husk project, in which beautiful and environmentally friendly and well-funded coal was produced by men in briefcases for the African market. This was meant to stop people burning charcoal. Problem was, the costs were high: big homes with twenty-four-hour security, broadband internet, private schooling at the international school, and so on had to be provided by the funding.

What is not said is that brown men with briefcases are readily available, downloaded from planes from Mumbai with fifty thousand dollars and the ability to live on a dollar a day while setting up the Kenya Coffee-Husk Charcoal Company, which will undercut the charcoal-dealing mafias.

It is for this reason that I am refreshed by the idea that the Chinese government built a mall as part of their trade mission in Nairobi. That they talk about doing business—and mean it. For when you hear our European Union-diplomat types talk, you would think all they do is donate and provide "partnership support"—we are not a market, we are a sort of kindergarten that needs a firm hand and bright, bold colors.

A raft of articles has come from concerned people in the West who talk about how China and India are exploiting Africa. But to me it seems that their motives are far more upfront, transparent, and sincere than the patronizing baby talk that issues from our partners with briefcases who want to start fail-safe businesses by getting pity grants.

I recently met somebody who trains Africans in "income-generating activities." She has never run a successful business. She took a course in development somewhere in Europe. She was flying business class to Amsterdam.

It's a good gig, if you can get it.

In Search of Coherence

It seems, despite the best efforts to manufacture our nations, that things will be built from the ground up. I have spent the past few months traveling around West Africa, and everywhere where people have created enclaves of coherence there is growth and progress.

I went to Touba, in Senegal—a city of nearly a million people. Here anybody of the Mouride movement (and others, I believe) can get a plot of land for almost nothing and not pay for water. There are no council taxes. The religious authorities build roads and supply free water. Welcome to West Africa's fastest-growing city.

Touba is built on the dreams of one man: Sheikh Ahmadou Bamba, the founder of the Mouride brotherhood. It is he who laid out the idea for a city in the desert; it is he who instigated trade-offs with the French to get them to give him the deed to forty thousand acres for his city. And it is he who demanded complete obedience from his adherents—an idea that scares me more than a little.

I don't know why it seems that Touba is a more egalitarian city than Dakar; it just does. It may be because the religious obedience demanded has more to do with work—immigrants are united in Touba by a phenomenal work ethic that is part of the movement. Maybe it is because most of the rules and laws that govern the city are tailored to make it work, and to make working and growing there easy. There is little bureaucracy, and most things are run by volunteer citizen groups.

Dakar, the city of colonial heritage, has been drowning for decades in fake ambitions. Abdoulaye Wade, the Senegalese

President, is keen to impress on the world the utter "world-classness" of his city. As you drive from the airport, monuments rise, groaning and heaving and announcing a new African renaissance. Massive highways are being dug, and the new streetlights look cheap, flashy, and unlikely to last more than a couple of years. Word has it that Wade is keen to impress representatives of the Islamic countries gathering in the capital sometime in 2008.

Dakar is beautiful in many senses: the live music, the massive wrestling bouts, the croissants, and the beautiful people. But Dakar is also the most expensive city I have been to on the continent. It is not clear to me exactly why. I suspect it has something to do with the high cost of needing to import things wholesale from France to maintain its sense of self.

Apart from the towers of the mosque, Touba is a more practical and lucid city. The roads in need of tarring get tarred, and there are wells everywhere. In the evenings, women come out and gather at the ends of their streets and clean up. There is no expectation that some city-council official will come and deal with anything outside of the gate. I can imagine a small-town person landing in Dakar with two thousand dollars in savings and soon finding himself on the street, broke and broken. But if he went to Touba he could end up owning a small garage or shop.

Maybe the question here has less to do with religion. In Lagos I met a man who told me he goes to all-night vigil parties at his church to gain the strength to go out on the streets every day and sell goods to people who are likely to insult him. You cannot survive the city without a kind of fever of hope.

I went to a city in the making, on the road to Ibadan, not far from Lagos. Redemption Camp is made up of thousands of hectares of Pentecostal lands that began as another idea for a retreat, with stories about pythons and demons and visions. Today—now that there are roads and Montessori schools and drains and crime-free, middle-class suburbs—church billboards talk less about demons and pythons and more about sexual health in marriage and investing in the stock exchange. One of Nigeria's biggest banks has announced it will help to build a new city there, where land is cheap and dreams seem possible.

Reason is built on harrowed ground.

While Dakar heaves and spins on the same axis, piling bureaucracy upon problem-solving bureaucracy, Touba names the simple things: what to do in the morning, how to do it, why we do it. It defines itself as much through its stated mission as through the daily transactions and interactions of its citizens.

Dakar insists on good manners and form and dictates them to everybody. It is much more fun than Touba, if you can afford it, but it does not make clear what it can do for you, unless you are arriving with French-expatriate hardship allowances. Or if, by the people you know or were born into, you find you need no coherence around you to thrive.

Goodwill Hunting with Monsieur Sarkozee

> The African peasant only knows the renewal of time, rhythmed by the endless repetition of the same gestures and the same words. In this imaginary world, where everything starts over and over again, there is no place for human adventure or the idea of progress.
>
> —Nicolas Sarkozy, President of France,
> July 26, 2007, Dakar

I am pleased to announce that a new species of bird, the African pheasant, was recently discovered by French wildlife enthusiast Nicolas Sarkozee.

After years of carefully observing pheasants from all over the world, he visited West Africa and spent time in the jungle, noting carefully the features of this curious bird. Last month in Dakar he delivered a paper on his findings, discussing the remarkable consistency of characteristics possessed by the African pheasant that make it unique among game birds worldwide.

Sarkozee spoke about the pheasant's "endless repetition of the same gestures." The eminent scholar, known for his careful research, observed the pheasants pecking on empty ground for several generations and concluded that they lived in an "imaginary world, where everything starts over and over again."

As game birds go, the African pheasant is tough, with rich dark meat. It has become more common in Europe, where it lives in vast, dark, multistory caves in the suburbs surrounding Paris and other cities. For generations African pheasants were taken to France, and now France has become part of their migration route. But environmental factors—walls and fences, wires and thorns, and police and soldiers, to say nothing of verbal threats—have caused problems in the pheasant's French habitat.

"Due to their particular nature, they benefited quite a lot from our control and benign influence," said the esteemed observer.

He was referring to the pheasants that managed, through careful and expert French training and general benevolence, to learn how to leave their homes and look for food to peck in France, where they became plump, put in cages outside Paris, and released for the pot every few months.

Monsieur Sarkozee, who for years was the French Pest Control Authority, criticized the reckless importation of African pheasants. This, he said, had resulted in the African birds acquiring European pheasant behaviors, and, as a result, the African pheasants in France were now spoiled, pecking and heckling and rustling their feathers angrily.

"Zey have become scum. And hooligans. Zis is why I have come to study ze African pheasant in hees own context. Here, he feeds in ze old time way, surrounded by green genocides and warm dictators and nuclear-power contracts. Here, zis species, so different from our own, knows only ze renewal of time and goes about rhythming everywhere—and zis, for me too, it ees a problem."

In a speech made before Africa's leading pheasant conservationists, notably Omar Bongo and Mu'ammer Gaddafi, he emphasized the need to create strong "Euro-African" partnerships to conserve the African pheasant.

Sarkozee was careful to use simple words to explain his complex analysis of the problem of African pheasants. "I want to speak in simple and rhythmic clichés about Africa, because I speak to the simple and rhythmic African pheasant. Working with ze migrant-pheasant populations in France, I learned to communicate appropriately. Zis for me is the most diplomatique and charmant way to get zee African pheasants to trust me."

When asked why he claimed to have discovered the African pheasant, when Africans had known about them all along, he said: "France will be by your side like an unwavering friend to develop ze African pheasant. Zis is my role. I do zis because I desire to help Africa develop. My rich friends in France will help."

Some analysts call Sarkozee's new conservation policy refreshing. Says one: "He is advocating for goodwill hunting, rather than old-school hunting, of African pheasants. He was keen to ally himself with prominent African pheasant conservationists like Professor Omar Bongo, who specializes in recycling Gabon's oil revenues to help maintain the condition of the African pheasant in its timeless and pristine way, removed from the polluting influence of other species."

Meanwhile, it has been suggested that the unique cry of the African pheasant, a cry at once rhythmic and repetitive and meaningless—Ugga Ugga Ugga Ugga—would make a good anthem for the Euro-Africa partnership.

Monsieur Sarkozee is also a musician and hopes to sample this rhythmic cry to raise awareness about the plight of the bird, which he intends to rescue. In support of this initiative, Bongo has volunteered his personal opera house, complete with a recording studio. Tens of thousands of pheasants will be shipped in from the suburbs of Paris, from the fields of Central Africa, from Sandton in Johannesburg and Gugulethu near Cape Town, from Cairo and the Rift Valley. Onstage they will gurgle in their repetitive, identical, and meaningless way, and the recording will be funded by the French ministry of culture's Marginalized Species Language Project.

The Perils of Truthism

In the fevered talk these days about religion and secularism, there is little room for the thing Africans like me most fear: religious or cultural rationalism.

Outside of tiny labs the general ignorance about science, even among people with good educations, is very high. I remember a famous Afrikaans rugby player, a medical doctor, saying in the 1990s that science had determined that Black people could not swim—something to do with muscles and heavy bones.

I once overheard a conversation in a coffee shop. A young African American woman in a gypsy peasant skirt was talking loudly to a Kenyan man twice her age. It was quickly apparent that she was his boss; it was also clear that he had been asking for either some sort of pay rise or leave. She was angry and a kind of stillness hung over the whole place as we all swung one ear in her direction. The man sat still in his immaculate suit, his face completely blank. He said nothing. Only nodding occasionally. At times you could see his eyes weighing things, kind of asking himself: "Does this tirade mean she is about to capitulate and give me the rise?"

She spoke about somebody called Vanessa, and about herself, and the sacrifices she had made, leaving good jobs to come to help in Africa. Sometimes I am in there until midnight! Because I care!

A few waiters started sniggering.

Soon enough she tripped: "We are here to help your people, and all you are interested in is money."

After this she went quiet. She had gone too far. He remained silent. His eyes gleamed for a moment: her transgression was a victory for him. Without saying a word, he had moved from being a greedy African patriarch to a victim of her bigotry. Her voice lowered, and she leaned forward, arms flapping about in retreat.

Poor woman. It was clear she felt that he was "local staff"—and therefore some kind of noble non-governmental ambassador for the suffering subalterns she cared for.

If you cruised the blogs of the newspapers with the most liberal and educated readerships in the United States and the United Kingdom after James Watson announced that Black Africans were doomed forever by their genes, a particular idea kept cropping up, especially in blogs in *The Guardian*.

Somebody would say, "Why is it okay to say Blacks are genetically superior on the racetrack and not okay to talk about their IQs?" Now the people saying those things are well-read people, who know their Kafkas, their Frappuccinos, and their Foucault.

In not a single one of all the blogs I cruised was the point made that Africa has more human genetic diversity than any other continent in the world. There is simply no easy case for building any common Black African platform of genetic similarities that can answer why Black African people are this way or that way. You start to stumble when you cross just one village market.

But—and here is where truthiness in science is more dangerous than all the marauding Osamas (remember Hitler)—the fact that we now have the human genome is only the beginning of a very long search. We still know next to nothing about our brains and how they work; we know very little about who we are and where we came from. People are still arguing about what the human mind is.

Our strong desire to select and highlight things from the slenderest evidence and to manufacture grand truths from these strands has come to polarize the world in many complicated ways of late. Everybody is an expert. Scientists are too far away from us to clarify things, and, when they do, they sound like they are saying nothing. So there is now a language of truthism.

I wonder if having a rational world, without religion, is sort of like having an America without a challenging superpower. We know from history that good scientists are quite capable of building edifices of absolute truths based on their visceral prejudices. If there is anything the twentieth century has produced, it is enough evidence to justify just about anything with some scientific authority. We are, however smart, still animals.

In a world where scientists are competing for funding and attention, we often know a lot about what they say they know, and less about what they do not know. I am all for science, but only in a world filled with irrationals and creatives; for Tibetan Methodists and Kikuyu Hippies, for cappuccino Mullahs and priests who beat themselves on the back, for Buddhist geneticists, for a white witch with a cat and sangoma beads in Woodstock. All I know for sure is that we do better when we are kept in check by competing differences.

Oxfamming the Whole Black World

Among white Americans the average IQ, as of a decade or so ago, was 103. Among Asian-Americans it was 106. Among Jewish-Americans it was 113. Among Latino-Americans it was 89. Among African-Americans it was 85. Around the world studies find the same general pattern: whites 100, East Asians 106, sub-Saharan Africans 70.

—"Created Equal" by William Saletan in *Slate*

Hello, kitty, kitty, kitty . . . Are you an orphan? Are you Sudanese? Chadian? Are you a sub-Saharan African suffering from mild mental retardation? Are you an African woman suffering from the African male? Would you like an Oxfam biscuit? Organic antiretrovirals? Have you been raped? You might not know it, but you are an orphan, a refugee. Can we fly 103 of you to France to be loved? We can breastfeed you. We can make you a Darfur orphan. Even if you are not. If you are Black and under ten years old, please come talk to us.

Come kitty, kitty.

We can save you from yourself. We can save ourselves from our terrible selves. Help us to Oxfam the whole Black world, to make it a better place.

We want to empower you. No, your mother cannot do this. Your government cannot do this. Time cannot do this. Evolution, it seems, cannot do this. Education cannot do this. Your IQ cannot do this.

No one can empower you except us. And, if you don't listen to us, our bad people, those RepublicanToryChineseOilConcessioningIanSmithing racists will come to get you: your choice is our compassionate breast or their market forces.

In our loving breast you will be a vegan. We will eliminate your carbon footprint, your testosterone, your addiction to religions. You will be kept away from bad, bad people, like ALL MEN.

We don't live in harmony with nature, and we are farting greenhouse gases all over the place. We will teach you how to live without farting greenhouse gases.

We will shut all your industries and build our organic Jeffrey Sachs–designed school inside your national parks, where you can commune with nature, grow ecologically friendly crops, trade fairly with eco-tourists, and receive visitors from the United Nations every month who will clap when you dance.

Instead of sweatshops, we will have Ubuntu shops where you can arrive in biodegradable loincloths to make bone jewelry for caring people who earn a million dollars a year, live in San Francisco or Cape Town, and feel bad about this. In our future world you will have three balanced meals a day.

In the afternoons Jeffrey Sachs will come and show the boys how to build a gender-friendly communal anti-poverty village where all base human emotions—lust, greed, and competition— will be sustainably developed out of your heads, along with truly dangerous ideas such as rebellion. After playing nonviolent games (rope-skipping and hugging), you will write letters to your loving step-parents in Toronto. For an hour a day we will teach you how to make clothes, shelter, and shoes out of recycled bottle tops in Ndebele colors.

We have learned from people and bonobos living in harmony in forests and deserts what your fate is and we will help you fulfill it. By the time we are done, you will all be having non-sexist multiple orgasms, you will be pacifists (we make and market organic pacifiers), you will dance and make merry with stone-milled, recycled mango wines that contain herbs to make you experience sudden and overwhelming universal love.

Some of us believe that if you all abandon industries and grow gentle herbs, your IQs will increase by thirty percent, because you are not eating toxins. Others believe that if the high IQ of the West is unsustainable, it is important to lower the level of world IQs.

Whatever side we are on here, we think you are special. If we are chimps, you are bonobos. Chimps are violent because they are smarter than bonobos.

For those of you with crude oil, we will help you use this resource—sustainably, mind you—to light your eco-candles and to make locally produced hair oil. The rest of the oil is bad, bad, bad. Leave it alone (we'll take it).

We will keep the Chinese out. Look how they are suffering because they abandoned Buddhism. We will allow only eco-tourists and poverty tourists in your countries.

Trust us. You can't do it yourselves. We have dedicated our lives to you. Come kitties, come to Mummy.

20

Beyond River Yei

Y ou may assume that a war-torn place is aware of the abnormality of its situation. That it will, for your own modesty, hide the graves, the torn clothes, the guns slung over shoulders, the raw animosity. It is possible that this happens in certain places. Not here. Surely, you think, your civilian Kenyan ego operating at full capacity, people will shoo you away, with a gun even, when faced by your scar-free self: fat and sleek, eyes unable to keep the pity out.

This is Sudan.

Do not mistake me: it was a relief, when we got to the outskirts of Yei Town, to see a lean, jaw-knotted teenager standing on the side of the road, a Kalashnikov slung over his shoulder, smiling and waving, and shouting.

"Kawaja!"

My fat sleek self has been granted a promotion. I sit in a large Land Cruiser; I speak English mostly, few people understand Kiswahili here; I smile awkwardly when I encounter somebody who may or may not be armed: I am a white man in a black skin. Kawaja.

Many years ago, as a child, I sat for days with my much-loved

atlas on the page that showed the NATURAL RESOURCES OF AF-
RICA. My project was simple: I needed a statistical analysis of
what Africa had to mine, grow, and sell to stop being poor. I
would measure this against everything I knew, and find a personally satisfying solution to our poverty.

The results were pleasant. Many, many squiggles:

. . . people

. . . oil

. . . gold

. . . sunshine

Which, I thought, would continue to make us interesting as
well as very rich. I needed those results because I could not find
a way to digest what had been leaked to me in the newspapers;
in weekly news programs like *Dunia Wiki Hii* (*The World This
Week*); and in conversations with my parents and family about
Uganda, the home of my maternal grandparents. For years, I
lived in a happy bubble, knowing that everybody was missing
the point. What we needed to do was to exploit these resources,
diligently, work hard, play canny, join this "world" game, and
fulfill our statistical potential.

Even this morning, somewhat further to the left, better read,
far more skeptical about the global-trade solutions we are offered, some little bit of me was still working with that elegant
model I designed so many years ago.

It took fifteen minutes in Sudan to kill this dream off for good.

There are no telephones in Yei; no electricity, except for gen-
erators owned by non-governmental organizations; no mobile
phones; no roads to speak of. There is no sign of any sort of serious trade in anything; no independent currency; no cars, other
than those run by donors or NGOs.

And Yei is said to be one of the better-developed towns in
South Sudan.

In Yei County, people were forced to move, by the stresses of
war, from their homes by the roadside. Everything became tem-
porary; you invest nothing permanent, because you know you
will lose it. You run inland to avoid rape, bullets, forced recruit-

ments, and the theft of all your produce, sometimes by the same soldiers you support.

No easy solutions. No solutions. No clear future. No way out.

Where do you start?

How quickly your intelligence fails you, when you are confronted with a reality that contradicts every point of reference you use to keep going; to have faith in a continent that was written off by many. I do not want to fall into this trap, because the next phase is predictable and depressing: "It is not my fault, it is theirs."

The colonizers, the Arabs, the Turks, the Slavers, the SPLA, the Donors, the Capitalist Military Conspiracy, the Russians, the People of South Sudan, America.

Oil Dependency, Muhammad, Garang, the OAU, the CIA, Tribalism, Racism, Middle Eastern Oil Money. The Dinkas.

The Tsetse Fly.

Anybody; anybody you can cede this shit to, so that you don't have to spend one more minute trying to understand it.

And your intelligence, or the shortage of it, starts to construct a million justifications, weaves an impenetrable theory, bits collected (only relevant to your theory) from unimpeachable sources; people who (you hope; you will insist) are in your boat; people whose ideas or ideals straddle the highest points of the issues you engage in; people who have SOLUTIONS, or maybe insights that place you so well in the context you desire (where responsibility is easily assigned), you are consoled by the fates they have set out: Fanon, Marx, Ngugi, Mamdani, Guevara.

Or

Kenyatta. Mandela. Kofi Annan.

Or

V. S. Naipaul. Keith Richburg. Colin Powell.

Or

The Bible. The Koran. *Economist* magazine. *Africa Intelligence. The East African.*

You will not be present in this story: it will be peopled by the scanty human evidence you have collected in two weeks, and fleshed out with language and terminologies, and histories and ideas approved by a consensus of your peers (or those you long to be your peers).

You have two weeks in Sudan. You will learn nothing that matters. You will, in fact, stop seeking because you will find you are drowning. The more you know, the more you know that what you know will offer no meaningful solutions.

Ultimately:

You will pick out from the (above) gospels only the strands that will make you leave Sudan feeling good about yourself.

Do not doubt the power of the mind to sort conveniently. Years later, you will read, watch the news, maybe even visit the place again. You have now designed eyes to see this place, and there is much material to affirm your eyes. Anything that diverts from this is sent to the trashcan.

If your sanity, or self-image, is sufficiently unstable, guilty, or disinterested, you may simply decide to draw a model such as this:

Sudan = Hopeless Civil War.

All information you receive will manage to find space within this brief phrase.

Fine. This may be a human way but remember: your eyes are working for you, not for Sudan.

Yei County

My eyes are half lidded with languor this third morning in Yei. We drive out of the compound into a dark avenue of giant mango trees; branches lean low, weighed down by rope mangoes. Shafts of light split the canopy of trees, torturing us with split-second tattoos of light and warmth. A young man wearing a tight muscle-top and a Kalashnikov walks hand in hand with a small child. An abandoned tank sits harmlessly by the side of the road, rendered impotent by the hordes of children who use it as a toy to clamber on.

Morning mist merges with light and rises like a wraith. I can smell earth.

Palm leaves are scattered all over the road; it was Palm Sunday yesterday, and many houses have a little palm cross on the door. Yei houses are mostly made of mud and thatch. People are afraid to invest in brick; they have been bombed too many times.

Three women sit on stones at a street corner, long fingers of falafels in plastic bowls in front of them. They turn to look at us, then laugh. Two children near them run alongside the car shouting, "Kawaja, kawaja."

Dr. Ajo's face is tense; it always seems to be when we set out on outreach programs. I imagine the mind gears clicking, checking, making sure everything is in place, every logistic managed. Little things can cause large dramas here. The rains started a week ago, and there is a sense of urgency with the lab crew. Much must be done before the roads are impassable.

I saw the team in full operation first last week, unpacking their lab—several large metal trunks—and placing the two or three hundred villagers into a conveyer belt of activity: checking blood, checking lymph nodes, checking lymphatic fluid for tryps.

By early afternoon, all must have been tested—sleeping sickness is notoriously difficult to diagnose—and all the patients must be transported back to the hospital.

The idea is to test as many people for sleeping sickness as possible. The only secure way to reduce the prevalence of the disease is to reduce the number of people infected by the parasite. Otherwise people will infect more tsetse flies, and the tsetse flies will infect more people. A full-scale epidemic would be disastrous. Yei borders the Democratic Republic of Congo and Uganda. Borders mean nothing to Trypanosoma.

Ah—but you ask, can't people just be given medicine? Yes. One medicine is a close relative of arsenic and kills quite a number of patients; the other one is sort of okay—it was developed in the seventies as a cure for leukemia but was not found effective enough. Then it was rediscovered in the nineties as a medicine to help rich American women remove unwanted body hair; then abandoned. Thank goodness for the person who rummaged through the trashcans of pharmaceutical companies and came up with this.

Who said garbage is useless?

Sleeping sickness is considered, in activist parlance, as a Neglected Disease. It isn't as sexy and Hollywood as AIDS, nobody in Europe or America gets it; there are no movies, full of wildlife and rugged compassionate American heroes, saving poor grateful Africans to make the Western world go, "Ohhhh, that is soo sweeet, Bruce Willis is so sensitive." And donate enough money for programs to run it. The Yei Hospital constantly has to fight for funds.

I am starting to sound like Ajo (Diktor) now. I found his book of poems in a dusty street bookshop, in Eastleigh, Nairobi, a year ago. Nothing about it called to me: the cover was lousy, a crude sketch of war (camouflage, a gun, khaki-green cover).

But the poems moved me, enough to spend months raising funds, finding any excuse to spend time in Sudan:

> *If you smile to your extremities*
> *You may be responding to:*
> *The giggles of a child*
> *Or the victory of your revolution.*
>
> *To the millimeter measurement of your mouth*
> *They may as well be the same thing*
> *Misery is different*
> *In those newspaper features of Sudan*
> *The sacrosanct assumption is that*
>
> *A millimeter measurement*
> *Of your misery*
> *Is possible*
> *You are*

They suggest
As miserable as
You are poor and fucked
But more people laugh in South Sudan
Than in Sweden
How about that?

Dr. Ajo has the face of a cherub with authority. I can see him dressed in nothing but a fresh nappy, waving a jewel-encrusted rattle and sitting on an enormous throne, masterminding a reluctant but fearful citizenry. His voice is soft and has no cracks; it never seems to waver, in tone or mood; whatever volume he speaks with is painted with a whisper. Everybody I have met so far respects him.

He has the strangest eyes. A dark blue-gray that is common here, especially in those with the darkest skins.

When they approached me in Nairobi to do this job, I had no idea the doctor I would be accompanying would be Ajo Diktor. I realized last night that he was the poet. We had gone out to a local bar, and he was talking to Peter, a know-it-all American from one of the Christian NGOs, who was saying, "It's hard, man. I'm, like, a people person, but people here, man, like they don't share, you know, they need to, like, learn to, like, talk about it."

Ajo: "Don't talk shit, Peter. We are all here to feed. If you want to believe that you are the savior and they are the recipients, feel free. But throwing that bullshit to me is a waste of your time."

Peter reddened, smiled like Jesus (Ye are forgiven, Ajo, for ye be wounded, and I feel compassion for ye, for ye are not a people person) and glided over to look for someone with more faith. Not hard here, where American Christian NGOs occupy vast compounds that are filled with unimaginable luxuries hidden behind electric fences, and propagated by rumor. The unspoken logo of this Christian public relation exercise is:

$!

Lurve gifts donated so the People of Sath Soo-Dan can get to have a prrrsonal relationship with Gaad.

Gaad promises secondhand basketball hoops, lurve, and last year's FUBU jeans. I have seen many people wearing T-shirts with the American flag in Yei.

It occurred to me, listening to him talk, that this Dr. Ajo could be Ajo (Diktor) that I met in that poetry book years ago.

Ajo started to drink glasses of *waragi* after this encounter. With each glass of clear alcohol, his eyes glazed more, and his voice remained whisper soft. He blacked out on the table. We carried him home.

Today, I decide to ask.

"I bought one of your poetry books in Nairobi many years ago: *Lies and Eyes*. I still have it."

Ajo turns to me, eyes blank, like they were in his stupor last night.

"Poetry book? I am not a poet."

Miles don't matter here, hours do—twenty miles can be a three-hour trip. When it rains, UN food trucks rush to distribute food to areas that will be cut off. They dig up the roads and turn them into fantastical features: gullies, canals, rivers, lakes, swamps, pools, ponds. New roads are created at the fringes of the features; the new roads become gullies (canals, rivers, roads) after a few days; and more roads are dug up by more trucks. Part of the sleeping sickness team's daily responsibility is to map the road, check new pools for depth, check the stability of new roads and the squishiness of swamps, and return this intelligence to camp for the other teams.

Although sleeping sickness does not get much attention in the world's media, large areas of South Sudan, Congo, and Uganda could be depopulated if the disease continues to spread without control. In many places it is spreading exponentially, and is not far from being out of control. In 1998 it was reported that, in Congo, more people died from Human African trypanosomiasis than from AIDS. In Tambura County in South Sudan, in 1997, there were areas that showed infection rates of forty-five percent. Without treatment, all the people infected with sleeping sickness will die. Because of the way it spreads, if consistent screening and treatment do not take place, an epidemic can develop very quickly.

Yei Town is the administrative headquarters of Yei County, New Sudan. The people who are supposed to inhabit a town like this are missing: the Vaseline-faced government servants of progress, scurrying about with such an ambience of tidiness around them, you are convinced that any regional trauma can be reversed; that the tentacles of an administration stretch far: paper punching into reality, stamping, filing, naming, listing, and roping all into a clear agenda. In another country, you might laugh at them with contempt, ridicule them and try to convince yourself that they are unnecessary, that they trade in setting your limits—that you can, and do, thrive despite them. But you have accepted the boundaries they have set, have internalized them, and never want to be reminded of their existence.

Until you go to a place where they do not exist.

Until yesterday, I found it difficult to digest the idea that managing an illness like sleeping sickness could possibly matter in a place like Sudan, where blood is fresh in the landscape around us; and dramatic problems, dressed in khaki camouflage and guns, reign supreme.

I broached this subject with Ajo Diktor, who darkened beyond possibility, and looked at me with contempt.

"You bewilder yourself with facile assumptions. Watch us do what we do every day. This disease is as much responsible for people choosing where to settle as the threats of war. When the British first came here, they found people dying like flies. That's why you see people living away from rivers; near the roadside. What we do does not have donor glamour; but, if we don't do it, we will have an epidemic the likes of which we have not seen in the Sudan, or Congo, or Uganda. The only way to do it is to manage it the way we are: making sure we link with other organizations that are treating sleeping sickness so we cover all possible areas; screen everybody; and treat all those infected. Any other situation does not bear thinking about."

There is an enormous patch of land, covered in grass, with a set of skimpy goal posts in the center of town. Puffs of glowing mist rise from the grass; there is a herd of cattle huddled together by the side of the road: large cows, with giant twisted horns, punching out in the air. I was told last night that Dinka youth run in military formations some mornings, hands in the air, announcing the shape of their cattle's horns. Each of the cattle has a burning log under its legs to keep it warm, and to keep insects away. A young Dinka man stands by the side, smoking strips of meat on a makeshift rack, body held high and tight. He stares at our car with disinterest and turns again to his meat.

We drive right through the center of this large town; we haven't yet encountered another car. We get to the center of the town, where the SPLM (Sudan People's Liberation Movement) offices are situated. A small group of men stand outside; a couple have military fatigues on—T-shirts, trousers, and sleeveless tops that seem more like secondhand-military-look clothes bought in secondhand markets.

Ajo turns to me. "You should have been here in 1997 when Yei was liberated. Bodies lined the road from here to the Uganda border. Civilians, caught between the SPLA forces who liberated Yei and those who liberated the border and were pursuing the Arabs who were headed back to Yei, not knowing that it had been captured. For months there were skeletons all along that road. But we got Yei back. I returned after two months: there were still skeletons lying everywhere; at one place I saw the remains of a person—all that was left was a flattened khaki uniform on the road. They told me it was the body of the commander of the Arab forces in Yei. He was shot on the road by the SPLA, and his body flattened over months by vehicles. Nobody touched it. That was Operation Thunderbolt."

Another poem!

Operation Thunderbolt Sandwiches (1997)
Many flavors are possible now
My brother
Grilled breast
Roast tongue
Bruised armpits
Twin drumsticks
Spread wide open for your enjoyment
And to have all these together
Flavored by blood
All you need to do
Is put one slice
In one hand
In Yei
Another in one hand
At the border
And slap them together
Viva la Revolución!

The car pauses on a thin, dusty crossroads, and Godwin, the driver, looks to the left nervously. The first sign of bureaucracy. The New Sudan Traffic Police Office. A tall traffic policeman stands, in a spanking new uniform, at attention near the building. It is always ominous when he decides to put on his uniform. Two days I have been here, and I know of him already.

Ajo puts on his seatbelt and motions for me to do the same. People have found themselves spending a night in Yei's notorious cells (situated in the former post office) after infringing some unwritten traffic law, in this town that has no traffic. Ajo spent a weekend there, a year ago. The town's only traffic policeman is at his most efficient on the rare occasion that he wears his uniform.

An angry conversation starts behind me, where Alfred and Godwin, the nursing assistants, are sitting. The conversation is in Kakwa, I don't understand anything except the word "Dinka."

Ajo laughs.

We are going to Pisak Village today, in the territory of the Pojulu.

We stop the car at the crest of an incline that leads to the River Yei. This is the border of Yei Town; a wooden barrier is manned by an SPLA guard.

Two women are standing by one side of the bridge, wringing a large, tattered blanket. Each stands on one side of the blanket, and they twist the blanket in opposite directions, and twist until the sheet becomes a hard cord, water spraying on to the ground.

It is around rivers like this that the tsetse fly thrives. It is a lazy, sluggish insect that waits for the blood of people or cattle when they come to fetch water.

Leni Riefenstahl would have camped out on the other side of the river and snapped away, the large protrusion on the front of her camera thrusting forward and back, forward and back: finding intimacy with the young man who stands in the shallow waters, parading heavy muscles, superlative arrangement of form and seamless black skin, scrubbing himself.

What power, to take control of rendition.

A disturbing phrase lodges itself in my mind, courtesy of Eldridge Cleaver: the Supermasculine Menial.

For centuries, occupiers of this land treated it like a supermarket of manageable muscle: slaves for the Middle East, for Khartoum; soldiers for British East Africa, for Khartoum; cheap labor for the Belgian Congo, for Khartoum; nude photographs for Europe, for Khartoum.

The young man turns to face us, and a broad grin tears his face open. He shakes his buttocks at us, and shouts, "Kawaja!"

Yei County is Kakwa territory. The Kakwa are known by the rest of the world mostly through the exploits of their most infamous citizen, Idi Amin. As it happens with most Africans, an incident, or a personage, is enough to brand your personality indelibly in the Western world's mind:

A Maasai is a noble savage who kills lions with his bare hands. Is thin and handsome.

A Nuba is an unspoiled giant, with fabulous muscles and great photographic potential if he remains unspoiled, which he refuses to do, so damn him.

A Nubian is a giant Black eunuch, with formidable sexual equipment, who inhabits the boudoirs of sheiks. A Nubian queen, an opposite reaction, inhabits the minds of identity-seeking people from across the Atlantic. Nubia is the category of the two extremes in the outside-Sudan imagination: fulfillment of the desire for an old empire to encourage a diasporic self-esteem; and the desire to own a man of near-animal characteristics, whom you can control—the Supermasculine Menial. In both cases, the situation of the people of Sudan is not the question, rather it is our own needs . . .

A Kikuyu (my tribe) is a brown-toothed fellow; avaricious (if you read George Thompson), loyal but childlike (if you read Blixen), untrustworthy (say Blixen, Thompson, and their heirs).

. . . and therefore Africa is a place where the usual human motivations and choices are somehow perverted.

Truth is, the Kakwa are farmers, people who have found themselves occupying three countries, as happens with many people who were divided by the casual pencils of European colonial bureaucrats. When they need to be, the Kakwa are formidable warriors.

They are the traditional occupants of Yei County, and are thought to have come from present-day Ethiopia. They were part of an ancient nation, the Eteka, which was situated between what is today Ethiopia and Somalia. Escaping drought, they fought their way southward, conquering a number of kingdoms along the way. They went as far as Turkana, at the northwest corner of Kenya, and settled there for a while. Northern Kenya is not a good place to grow crops, and pasture is scanty, so the ancestors of the Kakwa moved again, westward this time. They crossed the Nile, and over the years settled in their present location, in the three countries that share borders: Uganda, Congo, and South Sudan.

"Come, my friend, come to Maridi Road"

Maridi Road, driving to Pisak. More avenues of mangoes—do they end? A rock shaped like a beckoning finger, trucks stranded in the mud, a man weaves on the road: drunk, and singing a song to himself.

Graves: I lose count of the graves lining the road, all the way to Pisak, nestled beneath the mango and teak trees, surrounded by ripe, rich, brown earth.

Somebody is paying for the length and breadth of all those trees.

Pisak . . . She stands at the doorway to her family house, her baby leaning away from one hip. She doesn't have the curiosity, or the fluttering anxiety, other women have shown when we have come to visit. We sit in the spear-grass-thatched homestead, and watch her mother roasting coffee beans in an old tin pot. Her mother, Mrs. M, is telling us about manners: about how the umbilical cord is rubbed with ocher; about how God rules; about how liquor ruins; about war and death and the nobility of Any-anya One; about the fine old days, when girls were mannered; and men available to marry them.

Oh! Pojulu girls! The best in Sudan! Not lazy and slovenly like Dinka. Not fickle like the girls from Yei Town!

Their home is visibly poorer than others we have seen in Pisak. There are no men in her family to help with house building: husband died, son died. War. Graves by the road. All her three daughters have children but no husbands.

Mrs. M is embarrassed that she has nothing to offer us but coffee in this heat, from beans grown in her small plot. She is embarrassed that the three toddlers have spread last night's charcoal around the immaculately swept yard. She sweeps nervously, talking to us; then returns to the kettle of coffee, pouring in some of the sugar we have brought as a gift. Daughter doesn't lift a finger to help. Mother talks, one hand constantly covering the tear in her dress around her collarbone, and daughter stands, at the doorway to the family house, not eighteen years old, her eyes somber, then wistful, then just distant.

She is beautiful.

We walk through a weaving narrow path, surrounded by giant teak trees, heading back to the church, where the lab has been set up. George has appointed himself our guide as we visit residents, while the lab crew screen the villagers, calling all and sundry with a loudspeaker. I can hear the calls, bouncing off the trees, a beckoning from heaven.

George tells me about traditional medicine.

"Always, you carry this stick to chew for malaria. Especially when you are on a travel, it can strike abruptly."

I chew on the twig: it has a quinine taste, bitter. I cough. He laughs. I hear another laugh behind us. It is Mrs. M, walking behind us. She will follow us around for the rest of the day.

George tells me about the teak trees, the millions of them all over Yei County. The leaves are enormous, and people use them to sit on when gathered for a meeting. These will finance development here, he says, when the war is over. He talks of them lovingly, tells me how to trim, prune, chop even, and let it grow fresh, straight, and tall. Your children may fail you, die in battle and deliver no future for your old age; your teak will save you: fresh, straight, and tall.

He presents himself as an agent of "progress," sneering at those who have chosen to live near the rivers and risk being bitten by the tsetse fly; his face rearranges itself with concern when he talks about those that choose not to come for the screening.

I am different, his face says. I am different.

He produces his sleeping sickness card, shows me all the stamps. He was first in the queue this morning.

The path broadens: small pathlets fan out in various directions, and we find ourselves on the Maridi Road, two graves on each side of us marking our arrival.

When we left the lab team in the morning, people were milling about the grass-thatched church aimlessly; an occasion to gather and talk; a day free from school. Now the processing is taking place, a conveyer belt taking everybody through the tests required.

Ajo must have eyes at the back of his head; I see him throw comments at his team as he faces the wall, eyes focused on the microscope, looking for wiggly things.

Elders gather around us: George at the center; children are chased away. We sit in shade and talk, eating bananas.

Maridi Road is famous, they say. We aren't far from Mundu territory: the Mundu, they can sing, and they know medicine. What sort of medicine? I ask.

If someone has stolen from you or wronged you, all you need to say, when nobody wants to confess, is "I am going" and set off in the direction of Maridi Road. Before you are out of the door, the guilty will confess.

"Or you could die abruptically!"

It is a market day today. George excuses himself, pockets the Ugandan shillings I have given him, and heads off to buy some meat. Some Dinka have slaughtered a bull, and word has spread that there is meat for sale.

Minutes later, a group of women come through the gate of the church. They seem animated. They head straight for Godwin, and talk to him for a minute. He jumps into the car. I follow.

He briefs me on the way. We are going up Maridi Road, to get a woman who is very ill; we are not sure if she has sleeping sickness, but she is ill, and she must be seen to.

We arrive at the homestead. An old woman comes up to us. I am sure she is the ill one, but apparently it is her mother who isn't well; the mother speaks only Mundu.

They carry her out of her hut. I have never seen anybody so old: her eyes are milky, her hair wisps of frail white flapping in the wind. She can't talk, walk, or eat. She has not left her bed in months. Why hasn't she been seen to, we ask?

Silence.

Her daughter is quiet, then talks. Oh, we are in this homestead out of charity. My mother had only one child. Me. I never had children. So there is nobody to help us. The man who lives here cannot afford to take care of us. He is a second cousin.

Hidden in her talk is a quiet policy, applied to let the woman be, to die. But today some have defied this and seen the medical people. We drive back to the lab. As we unload the woman carefully, I catch sight of George stopping a few meters from the car. He sees me, waves halfheartedly and turns away, heading back from where he came, a package under his arm, his head bowed. The women whisper among themselves, eyes spread wide in alarm.

Godwin laughs and turns to me. "That is George's house we just came from."

The medics can't do anything for her; age is the problem. They suggest she goes back home.

While all this is taking place, the sky has surreptitiously lowered itself. We don't notice this until we hear a loud crack, which seems to come from somewhere too close to our heads to be comfortable. Clouds start to unfurl and spread their dark side all over the sky. We scatter.

Ajo stands up, and issues orders. Everybody, himself included, starts to pack up. Within half an hour all is loaded; the patients are in the car. One car will deliver them to hospital. The other car will stay behind; register those remaining and risk driving through the rain in a few hours.

The rain has other ideas. We are stranded in the church for four hours, as everything outside us seems to be pounded to submission. Godwin radio-calls from the other car, and says parts of the road will not be passable. The decision is made to spend the night in Pisak.

The rain has stopped.

Witches wander on nights like this, I am told, as we walk down to our homestead for the night. Silence is turgid and surrounds us like a solid thing.

Godwin has offered us his homestead for the night. He is from Pisak. He tells me about the history of the Pojulu.

Death comes in many ways. For centuries, *pongi,* the sickness of sleep, blighted the people of the region. At one point, it led to the region being deserted by people. Then a great healer suggested a ceremony to rid the area of the disease. A giant tree was cut down by the strongest of men. Incantations were made, and fires lit, and the tree dragged as far as possible, to the horizon—and tipped over the corner of the world, where it took with it this sickness.

There was great celebration. Clan leaders were called and told to tell their people to return. But this did not work, and in the history of these people, filled with the stories of great men and noble military victories, this tiny parasite remained the foe with the perfect strategy. Pongi always stays down for a while, then rises again and starts to kill.

It has started to kill again.

Gideon talks. "Many people died here when we went back to the bush. They are still dying of pongi. Always it goes away, then the hospital closes, and refugees start to move and pongi comes back."

Sultan Djata, of the ancient and legendary kingdom of Mali, was probably the first person written about who died of sleeping sickness. He was said to have died of lethargy in the fourteenth century.

In 1906, Under-secretary for the Colonies Winston Churchill reported to the British House of Commons that the disease had reduced the population of Uganda from 6.5 million to 2.5 million.

One old man talks. "The Belge, they were useless; but when the Britis they came, they made us cut bushes near rivers, and we were moved to be near the road, where we are now. They used to send people all over Sudan to check the collarbone and see if there were swellings; if there were fat swellings, they took you to hospital in Yei. They finish pongi, the Britis, but it came back when we went back to the bush to fight the Arabs."

Sleeping sickness has affected people in tropical Africa for thousands of years. It probably became epidemic only three or four thousand years ago, when Africans started to farm in tsetse fly territory. I believe this disease has had significant, and little researched, impact on the movement of people around the continent. Probably the worst epidemic occurred at the turn of the century, when colonial powers in Africa used forced labor to make Africans work in places that were full of tsetse flies.

In South Sudan and Uganda, populations of people were made to move out of tsetse fly areas. The epidemic was eventually brought under control. But war, poverty, and migration of displaced peoples have reintroduced the disease in many areas.

Four hours later, we sit in Godwin's homestead, surrounded by an enormous fire. It seems like the whole village is here. Yellow plastic jerry cans circulate, filled with various types of traditional alcohol. Godwin, Dr. Ajo, and I share a bottle of whisky, which some of the elders taste and reject with horror.

Mrs. M and the Pisak Temperance Society are seated primly near us, on teak leaves, while the men sit on stools. They serve food to us, on their knees, so their heads are never taller than ours. Other women have approached us and left with jugs of waragi.

Ajo is quiet, his face made fierce by the flames, he seems lost in some internal place.

A man arrives who introduces himself as Paustino—he is the music-man; his mother is a Mundari. He carries an *adungu,* a string instrument, with a tin base.

Since I arrived in Pisak, I have been held in this grip of a narrative that unfolds as we move; a narrative at once familiar and facile, it straddles the walls of my (pre)history, rubbing against them and ejaculating what is, for me, a common ecstasy:

Why can't we go back to BEFORE?

Well, Pisak Village, sitting in the cavernous silence of this night, is BEFORE as I have always dreamed it.

Cement, corrugated iron, plastic water tanks, and wire dominate the rural areas in my native Kenya.

These ingredients are practical, durable, but we do not have a knack with them. We do not yet know what makes these things look good; we just know how to make them work. We live in times when things are built in spare time: after work for an employer; after school. There is no community gathering to help you build. Hire labor and, if you can afford it, a contractor, Cousin Karanja from down the road that once worked as a bricklayer in Nairobi and knows the essentials.

Not here. This is housing that has acquired the poise of generations of finessing. Spear-grass thatch is waterproof, round is perfectly round, walls are freshly plastered. There is space—to walk, to sit, to cook in the open air, to dance around a fire, space for the whole village to turn up and sit hopefully near the jerry cans of alcohol. Everybody has their own hut; there is even a hut with walls reaching only halfway up the roof, whose purpose is for all to sit, avoid the sun, and talk. The only rugged structure, also perfectly symmetrical, is the chicken coop, a tiny rondavel that sits on top of a pole, with thatch untrimmed—it hangs over the round door like dreadlocks, when all other homesteads sport neat Afros.

The adungu tests itself in the air cautiously, lazy string sounds reaching out at the sluggish air. The focus shifts, and groups make their way around Paustino. He starts to play, and from the furthest corners of the compound voices reach out to join him.

"Bombolio"—a song from past days, when a line of young women stood opposite a line of young men, and each had to choose a partner to dance with. The song urges: choose the one, the sexy one, the charming one, the one with a sad smile. Poor teenagers, with their giant mountains of acne gleaming in the firelight; with knobbly knees, with stammers and endless hormonal throbs governing every thought. Many would not be chosen, and the entire village would laugh at them.

Oh, the songs we sing this night!

Godwin translates:

When they come
You will find your maize, your sorghum, all poured into the
    fire
When the deserters come, they will finish all your food

There in the bush, they are only eating belila
Which is uneatable
Let the musical instruments start singing
The youths are hiding themselves
You leave your bitter cassava soaking in the river
Overnight
When you go to collect the cassava
It is gone!
So sing loudly, so they can hear
Sing them to shame, so they come out of the bush

Oh, woman, you are so beautiful
Why do you always urinate inside the house?

But to fight wars is always about lice
Some lice you get from your hair
Others you get from your clothes
Since the war started
You do not wash
You have lice all over your body

Ajo has started to drink waragi again.

Elena, you are the beautiful lady
It would be better if my leg was amputated
So the recruitment won't take me away
So I can stay with you.

Everybody is dancing. All in a line, children weaving between our legs, shoulders bouncing up and down, smiles filling the air, lit to savagery by the fire. One person is not dancing: Mrs. M's beautiful daughter. She is standing among a group of women who are cooking, but her face is so held in she could be alone in the world.

I wonder, for a moment, what dreams she has, what legs have not been amputated for her, what legs have, who died and made her so sad.

Dr. Ajo
Make your thoughts count
Only numbers of your context
For numbers can justify anything

Haha
Wise advice
But Useless
(I) am individual,
Hitched my wagon to
(A star!)
I bought
Northern thought:
Arabic, European, Educated: what difference?
Contempt is necessary for sanity
Am as
Absurd as
Meursault
As
Far removed as
Fanon

They, not me, are the Wretched of the Earth
For I, like all in the north, am the savior and the
Devil.

This is Ajo's story.

In my language, we say when you have a hangover that you are "leftovers of yesterday's food."

It has been a long time since I spent a night in the village. I hate this: the begging, the way people have ceded all their needs to donors, to memories. Heroism has become nostalgia. I hate it that this Kenyan writer sees us like this. I don't like him: he is unlived, more hot-air vocabulary than life lived.

Why does this disease, sleeping sickness, occupy so much of my attention?

I fear the gun. I support its use; this struggle even; but I do not want to die.

So I try to save lives; try to avoid working as a doctor on the front line; always remain lubricated.

This Kenyan asks if I am Ajo Diktor. What does he want me to say? Eyes wagging hopefully, waiting for my "Yes!" before he takes liberties with me, assuming we have shared intimacies because he read my poems.

I was born in a hut by the side of Maridi Road, not far from Pisak. I remember an impossible memory, my navel spread with red ocher; my mother singing.

You know other things in similar ways: the first war of independence; the first war against the Arabs, which is so woven around your life by those who lived through it that it seems you did too. Like all wars, in retrospect, it is missed, much nobility is remembered; adrenaline is restless.

My father was a useless man. A former soldier in Amin's government. Selfish. My mother was his third wife.

His first wife had died. His second wife left him.

What I miss most about childhood is the sense that life is bursting with possibilities. For years, I carried in me the idea that there was an invisible life in the Earth, some creature of moist fumes that burrowed underground in the heat and came rising out of the Earth when it rained, revealing itself with a smell that always made me hungry to taste soil.

Before my mother died, I was fond of breaking things: not glass or bottles—those would mean too much of a beating. Bonds. I had the idea that people glided along railway tracks, doing what they do; and that out there, out of reach, there was a universe of interest. One day, carrying a basket of eggs to the homestead from the coop, I had this powerful desire to chuck them all up into the air: see how irrevocably my world would change with this small act.

Once, I set off on a journey; I walked as far as I could, trying to find the horizon. I wanted to find entry to another place—a soft-lit place, a far place, where life would not have stark realities. I was disappointed that the distant scenery became more and more real as I came closer. There was no vague magical place where reality blurred and I could slip through to elsewhere.

After a while, I could see my mother coming after me; the new thrill was to keep her far away; to keep them all so far away that for a while I could pretend that I could maintain distance forever.

I would let myself stretch and stretch, until I was contorted into an asymmetrical, illogical giant—comprising nothing but the complete fulfillment of my fancies.

This, of course, never happened. Not in this country. I was thrashed, and told I would be kidnapped: by the Arabs, by the SPLA as a child soldier; by wild animals or curses; or by pongi.

I did not enter vehicles often. Once we went to Arua, in Uganda, sitting on the roof of a lorry. How wonderful that was: a song that stuck itself like a wall in my mind, scraping through the solid wind the truck drove through. This song in my head would take on the sound of this wind.

I saw an acacia tree once, in Uganda. How strange it is, this tree! Her canopy is frizzy, like she was scribbled sideways with a sharp pencil, so she could cut her sharp edges into the soul of whoever looked at her from a distance and failed to feel a frisson. She doesn't ignore her bark, a considered color: the exact green of the flesh of an avocado, which when covered in dew shines like gold. You do not climb her: she has thorns. She is designed for dreams.

Then this war started when I was eight, and we moved away from the road, into the bush. It may have been while collecting water at the river one evening that the tsetse fly bit my mother. Two years later, my mother became mad. She would screech like a witch—sleep at odd hours, and wake up singing songs and crying. My father, now an elder of a religious organization that believed in demons, sought, endlessly, an evangelist of sufficient charisma to perform a successful exorcism. There is a part of me that believes that he preferred her mad—it made his efforts to get her "healed" saintly.

The tsetse fly is a fat, lazy fly, as flies go—it cannot fly further than two hundred meters from its base; but it will find somebody to bite at some point. This fly that bit my mother must have bitten somebody who carried trypanosomes; maybe one of the Dinka cattle-sellers, making their way to Arua, across the border; maybe somebody fleeing some conflict somewhere in Sudan, or Uganda, or Central African Republic, or Congo. Many possibilities.

So the fly released tryps into my mother's body. She had never been physically strong; they multiplied quickly.

This parasite has one supreme skill. Camouflage. When Mama's antibodies attacked this stranger, it changed its surface, causing much confusion in the immune system. Eventually, it made its way into my mother's brain, and she started to sleep during the day; my father prayed, surrounded her with praying men. He hit her several times, thinking this was just laziness.

Wind blew us away from our perches when the war for Yei started. We ran to Uganda, lived in a refugee camp, where I went to school. By the time the doctors got to her, it was too late. She had been suffering convulsions, then fell into a coma. She died.

Burial day. My cousin Eunice was charged to sit with me. She started to cry. I watched her from a far-off dream-place. Her sobs sounded like percussion: cacophonous, remote. Then they broke open my bubble, and I woke to find myself crying apace with her.

Father Gregory of the refugee chapel provided a car. I was able to look out of the window of the car: recognize the slow, persistent drizzle; notice that the sun was out too—beans had just popped out of the ground, more yellow than green, and shot with a shaking, sheer skin of light over the droplets of water.

I burned with joy and wanted to swell up, reach out and let myself go so I could be everything. The feeling was so intense I couldn't bear it for long, so I dived with my tears into a patch of moist dark soil, and let the food of growth seep into me, and goose bumps sprouted new shoots, cutting through me and mixing a tender pleasure with sharp pains. I was all cried out by the time we got to the church, and I was exhausted, and briefly content.

They say here, when the sun and rain occur together, a hyena is giving birth. In Uganda, they say, somebody important has died.

I can clearly remember standing in the rain/sun and rainbow, next to the coffin, surrounded by flowers, and seeing into an aspect of adulthood that only a child can see. How adults turn life into a third party and how this third party comes so naturally they aren't aware of its existence.

This one was flowers, a preacher of booming seduction, a coffin and suits, and nice shiny dresses and food cooking everywhere. The smell of bush meat cooking.

Despite the snarling, decomposing reality; despite the fact that not a single person there believed in things that they could not see, or hear, or prove—this was the third-party reality of death for them, and it had been made seamless by endless activity, and late-night meetings, and making sure all of us were always chaperoned, always consoled, always kept busy.

So the lie becomes a momentum, acquires a history, and a memory, and after a while it just seems like life.

Father was the busiest of all. Sorting, and welcoming, and conferring—his face drawn and brave: the long-suffering man of God.

Eunice was torn. She moved about in a bewildered now, but wasn't rendered useless by possibility like I was. She was able to smile shyly when father pulled her plaits; and held herself in a pose of long-dress, flowers-in-my-hand solemnity. A church expression.

I refused to abandon my stance. So I refused to greet, and paint the gaps with small talk. I refused to sit in front with the family, and dab my cheeks. I refused to join the other children—as was gently suggested by Aunt Margaret. I wandered around the church, sitting first with my class teacher, and then I joined the kids from my class. Then I stood and went to the back of the church and gazed at the stained glass, and made it hazy with my eyes, and shook my head so the singing around me would wobble and become ridiculous.

But this, this funeral, was my final rebellion. For in the days to come, I was rent apart with guilt at everybody's understanding. Even my father left me alone. For the first time in my life, they left me alone, cut me loose like a helium balloon and watched me stretch, saying nothing, just looking at each other with consternation. So there I was, being what I wanted to be, and, from my far, frothy place of grotesque things made normal, I yearned for lies, and third-party reality.

I failed to achieve this. Instead, I hitched my wagon to Father Gregory, and was banished by my father for rejecting his religion, which did not offer my sole possibility of escape: education. My father and I have not seen each other in twenty years. He lives five miles away from Pisak, and sends my stepbrothers regularly to the hospital to collect money from me.

I became a doctor, a captain in the SPLA (advancement not possible for skeptics like myself), and, sometimes, a poet. A bad one, I have been told.

I do not believe in God.

I like waragi.

A Place Called Addo

Fact is:
What you do
Reflects your philosophy
Not what you say
So:

Invent this thing called
A Legal Person
PharmaCorp!
To Do Your Dirty Work
Now PharmaCorp
Can safely say things
That could design genocide

Like:
"Only Potential Markets
Have a Right to Life"

More mango trees. These groan with the weight of unharvested fruit. The road is little more than a track; the car rattles through, and rotten mangoes drop on the roof at every bump, some land with a splat! and spray strings of soggy flesh out of our windows.

We are going to Addo. A place Ajo believes has many sleeping sickness patients. He is quite crabby today. Hangover, I think. One young man turned up at the Pisak screening and told of pongi, how chameleons are used to cure sleeping sickness in this place called Addo. He promises to take us there. His name is Luka.

The further inland from Maridi Road we drive, the more time rolls away. There are few people on the road; most of them dive into the bushes with fear when they see the car. We meet one man, several largish ratlike animals hanging in a string in his hands. We stop twice to cut away trees that have fallen across the road.

There are little surprises: a bridge, better than any I have seen on Maridi Road, concrete. We cross. Luka tells us that Addo was once a huge refugee camp for Ugandans, fleeing after Amin's government fell. Idi Amin was Kakwa, from Uganda, and people feared repercussions.

The Ugandan refugees here were doing well. The land was fertile; they cultivated much food and supplied markets, even Khartoum, with food. They did not want to go back to the uncertainties of Uganda. But they were forced to go back.

We drive past a giant church. The first stone-built church we have seen outside Yei. It stands, imposing and forlorn, with a woman in front of it.

Half an hour later, we park the car in Ado Village Square. It is deserted.

A brick and stone village. The corrugated-iron roofs have

been disassembled and carted away for other uses. To our left and right is the school. We park and get out of the car.

There is a giant anthill in the classroom I enter, right in the center of the room, stretching sideways to one of the window-panes. White walls are full of charcoal scribbles. On the black-board: the last lesson, December 1996. Multiplication. Mr. James Dada, who writes in rounded Catholic school script. On the walls, scribbled in charcoal: a beetle-sized tank, sketched out of char-coal, nose pointed at giant lettering: *La illah ila Allah* ("There is no Allah but Allah").

An archive of messages:

"*Rambo III.*"

"A drowning man will catch at the grass. He that is down need fear no fall. He is my son, out of sight out of mind, sorry, Yei people."

"I am John; bye bye, brothers and sisters. June 1996."

"Phantom Soljas"

"Juba is calling brother."

"Idi Amin Dada"

"Ha, ha, John Garang kill, bu, make sure that your (life is) also in danger, my friend."

"Leah, we have gone home—God b with yu."

Luka returns with the Chief, who has just come back from a four-day hunting trip, looking for bush meat. He translates: "After the UN left, we stayed by the road, but always they would rape our daughters and rob us. The soldiers. Many died here, so we moved into the bush . . . ten children have died of measles this past month. Life is hard, there is much pongi here. People they die every day."

We talk for hours. Plans are made to screen here next week. As we pack up to head back to the hospital, a group of people arrive, carrying a man. He is laughing, his eyes lit to fire. His hands are tied together. His legs held firmly, as he squirms in their firm grip. They come closer. We see bruises on his wrists and legs. He moans and then screams and starts to struggle.

Ajo and the team rush to them. He is sedated. Ajo is sure he is a Stage 2 sleeping sickness patient. His name is John. We call him Crazy John.

Epilogue

Guerillas,
Protozoa: battling and breeding their way into your brain,
changing skin to deceive your body's army
You will sleep, odd hours; have dreams filled with fear, as the
guerrillas eat the stuff of your brain:
"Terrorists!" you will scream.
"War against terror," replies Diktor, pumping you full of
medicine. "Removing Weapons of Mass Destruction"
In these days, when Lab Mice Have Rights Too
Who is agitating for the right of the
Trypanosome
To feed on our brain cells?

Crazy John's antics keep the hospital staff busy. They all complain about him, but he makes the shifts interesting for everybody. He is a little better, has even found a voice of sorts: he sounds less and less like Jimi Hendrix's guitar. He needs to be held down often.

On the wall of the ward, there is a large poster that reads: NOBODY LOSES SLEEP OVER SLEEPING SICKNESS.

Except sleeping sickness patients, I think.

I saw death today: a patient was brought to the hospital a few days ago, James Lugala. He had Stage 2 sleeping sickness, but was too far gone. I walked into the wards this morning and found the man's son sitting next to him, bewildered. He told me his name was Gideon.

James had died that morning. A soft morning light seemed to carry streams of the man's soul away from his face. I could hear Ajo barking orders in the distance, his voice angry.

The sleeping sickness hospital is situated in front of the church.

Coming from Yei Town this evening, just before sunset, I saw a man kneeling by the doors of the church, head bobbing animatedly, hands in the air, praying, his axe sitting by his side.

It was Gideon.

Something in my stomach relaxed and a fluid feeling flooded the base of my chest. Ajo looked away from the man, turned to me, his face blank. "Let's go back to Yei. I feel like a beer."

Drink beer when the sun shines
And waragi in the dark
For your engine
To perform efficiently
Always
Remain
Lubricated

21

The Most Authentic, Blackest, Africanest Soccer Team

I meet Alex at breakfast in Accra. He is a carver of wooden curios who keeps a small shop at the hotel. His uncle owns the hotel. He spends his days at the gym, playing soccer, and making wooden sculptures of voluptuous Ghanaian women. For tourists. He shines with beauty and health and fresh-ironedness. He seems ready; fit and ready. I am not sure for what. We chat. He doesn't speak much. I ask him if he can help get me somebody to take me to Lomé. He plays finger football on his mobile phone and finds me somebody.

Later, in the evening, we get in his uncle's Peugeot and he drives me to meet my guide. I am struck, again, by the fluidity of his body language, and even more by his solemn maturity. There does not seem to be anything he cannot handle.

But his attitude toward me is overly respectful. He plays boy to my man. Does not contradict anything I say. It is disturbing. Before we get to the suburb where his friends are hanging out, he turns to me and asks, his face awed, and suddenly boyish, "So, how is life in New York?"

We find them, Alex and me, at dusk: a group of young men sitting by the road, in tracksuits and shorts and muscle tops. They are all fat-free and pectoraled, and look boneless, postcoital, and gray, after a vigorous exercise session at the beach, and a swim and shower. One of them has a bandage on his knee and is limping. They are all fashionably dressed.

I ask around. They all come from middle-class families. They are all jobless, in their twenties, not hungry, cushioned in very small ways by their families, and small deals here and there.

Hubert is a talented soccer player. Twenty-one years old, he is the star of a First Division team in Accra. In two weeks he will go to South Africa to try out for a major soccer team. His coach has high hopes for him.

"I am a striker."

He looks surprisingly small for a West African football player. Ghanaians are often built like American footballers. I conclude that he must be exceptionally good if he can play here with people.

"Aren't you afraid of those giant Ghanaian players?" I say, nodding my head at his hulking friends.

He just smiles. He is the one with the international offers.

Hubert agrees to take me to Lomé for a couple of days. He is mortified by my suggestion that I stay in a hotel. We will sleep in his mother's house in Lomé. His father died recently. Hubert is in Accra because there are more opportunities in Ghana than in Togo.

"Ghana has no politics," he says.

I offer Alex a drink. To say thanks. We end up at a bar by the side of a road. A hundred people or more have spilled on to the road, dancing. Talking and rowdily staggering. Alex looks a little more animated. They are playing hip-life, Ghana's version of hip-hop merged with highlife. It is a weekday, and it is packed with large good-looking men, all in their twenties, it seems. There are very few women. We sit on one side of the road and chat, watching people dance on the street. This could never happen in Nairobi—this level of boisterousness would be assumed to lead to chaos and anarchy, and would be clipped quickly. Three young men stagger and chase each other on the road, beers in hand—laughing loudly. Alex knows a lot of the guys here—and he joins in a little, in his solemn way.

I notice there are no broken bottles, no visible bouncer. No clues that this level of happiness ever leads to meaningful violence.

After a while, we find a table. I head off to the bar to get a round of drinks—some of Alex's friends have joined us. (You don't drink Guinness? they ask, shocked. Guinness is MAN-POWER.)

When I get back, I find a couple have joined the table. A tall man with large mobile lips and a round, smooth baby face, and a heavily made-up young woman with sharp breasts and a shiny, short dress.

The rest of the table is muted. They do not meet the woman's eye—although she is their age. The man is in his thirties. He shouts for a waiter, who materializes. His eyes sweep round, a string of cursive question marks. People nod assent shyly. He has a French African accent.

Alex introduces us. He is Yves, from Ivory Coast. He is staying at the same hotel that I am.

Yves laughs, his eyes teasing, "Your uncle's hotel. Eh."

Alex looks down. Nobody talks to me now. It is assumed Yves is my peer, and they must submit. They start to talk among themselves, and I turn to Yves.

"So—you are here on business? Do you live in Côte d'Ivoire?"

"Ah. My brother, who can live there. I live in South London. And in Chad. I also live in Accra sometimes."

"Oh, where do you work?"

"I am in oil—we supply services to the oil companies in N'Djamena."

We talk. No. He talks. For a full hour. Yves is thirty-three. He has three wives. One is the daughter of the President of Chad.

The other is mixed race—a Black Brit. The third lives here in Accra. I look for him to turn to cuteface by his side. He does not. And she does not react. It is as if she is worried her makeup will crack if she says anything. Every so often, he breaks from his monologue to whisper babyhoney things in her ear.

Yves knows Kofi Annan's son. He is on retainer for a major oil company seeking high-level contacts in Africa. He looks at me, eyes dead straight and serious, and asks me about my contacts in State House. I have none to present. He laughs, generously. No problem. No problem. Kenya was stupid, he says, to go with the Chinese so easily.

This is the future. But most people do not see this . . .

He turns to Alex. "See this pretty boy here? I am always telling him to get himself ready. I will make it work for him . . . but he is lazy."

Yves turns to the group. "You Ghana boys are lazy—you don't want to be aggressive."

The group is eating this up eagerly, smiling shyly and looking somewhat hangdog. The drinks flow. Cuteface now has a bottle of champagne.

Later, we stand to head back. Yves grabs Alex's neck in a strong chokehold. "You won't mess me in the deal, eh, my brother?"

Alex smiles sheepishly. "Ah, no, Yves, I will do it, man."

"I like you. Eh . . . Alex? I like you. I don't know why—you are always promising, and nothing happens. You are lucky I like you."

Alex looks very happy.

We separate at the hotel lift, and Yves slaps me on the back. "Call me, eh?"

Early the next morning, we take a car from the Accra bus rank at dawn. It is a two-hour drive to the border. You cross the border at Aflao, and you are in Lomé, the capital of Togo.

Lomé is hot, dry, and dusty. People look dispirited, and the city is rusty and peeling and bleached from too much brine, sun, and rough times. Hubert points out a tourist hotel to me. It looks like it has been closed for years—but the weather here can deteriorate things rapidly. The tourist industry collapsed after the pro-democracy riots of early 2005.

The Ewe, who are the largest ethnic group in both Ghana and Togo, settled in the Lomé area in the early 1600s. The region had plenty of trees that provided fragrant and healthful chewing sticks, traditional toothbrushes. So, it is said, they called the place Alo Mé, meaning "among chewing sticks."

For two hundred years, the coastal region was a major raiding center for Europeans in search of slaves. To Europeans, what is now Togo was known as "The Slave Coast." Gnassingbé Eyadéma was a Kabye, the second-largest ethnic group in Togo. The Kabye homeland around the northern city of Kara is arid and mountainous. In the first half of the twentieth century, many young Kabye moved south to work as sharecroppers on Ewe farms. The wealthier Ewe looked down upon the Kabye, but depended on them as laborers. Eyadéma made sure to fill the military with Kabye loyalists. It was called "The Army of Cousins" and was run by the French.

So Eyedéma had the loyalty of most Kabye—and was happy, when threatened, to make much of the differences between the two ethnic groups. Ewe protesters were imprisoned or harassed in the 1990s. The Kabye who were not directly related to the President benefited very little from his rule—but he held them hostage through fear. Like Kenya's former President Daniel Arap Moi, he had so offended the rest of the country over the years that the Kabye were terrified that they would be victimized if his family ceased to rule.

In 1974 Eyadéma decided to stop calling himself Étienne. He Africanized his name and became General Gnassingbé Eyadéma—the title "General" was not Africanized. He survived a few assassination attempts and was well known for having "powerful medicine."

He threw political opponents to the crocodiles.

When Eyadéma died, while on his way to seek treatment

"abroad," the military forcibly installed one of his sons as President.

Faure Gnassingbé, thirty-eight years old, was the son who most resembled his father, the son known to be sober, and the son who had earned an MBA at George Washington University in America before returning to Togo to manage his father's businesses.

After Faure was installed as President by the military, there were riots in the streets, arrests, and deaths; other states refused to recognize his government. But his late father's machinery organized new elections, which he won. He immediately began to appeal to young people for support, saying his door was open to them.

He has had good fortune on his side: his younger brother Rock, a former parachute commander, was in charge of Togolese football, and amid all the unrest delivered to Faure the best gift his family may have received since his father took over the government in 1967.

Togo qualified for the World Cup.

They swept away a series of African soccer giants—Senegal, Mali, Congo, Zambia, and Morocco—and thrilled the country. The Togolese yellow jersey flapped about Lomé's markets like a new flag.

Rock Gnassingbé was recently made a Commander of the Order of Mono. France is in the group Togo has drawn—an encounter many Togolese are looking forward to, especially after Senegal, which had many old grudges to settle and beat France in the opening match of the last World Cup.

Hubert, my companion, is not Ewe. And he supports Faure. "He understands young people." It turns out that his family is originally from the north.

We take a taxi into town and drive around looking for a bureau that will change my dollars to CFA francs. One is closed. We walk into the next one. It has the characterless look of a government office. It smells of old damp cardboard. They tell us we have to wait an hour to change any money.

In the center of the city, buildings are imposing, unfriendly, and impractical. Paint has faded, and their plastic fittings look bleached and brittle. I have seen buildings like this before—in South African Homeland capitals of yore, in Chad and Hungary. These are buildings that international contractors build for countries eager to show how "modern" they were. They are usually described as "ultramodern"—and, when new, they shine like the mirrored sunglasses of a presidential bodyguard. Within months, they rust and peel and crumble. I see one called Centre des chèques postaux, and another called Centro nacional de perfeccionamiento profesional.

There are International Bureaus of Many Incredibly Important things, and Centers Internationals of Even More Important Things. I count fourteen buildings that have the word DÉVELOPEMENT on their walls. In Accra, by contrast, the shop signs are warm, quirky, and humorous: HAPPY DAY SHOP, DO LIFE YOURSELF, DIPLOMATIC HAIRCUT.

Everywhere, people are wearing yellow Togo team shirts.

We decide to have lunch. Hubert leads me to a small plot of land, surrounded on three sides by concrete walls. On one side of the land, a group of women are stirring large pots. On the other, there is a makeshift thatch shade, with couches and a huge television. A fat gentleman, who looks like the owner of the place, is watching *Octopussy* on satellite television. There are fading murals on the walls. On one wall, there are a couple of stiff-looking white people waltzing, noses facing the sky. Stiff, awkward, white people. An arrow points to a violin, and another arrow points to a champagne bottle. It is an ad for a hotel: L'HÔTEL CLIMON. 12 CHAMBRES. ENTIÈREMENT CLIMATISÉS. NON LOIN DU LYCÉE FRANÇAIS.

On another wall, there is an ad for this restaurant. A topless Black woman with spectacular breasts—large, pointy, and firm—serves brochettes and a large fish on a huge platter. A Black chef grins at us, with sparkling cheeks. A group of people are eating, drinking, and laughing, fluent, affluent, and flexible. I order the fish.

We make our way out and look for a taxi. There are more taxis than private cars on the road. Hubert and the taxi driver have a heated discussion about prices: we leave the taxi in a huff. Hubert is furious. I remain silent—the price the taxi driver quoted seemed reasonable—but what do I know—Nairobi taxis are very expensive.

"He is trying to cheat us because you are a foreigner."

I assume the taxi driver was angry because Hubert did not want to be a good citizen and conspire with him to overcharge me. We get another taxi, and drive past more grim buildings. There are lots of warning signs: INTERDIT DE . . . INTERDIT DE . . .

There are several hand-painted advertisements of women serving things, topless, with the same spectacular breasts. I wonder if they are all by the same artist. Most Ghanaian hand-painted murals are either barbershop signs or hair salon signs. Here, breasts rule. Is this a francophone thing? An Eyadéma thing?

It could be that what makes Lomé look so drab is that, since the troubles that sent tourists and donors away, there have not been any new buildings built. The licks of paint, the gleaming automobiles of a political elite, the fluttering flags on the streets, and presidential murals; the pink-and-blue tourist hotels with pink-and-blue bikinis on the beach, sipping pink-and-blue cocktails— these illusions of progress no longer need to be maintained. The dictator who needed them is dead. The tourists have gone; the French are too busy Eurogizing to remember Togo as well as they did.

We drive past the suburb where all the villas are, and all the embassies. Nearby there is a dual carriageway, in sober charcoal-gray, better than any road I have seen so far. It cuts through bushes and gardens and vanishes into the distance. This is the road to the presidential palace that once housed the dictator Gnassingbé Eyadéma. It is miles away. It is surrounded by lush parkland, and Hubert tells me the presidential family has a zoo in the compound. Eyadéma was a hunter and loved animals.

We drop my luggage at Hubert's home. His mother lives in a large compound in a tree-lined suburb. The bungalow is shaped like a U, with rooms that open to a corridor and face a courtyard where stools are set. His mother and sisters rush out to hug him—he is clearly a favorite. We stay for a few minutes, have some refreshments, and take a taxi back to the city center.

Driving past the city's main hospital, I see the first signs of sensible commerce: somebody providing a useful product to individuals who need it. Lined along the hospital wall are second-hand imported goods in this order: giant stereo speakers, some very expensive-looking, a drum set, bananas, a small kiosk with a sign on its forehead: TELEPHON INTER-NATION, dog chains, a cluster of secondhand lawn mowers, more dog chains, five or six big-screen televisions, more dog chains, crutches, a row of secondhand steam irons, and a large, faded, oriental carpet.

An hour later, we reach the market in Lomé, and finally find ourselves in a functional and vibrant city. Currency dealers present themselves at the window of the car, and negotiations are quick. Money changes hands, and we walk into the maze of stalls. It is hard to tell how big it is. People are milling about everywhere; there are people selling on the ground and in small rickety stalls, taking up every available space.

There are stalls selling stoves and electronic goods, there are currency changers and traders from all over West Africa, and tailors and cobblers and brokers and fixers and food and drink. Everything is fluent, everybody in perpetual negotiation, flexible and competitive. Togo's main official export is phosphates—but it has always made its money as a free-trade area, facilitating traders from all over West Africa.

Markets like these have been in existence all over West Africa for at least a millennium, and there are traders from eight countries here. Markets in Lomé are run by the famous "Mama Benz"—rich trading women who have chauffeur-driven Mercedes-Benzes. These days, after years of economic stagnation, the Mama Benz are called Mama Opel.

The stalls are bursting with fabrics. I have never seen so many.

There are shapeless splotches of color on cloth, bold geometries on wax, hot pinks on earth brown, ululating pinstripes. There are fabrics with thousands of embroidered coin-sized holes shaped like flowers. There are fabrics that promise wealth: one stall-owner points out a strange design on a Togolese coin and shows me the same design on the fabric of an already busy shirt. There are fabrics for clinging, for flicking over a shoulder, for square-shouldering, for floppy-collaring, for marrying, and some, surely, to assure an instant breakup.

We brush past clothes that lap against my ear and whisper into it, while others lick my brow from hangers above my face.

Anywhere else in the world the fabric is secondary; it is the final architecture of the garment that makes a difference. But this is Lomé, the freeport capital of Togo, and here it is the fabric that matters. The fabric you will buy can be sewed into a dress, a shirt, an evening outfit consisting of a headband, skirt, and top in one afternoon, at no extra cost. It is all about the fabric. There are fabrics of silk and cotton; from the Netherlands and China; as well as mudcloth from Mali and Kente cloth from northern Togo.

It is the stall selling bras that stops my forward motion. It is a tiny open-air stall, and there are bras piled on a small table, bras hanging above, bras everywhere. Years ago, I had a part-time job as a translator for some Senegalese visitors to Kenya. Two of the older women, both quite large, asked me to take them shopping for bras. We walked into shop after shop in Nairobi's biggest mall. They probed and pulled and sighed and exclaimed, and I translated all this to the chichi young girls who looked offended that women that age could ask questions about a bra that had nothing to do with its practical use. We roamed what seemed like hours, but these francophone women failed to find a single bra in all the shops in Sarit Center that combined uplifting engineering with the right aesthetic.

They could not understand this anglophone insistence on ugly bras for women over twenty-five with children.

Open-air bra-stalls in my country sell useful, practical, white bras. All secondhand. Not here. There are red strapless bras with snarling edges of black lace. A daffodil-yellow bra with curly green leaves running along its seam. Hanging down the middle of the line is the largest feeding bra I have ever seen— white and wired and ominous—that looks like it may contain pulleys, pistons, and a flying buttress or two. One red bra has bared black teeth around a nipple-sized pair of holes. Next to it is a corset in a delicate ivory shade. Honestly, I did not know people still wore corsets.

A group of women start laughing. I am gaping. Anglophone. Prude.

It takes an hour for us to move a hundred meters or so. Wherever I look, I am presented with goods to touch and feel. Hubert looks grim. I imitate him. Heads down, we move forward. Soon we see a stall specializing in Togo football-team jerseys. There are long-sleeved yellow ones, short-sleeved ones, sleeveless ones. Shirts for kids. All of them have one name on the back: the name of Togo's super-striker, Sheyi Emmanuel Adebayor.

I pick out a couple of jerseys, and while Hubert negotiates I amble over to a nearby stall. An elegant, motherly woman, dressed in pink lace, an image of genuine Mama-Benzhood, smiles at me graciously. Her stall sells shirts, and looks cool and fresh. She invites me in. I come and stand under the flapping clothes to cool down. She dispatches a young man to get some cold mineral water. I admire one of the shirts. Too small for you, she says sorrowfully. Suddenly I want it desperately, but she is reluctant. Okay. Okay, she says. I will try to help you. When are you leaving? Tomorrow, I say. Ahh. I have a tailor—we will get the fabrics and sew the shirts up for you, a proper size.

It is here that my resolve cracks, that my dislike of shopping vanishes. I realize that I can settle in this cool place, cast my eyes about, express an interest, and get a tailor-made solution. I point at possible fabrics: she frowns and says *nooooo*—this one, without fancy collars. We will make it simple—let the fabric speak for itself. (In French, this opinion sounds very authoritative.) Soon, I find, I have ordered six shirts. A group of leatherworkers present an array of handmade sandals: snakeskin, crocodile, every color imaginable. Madam thinks the soft brown leather ones are good. She bends one shoe thing into a circle. Nods. Good sole.

Her eyes narrow at the salesman and ask, "How much?"

His reply elicits a shrug and a turn—she has lost interest. No value for money. Price drops. Drops again. I buy. She summons a Ghanaian cobbler, who reinforces the seams for me, as I sit glued to the edges. In seconds, all is ready. She looks at me with some compassion. What about something for the woman you love? I start to protest—no, no, I am not into this love thing. Ahh. Compassion deepens. But the women's clothes! I see a purple top with a purple fur collar. A hand-embroidered skirt finished with white cotton. It is clear to me that my two sisters will never be the same again if they have clothes like this. They each get two outfits.

Hubert and I make our way to a beach bar. On the way out of the center of Lomé, I see an old sign by the side of the road. Whatever it was previously advertising has rusted away.

Somebody has painted on it, in huge letters: TOGO 3—CONGO 0.

The beach runs alongside a highway, and hundreds of scooter-taxis chug past us with 5 P.M. clients—mostly women, who seem very comfortable. One woman sits in the passenger seat, at a right angle to the scooter. She is holding a baby and groceries, and her head is tied into one of West Africa's ubiquitous knots of cloth. She seems quite unbothered by the risk of two wheels. We sit on some rickety plastic chairs and discourage a guitar-playing crooner who wants to play us a personal soundtrack for sunset. We order beer.

"Look," Hubert says, pointing at the fishermen. "They are about to pull in the nets."

There must be fifty people all dragging one long, long net in.

"They do this every evening—then you will see people coming to buy fish for home and for the market."

It takes at least half an hour for the net to come in. Hundreds of people gather to buy fish. The crooner starts up again, and a group of Sierra Leonians sitting next to us shout at him to leave.

After sunset, we return to Hubert's house. Hubert's mother and sisters are happy to see him home, and have cooked a special sauce with meat and baobab leaves and chili. Hubert's mother, a retired nurse, is a widow. Hubert is the last born, and it is clear he is the favorite of his sisters. The front of the house opens to the garden, and it is where some of the cooking takes place to take advantage of the cool breeze.

After dinner, I find out I am to sleep in his room.

It is very neat. There is a fan, which does not work. There is a computer, which does not work. There are faded posters of soccer players. There are two gimmicky-looking pens arranged in crisp symmetry on the table, both dead. There is a cassette player plugged in and ready to be switched on, but no cassettes. There is also no electricity; I am using a paraffin lamp. The bedroom is all aspiration.

In the morning, I make the bed. I lift the mattress and see, in a corner, a heavy gray pistol, as calm and satisfied as a slug.

The 2010 World Cup is over. I am in Kenya. I have spent the last week sitting on a balcony, surrounded by coconut trees and cute gray monkeys with large blue testicles, trying to write this.

I wish I had read Ahmadou Kourouma before I went to Togo.

I wish every African in the world would read Ahmadou Kourouma.

For the late Kourouma's rage is magisterial. *Waiting for the Wild Beasts to Vote* measures, with an exactitude I have not encountered anywhere else, the farce: the history, the rumor, the myth, the praise, the double-eye, the flapping ears operating on four registers, the crocodile-grinning farce of the giant blue balls of our monkeyish leaders, who are rendered at once more and less than human by the seriousness with which their administrations take the fake independence they have been given.

If it is said that Big Men survive because they cultivate mystery, readers of *Waiting for the Wild Beasts to Vote* will find themselves immune to any of the psychological fetishes that have been ruling us. The fetishes are rendered mute by exposure.

The book is a thinly disguised attack on Eyadéma's Togo. Here, he is called Koyaga, of the totem of the falcon; he is a hunter, and Dictator-President of the République du Golfe. When Koyaga goes to visit his brother dictator, he gets this advice: "Other African presidents are dishonest, hypocritical. They begin the tour of their republics at the National Assembly or at some school. The most important institution in any one-party state is the prison."

Democracy is a negotiable object, but soccer is not. Treasuries, French government loans and grants, the lives of every citizen, the wombs of all women—all these things can bend comfortably to the will of the First Family, but the fate of the National Soccer team is in the hands of the people.

Nobody has ever successfully banned the playing of soccer in Africa.

It is easy to see why: soccer is a skill one can cultivate to the highest levels with nothing but plastic and string and will.

What makes billions of poor people around the world froth at the mouth about this game is that so many formidable countries can be rendered mute by the feet of one man.

Togo meets South Korea in their opening match of the World Cup.

The entire continent, almost every man and woman, all nine hundred million of us: from small towns in Germany to musty dormitories in Moscow, dusty and tired and drunk, living among abandoned warehouses and dead industries of New Jersey, in well-oiled board rooms in Nairobi, and Lagos and Johannesburg, in cramped tenements in the suburbs of Paris, inside the residences of the alumni of the Presidential School of Lomé, in the markets of Accra, and behind the corrugated-iron bars of Lusaka, in school halls and social halls, in the giant markets of Addis Ababa, in ecstatic churches dancing in Uganda, on wailing coral balconies in Zanzibar, in a dark rhumba-belting, militia-ridden bar in Lubumbashi, in rickety video shops in Dakar, in prisons in the Central African Republic, in miniskirts on red-lit street corners in Cape Town, in SuperSport bars, in school halls in Cherang'any, in parliament cafeterias in Harare—we all jump up and down, and shout, and sing, when, in the thirty-fourth minute of the game, Mohamed Kader gives Togo the lead over South Korea, with a blistering shot from a very difficult angle.

For one and a half hours, the continent is a possible place.

A Continent of Satire

I feel like the original Granta piece now belongs to somebody else. I have enjoyed desecrating it—and the sanctimoniousness that sometimes surrounds it. I want to be contrary about "How to Write About Africa."

—Binyavanga Wainaina, in an interview with
Rob Spillman, *BOMB*, 2011

In 1964, the United States Supreme Court was tasked with deciding whether the French filmmaker Louis Malle's new work, *The Lovers,* constituted "hard-core pornography." Potter Stewart, one of the justices on the bench, confessed his inability to precisely define the category, but added, somewhat famously, that he would know it when he saw it.

To collect Binyavanga's satire, then, and label it so, might seem like a perverse variation of this exercise. Nevertheless, here we are. Consider the problem: yes, we may know what satire is, but when it comes to satire from Binyavanga Wainaina, the Great African Writer, would we believe it when we saw it?

It isn't clear why Binyavanga's humor caused such confusion.

Perhaps it is because no one quite believes that serious writers can be funny, and certainly not if they are from Kenya. Any understanding of him, however, would be incomplete without an acknowledgment of his love of satire. It was the way he saw, and lived, and spoke. It was in his blood. And it was essential to his survival.

When you think about the body he lived in, the places he was from, and the lives he led, he had no choice, really. Binyavanga mocked the world because he had to: how else could he survive the indignity of having to take it seriously?

22

How to Be a Dictator

Rule 1

Be the richest man in your country (Daniel arap Moi, Robert Mugabe, Uhuru Kenyatta). If you are a second-generation dictator, this is not hard—just blackmail the guy who came before you (Frederick Chiluba). If you come from an oil-producing country, this is even easier (many Nigerians and Angolans, Chad). If you are a Kenyan, the National Social Security Council is good for a few billion. Defense contracts are even better (all presidents). Money-printing contracts, the best (all presidents). In South Africa, anything with the words "Black Empowerment" works fine (Jacob Zuma).

Rule 2

Find poor, stupid, and brutal men from every corner of your country and make them rich (Julius Malema). Do not give them money. Give them a place to steal from. Give all women's church groups money. They are the most powerful groups in your country.

Rule 3

Make America and China happy. Make Israel and Saudi Arabia very happy. Do not mess with the Muslim Brotherhood (Hosni Mubarak, Gaddafi). Blame all internal conflict on al-Qaeda. Blame all external conflict on American intervention.

Rule 4

Be very, very nice to your army. Be very mean to your police. Expand your private and state spy service with the most violent and loyal people who come from your village. Make sure you have private security imported and well lubricated. Brandy and hard cash. South Africans are excellent for this.

Rule 5

Allow all international NGOs and donors free access to starving rural people, so that they vote for you because they got Food Aid (most African countries). Arrest all the same whenever they tweet the following hashtags: #Occupy, #Dictator, #Democracy.

Rule 6

Colonial countries expected little of Africans. Maintain this illusion. Keep your citizenry ignorant and unproductive. For their food needs, see Rule 5 above.

Rule 7

Make sure you become your tribal leader (Kenyatta and son, Odinga, Goodluck Jonathan, Moi, Zuma). Even if you do not speak the language (Jerry Rawlings). Meet important people in your tribe every month and emphasize how the other tribes are going to kill you all if you leave power (Moi). When the shit hits the fan, your people will wield machetes for you. In Africa, "tribe" means anybody who speaks your language to whom you give money and civil service jobs. Just like the colonials.

Rule 8

Destroy or infiltrate all workers' unions and civil organizations that have a constituency of educated Africans. This way, you have no organized civil society that works. All farmers' associations, parents' associations, and teachers' associations. Also church groups—especially the Catholics, who have a dictator in the Vatican who is richer than you.

Rule 9

Allow all civil-society groups that do not have any sizable membership or constituency among your citizens. This way, you can shrug your shoulders and say you are happy to be criticized, but what noise they make means nothing.

Rule 10

A free press is important. But have shares in all major media and make sure that you allow them to be very critical of everything, except you. You can, these days, secretly pay bloggers. They can say, for example, that your economic policy is Keynesian, but they should never say you are a "corrupt Zulu warlord."

Rule 11

Do not send all the money you steal to Switzerland and do not give it to your wife. Do not have businesses in your wife's name.

Or in your children's names. Deal in euros, Krugerrands, and diamonds.

Rule 12

Be nice to your fellow world dictators; you may need them to give you a home someday. Join NEPAD (Abdoulaye Wade). Attend all African Union (AU) meetings. The AU is the dictator's best friend (Idi Amin). For presents to colleagues, cash is good, gold is better, and treasury bonds are best. No Ndebele prints please. Always make sure you have a direct line to Syria and North Korea.

Rule 13

Buy ten thousand drones and get a huge anti-terrorism grant from Obama to increase surveillance on all your political threats. Say yes to Africa Command and the Americans will defend you.

Rule 14

Be seen in a Pentecostal church every Sunday and you will be forgiven. Any Saudi-financed mosque works well too when relevant. Give noisy imams land and money.

Rule 15

Do not fuck with any drug dealers or, if you are francophone (all francophone countries), with the government of France (Rwanda, Ivory Coast).

Rule 16

Love China.

23

How to Be an African

Being a Partial Account of the Meeting of the Brooklyn Association of Pan-African Seekers and Thinkers and Queens (PAN-AFRISTQ). Panel II, presentation, hosted by Professor Brother (MC) Uhuru.

My brothers and sisters.

We all know that Leo was an African, do we not?

So was Tut, Cleo, and Janis Joplin. Rock and roll comes from Bamako.

My brothers, I lead you to the debate, held last summer in Boston, "Is a Grain of Wheat a Eurocentric Title"? Why not a grain of sorghum? Or a grain of millet? But Brother Ashanti made the valid point that wheat is Egyptian. And in Egypt the wheat was black.

The translation of the Ancient Egyptian symbol for wheat is "black grain that nourishes us."

We here know it all started with the royal calabash. In ancient times the calabash became the tray, the plate, the saucer, and, ultimately, the Tupperware container, which comes from Guinea Bissau, and which to this day women talk about when they say:

"Oh! Go and buy some Tupperware containers from the market, the one with a suction-seal top, like our ancestors loved." We invented the wine bottle—look at the gourd of the Kikuyu people—used to store millet wine. My brothers and sisters, we come from great people—look how ancient European queens wore wigs of Afro; powdered white like our ancient Africanist elders and shamans.

My sons and daughters, the twelve tribes of Israel are, in fact, eight: the Igbo, the Amhara, the Kalenjin, the Maasai, the Baganda, the Venda, the Tutsis, the Swahili (in Kiswahili, *juu* means "up," which comes from our people pointing up to Israel, where the Juus, the real Juus, came from). The Kalenjin still speak an ancient form of Hebrew. The Tutsis were ancient Phoenicians and Greeks. No, no. Sorry. Ancient Greeks and Phoenicians were Tutsis.

The nose of the Sphinx was cut to spite us.

Luo elders had the same pointy beard as King Tut.

Have you heard about the Black Irish?

Jesus was an African, you know.

We invented coffee.

All of us, every single one of us, are descended from kings and queens. We all wore kaftans of old and wraparound headscarves woven out of genuine Erykah Badu. Africa had no peasants.

Pushkin's great-grandfather was from Cameroon. Alexandre Dumas's grandmother was a Black woman from Saint-Domingue. (She did not call herself Black, but what does she know.)

My brothers and sisters, we need to talk about Angelina Jolie. Look at the syntax of the lips, the linguistics of the adoptions; notice the grammatical arrangement of the sarong, the Nefertiti nose. She is an African.

All of this information can be found in the great African library of Alexandria, which burned down.

My son, my daughter, vault yourself to esteem through these maybes; these almost-becames.

Create whole university departments of rejoinders. Take ownership of all empires.

Now, my brothers, a Dr. Brace, of the University of Michigan, tells us that Nubians and Egyptians were not Black Africans. He says they had black skins and Danish craniums—and it is indeed the cranium that makes the European. We are told that their skin "eventually adapted to the harsh rigors of the tropical sun."

They will find an Aryan in a toenail.

Professor Kwame Tut and Dr. Nefertiti Dakar have agreed to draft a strategy to counter this, and at our next gathering, again at the Kenteccino Chipotle Coffee Bar in Brooklyn, we will discuss this further.

Now let us take a break and listen to the beautiful words of Ashanti Nkrumah, a praise-singer and proet.

ASHANTI: Everybody say *Mamaaaaa.*

EVERYBODY: Mamaaaaa.

ASHANTI: Everybody say *Africaaaaaaaaaa.*

EVERYBODY: Africaaaaaaaaaaaaa.

ASHANTI: Okay, when I lift my hand in worship, brothers, sisters, shamans, and elders, I want you all to say, *Mamaaaaa Africaaaaaaaaaaa.*

EVERYBODY: Mamaaaaa Africaaaaaaaaaa.

ASHANTI: I am a Nubian Queen
    SexGoddess of Pride
    Ride

EVERYBODY: Mamaaaaa Africaaaaaaaaaa.

ASHANTI: My hide
    My black hide
    Ride

EVERYBODY: Mamaaaaa Africaaaaaaaaaa.

ASHANTI: Me to Bamako
    Play my blues
    In Cotonou

EVERYBODY: Mamaaaaa Africaaaaaaaaaa.

ASHANTI: Call the anSISTERS
        You GOD, girl

EVERYBODY: Mamaaaaa Africaaaaaaaaaa.

PROFESSOR BROTHER (MC) UHURU: Let's give it up for Ashanti
   and Mamaaaaa AfRicaaaaaaaaaa!

Now, let's have a break for a Kenteccino before we listen to
Brother Kente dia Kente rap some Bamako soul from his new
album, *The Nubian Soul of Bamako Griots*. After that, our
brother, Dr. George Hannington Kibwana, will deliver a lecture
on the Oral Literature of the Maragoli.

24

The Senegal of the Mind

The Senegal of the Mind is especially lovely this time of year. Its capital is Dakar, the Paris of Africa, where the ancient Moorish civilization of Black Africa speaks French to power. The Senegalese of the Mind is also very fond of Beirut (the Paris of the Middle East), as well as Buenos Aires (the Paris of South America) and Paris (the Paris of France).

The Senegal of the Mind was discovered by Tracy Chapman in the 1980s. Also present at the founding were Gil Scott-Heron, Jean-Michel Basquiat, the Joseph-Désiré Mobutu shirt and horn-rimmed glasses, the Kaunda suit, the Badu twist, the Indonesian tie-dye, various Yoruba goddesses, the music of the anti-apartheid movement, Fela Kuti's sweaty abs, and a guy called Enrique who makes hats in Brooklyn.

Zap Mama was not present at the founding, though she would become the mother of the nation in the late nineties, by conquering it.

Marie Daulne, or Zap Mama, was born of a Belgian father and a Zaïroise mother. Her father was killed during the riots that led to independence. Her mother fled, with Marie in her stomach, to the Congo forest, where they were rescued by Pygmies. She was born in the forest without anesthetic, and she was named »«¿¿¿, which means "the Queen with colliding arrows and upside down question marks." (In French, this translates as Marie Untoilette.)

Decades later, she made a pilgrimage back to Africa to meet the Pygmies, and they treated her specially because she could sing like them. Her Congolese homecoming was only the beginning of her Afropudlian idyll. In 1997 she had a baby she named Kesia, and she went to Mali. "A man in Mali told me that there are seven senses," she said. "Everyone has five, some can use their sixth. But not everyone has the seventh. It is the power to heal with music, calm with color, to soothe the sick soul with harmony. He told me that I have this gift, and I know what I have to do with it . . . I'm looking for instruments that have vocal sounds, forgotten instruments like the *guembri*." She had embarked on a Pan-African search for some quality me-time, a quest that could end only in Senegal.

Marie Untoilette started to recruit revolutionaries for the attack on Fort Greene, Brooklyn, the heartland of the Senegal of the Mind. She worked with Michael Franti, Limp Bizkit, the Butthole Surfers, Rob Zombie, the Foo Fighters, Erykah Badu, and the Wizards of Ooze to make the soundtrack. Luckily, she had studied "polyphony in Asian, Arabic, and African contexts," which came in handy during the fighting. One fine morning Marie and her shock troops (including a contingent from HEMP: Hair Empathy Messes Patriarchy) descended on DeKalb Avenue wielding Vodoun essential oils and Candomblé drumbeats, beating up people with perms. Some of the extremists pulled women out of their storefronts and gave them jojoba scalp rubbings. Afterward, negotiations with the long-haired pimp look of Fulton Mall were dreadlocked for months, until Marie went directly to the Taiwanese Mafia and made them pull all lye-based products from all shelves and replace them with shea butter, Rita Marley Pancake Mix, Wyclef Jeans, and Goree Hand Cream.

"Now, my massage is that we need to go down to our roots!"

she said, strumming her endangered instrument as the crowds cheered.

She declared independence in 2000 and was registered by the United Nations World Music Council.

Location: within five hundred yards of any outlet that sells Putumayo products to Black people in every major city in the world.

Credit rating: above seven hundred.

Border countries: Ali Farka Touré, Bahia, Jamaica, Toronto, Salsa, and Yassa rice.

Maritime claims: all offshore territories in the world where Black people look beautiful and are artisanal and musical.

Terrain: generally low, rolling voices with riffs and instruments made of earthy products, set to a retro beat by a DJ who is very cool.

Elevation extremes:

Lowest point: Michael Franti.

Highest point: Salif Keita, Youssou N'Dour.

Irrigated land: ten million scalps, furrowed and oiled.

Natural hazards: lowlands seasonally flooded by gentrifying white people.

Main exports: polyphonic a cappella, jojoba oil, World Music CDs, plantain facemasks.

25

How to Write About Africa

Always use the word "Africa" or "Darkness" or "Safari" in your title. Subtitles may include the words "Zanzibar," "Maasai," "Zulu," "Zambezi," "Congo," "Nile," "Big," "Sky," "Shadow," "Drum," "Sun," or "Bygone." Also useful are words such as "Guerrillas," "Timeless," "Primordial," and "Tribal." Note that "People" means Africans who are not Black, while "The People" means Black Africans.

Never have a picture of a well-adjusted African on the cover of your book, or in it, unless that African has won the Nobel Prize. An AK-47, prominent ribs, naked breasts: use these. If you must include an African, make sure you get one in Maasai or Zulu or Dogon dress.

In your text, treat Africa as if it was one country. It is hot and dusty with rolling grasslands and huge herds of animals and tall, thin people who are starving. Or it is hot and steamy with very short people who eat primates. Don't get bogged down with precise descriptions. Africa is big: fifty-four countries, nine hundred million people who are too busy starving and dying and warring and emigrating to read your book. The continent is full of deserts, jungles, highlands, savannas, and many other things, but your reader doesn't care about all that, so keep your descriptions romantic and evocative and unparticular.

Make sure you show how Africans have music and rhythm deep in their souls, and eat things no other humans eat. Do not mention rice and beef and wheat; monkey-brain is an African's cuisine of choice, along with goat, snake, worms, and grubs, and all manner of game meat. Make sure you show that you are able to eat such food without flinching, and describe how you learn to enjoy it—because you care.

Taboo subjects: ordinary domestic scenes, love between Africans (unless a death is involved), references to African writers or intellectuals, mention of school-going children who are not suffering from yaws or Ebola fever or female genital mutilation.

Throughout the book, adopt a *sotto* voice, in conspiracy with the reader, and a sad *I-expected-so-much* tone. Establish early on that your liberalism is impeccable, and mention near the beginning how much you love Africa, how you fell in love with the place and can't live without her. Africa is the only continent you can love—take advantage of this. If you are a man, thrust yourself into her warm virgin forests. If you are a woman, treat Africa as a man who wears a bush jacket and disappears off into the sunset. Africa is to be pitied, worshipped, or dominated. Whichever angle you take, be sure to leave the strong impression that without your intervention and your important book, Africa is doomed.

Your African characters may include naked warriors, loyal servants, diviners and seers, ancient wise men living in hermitic splendor. Or corrupt politicians, inept polygamous travel guides, and prostitutes you have slept with. The Loyal Servant always behaves like a seven-year-old and needs a firm hand; he is scared of snakes, good with children, and always involving you in his complex domestic dramas. The Ancient Wise Man always comes from a noble tribe (not the money-grubbing tribes like the Kikuyu, the Igbo, or the Shona). He has rheumy eyes and is close to the Earth. The Modern African is a fat man who steals and works in the visa office, refusing to give work permits to qualified Westerners who really care about Africa. He is an enemy of development, always using his government job to make it difficult for pragmatic and good-hearted expats to set up NGOs or Legal Conservation Areas. Or he is an Oxford-educated intellectual turned serial-killing politician in a Savile Row suit. He is a cannibal who likes Cristal champagne, and his mother is a rich witch-doctor who really runs the country.

Among your characters you must always include the Starving African, who wanders the refugee camp nearly naked and waits for the benevolence of the West. Her children have flies on their eyelids and pot bellies, and her breasts are flat and empty. She must look utterly helpless. She can have no past, no history; such diversions ruin the dramatic moment. Moans are good. She must never say anything about herself in the dialogue except to speak of her (unspeakable) suffering. Also be sure to include a warm and motherly woman who has a rolling laugh and who is concerned for your well-being. Just call her Mama. Her children are all delinquent. These characters should buzz around your main hero, making him look good. Your hero can teach them, bathe them, feed them; he carries lots of babies and has seen Death. Your hero is you (if reportage) or a beautiful, tragic international celebrity/aristocrat who now cares for animals (if fiction).

Bad Western characters may include children of Tory cabinet ministers, Afrikaners, employees of the World Bank. When talking about exploitation by foreigners, mention the Chinese and Indian traders. Blame the West for Africa's situation. But do not be too specific.

Broad brushstrokes throughout are good. Avoid having the African characters laugh, or struggle to educate their kids, or just make do in mundane circumstances. Have them illuminate something about Europe or America in Africa. African characters should be colorful, exotic, larger than life—but empty inside, with no dialogue, no conflicts or resolutions in their stories, no depth or quirks to confuse the cause.

Describe, in detail, naked breasts (young, old, conservative, recently raped, big, small) or mutilated genitals, or enhanced genitals. Or any kind of genitals. And dead bodies. Or, better, naked dead bodies. And especially rotting naked dead bodies. Remember, any work you submit in which people look filthy and miserable will be referred to as the "real Africa," and you want that on your dust jacket. Do not feel queasy about this: you are trying to help them to get aid from the West. The biggest taboo in writing about Africa is to describe or show dead or suffering white people.

Animals, on the other hand, must be treated as well rounded, complex characters. They speak (or grunt while tossing their manes proudly) and have names, ambitions, and desires. They also have family values: *see how lions teach their children?* Elephants are caring, and are good feminists or dignified patriarchs. So are gorillas. Never, ever say anything negative about an elephant or a gorilla. Elephants may attack people's property, destroy their crops, and even kill them. Always take the side of the elephant. Big cats have public-school accents. Hyenas are fair game and have vaguely Middle Eastern accents. Any short Africans who live in the jungle or desert may be portrayed with good humor (unless they are in conflict with an elephant or chimpanzee or gorilla, in which case they are pure evil).

After celebrity activists and aid workers, conservationists are Africa's most important people. Do not offend them. You need them to invite you to their thirty-thousand-acre game ranch, or "conservation area," and this is the only way you will get to interview the celebrity activist. Often a book cover with a heroic-looking conservationist on it works magic for sales. Anybody white, tanned, and wearing khaki who once had a pet antelope or a farm is a conservationist, one who is preserving Africa's rich heritage. When interviewing him or her, do not ask how much funding they have; do not ask how much money they make off their game. Never ask how much they pay their employees.

Readers will be put off if you don't mention the light in Africa. And sunsets, the African sunset is a must. It is always big and red. There is always a big sky. Wide empty spaces and game are critical—Africa is the Land of Wide Empty Spaces. When writing about the plight of flora and fauna, make sure you mention that Africa is overpopulated. When your main character is in a desert or jungle living with Indigenous peoples (anybody short) it is okay to mention that Africa has been severely depopulated by AIDS and War (use caps).

You'll also need a nightclub called Tropicana, where mercenaries, evil nouveau riche Africans, and prostitutes and guerrillas and expats hang out.

Always end your book with Nelson Mandela saying something about rainbows or renaissances. Because you care.

Afterword

One day in September 2006, three visitors to London walked up to the door of The Village, a gay bar in Soho. Two of the three were men, one of whom had just flown in from India, the other from Kenya. Earlier that evening, they had both endured dinner with a pompous American law professor who would, years later, mount a forgettable run for President. After dinner, they walked along the river to the Tate Modern museum to pick up the third of their trio, an Indian woman who had just staged a performance involving a Palestinian mime artist and Bombay electronica. They proceeded to join a mutual friend's birthday party, which is how they ended up at The Village.

Now it just so happened that each one of them was dressed in non-Western clothes. The Indian man wore a cotton kurta that went below his knees; the Indian woman was dressed in a silk saree, fresh flowers in her hair; and the Kenyan man wore a full-length kaftan with dramatic bell sleeves that he had gotten made in Dakar. (He insisted on calling this a boubou.) At the door of The Village, they were met by a kindly bouncer, who drew them aside and gave them the chance to admit they were hopelessly lost. This is a gay bar, he said. At that very moment, behind a window to their side, a go-go dancer vigorously bounced against the glass, his groin only a few inches away from their faces. Yes, thanks, they replied. Look, the bouncer pleaded, shaking his head. It's a *gay* bar. It's *five* pounds entry. Are you *sure* you want to go in? Yes, they said again, and here is fifteen pounds for the three of us. It went on like this for a bit, until the bouncer threw his hands up in the air and let them through.

In the basement of The Village, the party was in full swing. The Kenyan leaned back against the bar, under a thundering cloud of disco and smoke, like a grand Sufi mystic. Naturally, all eyes turned to him. A stranger walked up and said, Are you that . . . and the Kenyan smiled. You must sign my copy, he continued. It's right here, in my bag. But, of course, it was not. Whereupon the stranger unbuttoned his shirt and said, Write anything! The Kenyan motioned for a pen and wrote his name down on the stranger's chest. He inscribed the letters carefully so as not to hurt: BINYAVANGA. Then, he looked around, delighted, as if it had just dawned on him how much he enjoyed generating this peculiar mix of bewilderment and adoration. It's true. I know, because I was there—I was the Indian chap with him that night.

Binyavanga Wainaina was born in 1971 in Nakuru, the agricultural capital of Kenya. At this time, the country of his birth was only eight years older, having just wrested itself free of the British Empire. His mother, Rosemary, who trained in secretarial studies, ran several businesses, including a hair salon, and his father, Job, headed a government-owned company that produced pyrethrum, a natural insecticide harvested from chrysanthemum flowers. He was their second child, and, in his mother's eyes, her favorite—the shy one. To her, he was KenKen; to the rest of his family, Ken; to his siblings, sometimes, also SweSwe.

He went to primary school in Nakuru. When he turned twelve, he went to an all-boys boarding school, as one did. His first attempt at high school was disastrous: an ill-fated one-year stint at a school called Njoro Boys, where he was savagely abused. His sister Ciru remembers him coming home depressed, anxious, and also missing two full thumbnails as a result of bullying by fellow students. Binyavanga's horrified parents pulled him out at once. They enrolled him at Mang'u, a better-regarded school that provided him with an altogether happier experience, and, finally, at Lenana, among the most prestigious schools in the country.

Ciru's most consistent memory of her slightly older brother is that his kindness attracted other students to him like a magnet.

At Lenana, he made a lifelong friend in Martin, whom he roped into the high-school production of a play he wrote. Binyavanga himself played the lead character, a femme fatale named either Désirée or Jacqui—on this point, recollections differ—dressed in a Tina Turner wig, a shimmering ballgown that belonged to his mother, and stilettos "borrowed" from his sister Ciru. Martin remembers his friend as someone who clearly understood the power of words. In their late teens, they once went to a Wimpy's, a fast-food restaurant, and got into a fight with a waiter over the food and service. They demanded to see the manager, who came and promptly asked them to leave. Binyavanga protested in the poshest voice he could summon. "Do you know who I am?" he said. "I am the editor of the student magazine. I can break your restaurant with one story." The manager threw them out anyway.

Chiqy, his youngest sister, remembers one trauma they had in common. They were both naturally left-handed infants who were forced by their teachers to become right-handed in nursery school.

She remembers all the younger siblings growing up in the shadow of the eldest one, Jimmy, who was perfect. He was the all-rounder and star basketball player whom every girl adored. In fact, Chiqy built a whole economy around Jimmy, providing advice to girls who were interested in him in exchange for snacks and treats. Binyavanga, the sensitive lover of the arts, was of no such practical value. Regardless, he remained his mother's favorite child. Chiqy remembers her mother handing her the very worst job in the kitchen—to slaughter chickens, dunk them in boiling water, and pluck them clean—while giving Binyanga money to go into town and swap books, in lieu of housework. "He's a reader," her mother would explain, much to Chiqy's chagrin. "Let him read." Chiqy took her revenge by hiding raw chicken feet under Binyavanga's bedsheets before he went to sleep, and listening with satisfaction as he screamed the house down upon discovering them.

Jimmy's earliest memories of his younger brother are of a gentle child, lost inside his head. A loving little fellow. Except perhaps for that one time when Binyavanga was seven, and Ciru, who was a year younger and something of a child prodigy, was upgraded to the same class as him, leading to a serious case of status anxiety: he was outraged beyond belief that she had become his equal.

Jimmy's physical resemblance to Binyavanga is uncanny; they even speak almost identically, with the same cadence, the same rhythm, and in the same precise accent that is exclusively their own.

In 1991 Binyavanga moved with his sister Ciru to a small town called Mthatha in South Africa, to study for a bachelor's degree in accounting. They enrolled at the University of Transkei, which has ceased to exist, as has the eponymous region. Ciru sailed through her courses, but her brother found that accounting—or, indeed, getting out of his dormitory room, going to class, passing exams, or extending his visa—was not for him. After a few tortured years of trying and failing, he fled to Cape Town, South Africa's second-largest city, a bona fide metropolis, to reinvent himself—in a city and a country that were doing much the same.

It was the late 1990s. South Africa had liberated itself from three hundred and fifty years of settler colonialism, and it was a time of new beginnings and opportunities. At first, with the help of the son of a family friend, he took over the café at the Pan-

African market. A few years later they ran a restaurant called Waka Mundo. When both ventures failed, they set up a catering service specializing in African food. Through this time, Binyavanga had been writing too, and soon he found editors willing to publish him. Some of his earliest essays were published by the country's leading newspapers—the *Sunday Times, Cape Times,* and *Cape Argus.* Often, these essays were about food, but just as often he appeared in these papers as an authority on food.

"If you've been visiting the same-old-favorite restaurants and eating the same-old-food and getting the same-old-vibe, and you're dying for a change, give Ken the Kenyan a call," a columnist wrote in the *Cape Times,* in September 1998. Speaking to a reporter for the same newspaper later that year about his catering outfit, the cheerily named Ubusuku Be Africa, or African Nights, Binyavanga declared he was tired of hearing that traditional African cuisine didn't exist. "Of course it does," he said, "but no one ever asks for it, especially in Cape Town."

In due course, Binyavanga met Graeme, a DJ and designer, who in turn introduced him to his friend Rhoda, a music producer. The three of them became instantly inseparable, and moved into a house together. Rhoda remembers that time, in that house, in the vibrant, student-dominated, bookshop-filled area called Observatory, as the happiest household she has ever lived in. They were young and free. There was music, there was dancing, and there were people dropping in every hour of the day to stay late into the night. And Binyavanga, writing furiously in a room that was a chaotic mess of cigarettes and clothes and papers, from which he emerged once in a while to cook something wonderful, especially when he was dissatisfied with the words he had written.

At the end of that decade, as the world gave itself over to a new century and a new millennium, Binyavanga received devastating news: his mother's life had ended too. He fought the tears and scrambled to leave. Graeme made him a mixtape as an expression of love, for him to comfort himself with on the journey home. He labeled it "For Rosemary's Baby."

Nearly two decades later, Binyavanga wrote a love letter back to the country in *Business Day,* a South African newspaper. "I thank you and love you deeply for looking out for a lonely young man, confused, lost and depressed," he wrote. "I am writing to you to thank you for loving me when I lived in your country for ten years. Illegally. I thank you for taking care of me, for growing my mind. For stretching my heart. For building an African."

Binyavanga returned to Kenya a writer. With new eyes to survey the country of his growing up, he wasted no time. He was an irresistible gravitational force, pulling a whole generation into his orbit. "We could taste it, the freedom to come. We wanted to be the new, unshackled Kenyans—our whole selves and not the staid old Kenyan selves epitomized by the then literary space whose walls he was determined to bring down," the political scientist Muthoni Wanyeki wrote in *The Elephant,* of Binyavanga's role in the new wave. "He moved into my flat. As did, for a while, all the people he was gathering around him. There was food—he loved to cook, messily, things full of butter and cream and everything as artery-clogging as it could be. There was drink—a lot of it—fueling all the passionate conversations about writing and life."

Two years into his return, he had gathered enough momentum to take a shot at the Caine Prize for African Writing. There were the online writing communities he had enthusiastically signed up to, the newspapers in Kenya and South Africa that wanted to publish him, and there was his new friend Rod Amis, the editor of an internet-only literary magazine called *G21.* He wrote an essay, called it "Discovering Home," published it in *G21,* and sent it to the Caine Prize. They declined to accept it, explaining that they were a serious prize and could therefore accept only serious writing in serious journals. "Now, in the last twelve months, if not a single collection of writing or short stories has been published in Africa, where do you think you're going to get submissions from?" he protested. They relented. He won the prize. And used the money—and the tornado-level energy surrounding him by this point—to start the literary magazine he wanted to read.

He called it *Kwani?*, which means "So what?"

The very next year, Yvonne Owuor won the Caine Prize for her short story "The Weight of Whispers," which was published in this defiant upstart of a magazine.

Then came that essay. It started out as an angry email driven either by low blood sugar or by a passionate hatred of the Polish journalist Ryszard Kapuscinski, or by both. It ended up with Binyavanga being courted by at least two European heads of state and Bono. (And that was just the beginning.) The publication of "How to Write About Africa" in 2005 was a turning point. For one thing, it was because of the astonishing velocity of the essay, which remains, to this day, *Granta*'s most-circulated article ever. For another, it was because of that voice: that singular, hilarious, worldly, biting, flippant, and meaningful voice that set fire to a whole millennium's worth of assumptions about what a writer in Binyavanga's position was supposed to do.

Mainly, however, I think the essay was a turning point because it made Binyavanga possible. I met him for the first time only a few months after the essay was published, exactly at the time it was circling the planet. To be sure, I grew up thousands of miles away from him, in another country on another continent. But I recognized his predicament, because it was mine too: the impossible and almost civilizational chasm that separated expectation and circumstance. The ambition to prove here is just as significant as there without enough power to; the desire to engage the world without anywhere near the means to.

At the time of Binyavanga's early wins, all of which happened in quick succession—the Caine Prize, the launch of *Kwani?*, and the *Granta* essay—it seemed like he could do just about anything. I certainly thought so when we first met. He had an assured air about him that suggested he was in no hurry. At the same time, he left no doubt that he wanted to remake the world in a hurry. And why not? The world waited, with arms outstretched. Finally, everything was possible. *He* was finally possible. I can't fully convey what a heady feeling it was to be around him then. It was his time. He knew it—and loved it. KenKen had made the jump to Binyavanga Wainaina. He had found the world he had been waiting for, the sky was the limit, and the future was wide, wide open.

Glossary

NOTE ON THE TEXT. *Throughout the book, words in the languages of the African continent are italicized at first mention and romanized thereafter, with the exception of proper nouns and place names.*

abakwetha: a young man undergoing initiation into manhood

ai: that; I'm sorry, what?; um-hmm

Ambi: skin cream to fade dark spots

Anyanya One: a Southern Sudanese separatist army that operated in the First Sudanese Civil War

apana: no

belila: boiled grains; porridge

bhuti: brother

buibui: black shawl-like head covering

bundu: wilderness

bwana: boss; sir; mister

chubana ndebe: tin-and-bottle man

cūcū: grandmother

dawa: medicine

fungua: open

guembri: sintir; a stringed instrument

haki: truly

kaa mũcĩĩ: stay home

kanga: sarong or wraparound

karibu: welcome

kawaja: white man; honorific

kinyozi: barber

Kwani?: So what?

kwaruza: scratch

lakini: but

Leo: Leo Africanus, Islamic scholar, writer, and traveler; author of *Descrittione dell'Africa* of 1550 (*A Geographical Historie of Africa,* 1600)

malaya: prostitute

maneno: words; thing

manyatta: homestead consisting of huts, especially of the Maasai

mayai: eggs

mi ni: I am

mieiles: corn on the cob

miraa: khat

mkokoteni: hand-cart

moran: a young man, initiated into manhood; literally "warrior"

mtukufus: nobles

muguu wazi: open legs

mursik: yogurt

muti: black magic

mwananchi: person on the street

mzungus: white people

NEPAD: New Partnership for Africa's Development

nsa-nsa-nsa: cool dude

orkoiyot: spiritual and military leader

oyinbo: light-skinned person; white person

pole: sorry

sawa: okay

shamba: farm

shoga: gay male—pejorative

shuka: shawl; scarf; bedsheet

Si: "Is it not the case?"

siasa: politics

toboa: puncture

urugwagwa: homemade banana liquor

waragi: domestic gin distilled in Uganda

Acknowledgments

The editor and publisher would like to thank Melissa Wainaina, June Wainaina, and James Wainaina for their support and encouragement in the process of making this collection; Ed Pavlić and Rhoda Isaacs, among others, for contributing personal records; Billy Kahora and the team at *Kwani?* for excavating their archives; the editors who originally brought many of these essays and stories to life—Andrew Unsworth, Rod Amis, Ntone Edjabe, Michael Vazquez, Ferial Haffajee, and Matt Weiland, and, finally, Binyavanga Wainaina's loving network of family, friends, and readers who made his career, and this collection, possible.

1   Binguni!: First published in *Pure Fiction*, www.purefiction.com, 1996.

2   A Foreigner in Cape Town: First published in *G21*, www.g21.net, 1998–2002.

3   Food Slut: First published in *G21*, www.g21.net, 1998–2002.

4   Cured of England: From private correspondence with the author.

5   Circumcision: First published in *G21*, www.g21.net, 1998–2002.

6   Discovering Home: First published in *G21*, www.g21.net, 1998–2002. Winner of the Caine Prize for African Writing, 2002.

7   Joga of Mathare Valley: First published in *G21*, www.g21.net, 1998–2002.

8   Hair: First published in *G21*, www.g21.net, 1998–2002.

9   Travels Through Kalenjinland: First published in *Kwani?*, 2003–10.

10 I Hate Githeri: First published in *Kwani?*, 2003–10.

11 Who Invented Truth?: First published in *Kwani?*, 2003–10.

12 Inventing a City: First published as "Nairobi: Inventing a City" in *National Geographic*, September 2005.

13 She's Breaking Up: From private correspondence with the author.

14 All Things Remaining Equal: First published in *Kwani?*, 2003–10.

15 Hell Is in Bed with Mrs. Peprah: First published in *Chimurenga 3: Biko in Parliament*, November 2002. Reprinted by permission of *Chimurenga*.

16 An Affair to Dismember: First published in *Wasafiri*, 2002. Copyright © *Wasafiri*, 2002, reprinted by permission of Taylor & Francis Ltd, www.tandfonline.com on behalf of *Wasafiri*.

17 According to Mwangi: First published in *New Writing 12*, edited by Diran Adebayo, Blake Morrison, and Jane Rogers, Picador, 2003.

18 Ships in High Transit: First published in *Virginia Quarterly Review*, December 2005. Finalist for the U.S. National Magazine Award for Fiction, 2007.

19 The Continental Dispatch: Selected columns first published in the *Mail & Guardian*, South Africa, 2006–9. Copyright © *Mail & Guardian*. Reprinted by permission of the *Mail & Guardian*.

20 Beyond the River Yei: Published in "Beyond the River Yei: Life in the Land Where Sleeping is a Disease" in *Kwani?*, 2004.

21 The Most Authentic, Blackest, Africanest Soccer Team: A version of this essay was first published in *The Thinking Fan's Guide to the World Cup*, edited by Matt Weiland and Sean Wilsey, Harper Perennial, 2006.

22 How to Be a Dictator: First published in *Chimurenga*, 2008; *Chronic* edition, August 2013. Reprinted with permission of *Chimurenga*.

23 How to Be an African: First published in *Transition*, 2006. Copyright © Indiana University Press, 2006. Reprinted by permission of Indiana University Press.

24 The Senegal of the Mind: First published in *Bidoun 11: Failure*, 2007. Reprinted by permission of *Bidoun*.

25 How to Write About Africa: First published in *Granta*, 2005. Copyright © *Granta*, 2005. Reprinted by permission of *Granta*.

About the Author

——————

Binyavanga Wainaina was a Kenyan author, activist, and journalist, and the 2002 winner of the Caine Prize for African Writing. His debut book, the memoir *One Day I Will Write About This Place,* was published in 2011. *Time* magazine included Wainaina in its list of the 100 Most Influential People in the World in 2014. He died in 2019.

About the Type

This book was set in Sabon, a typeface designed by the well-known German typographer Jan Tschichold (1902–74). Sabon's design is based upon the original letter forms of sixteenth-century French type designer Claude Garamond and was created specifically to be used for three sources: foundry type for hand composition, Linotype, and Monotype. Tschichold named his typeface for the famous Frankfurt typefounder Jacques Sabon (c. 1520–80).